The KLC Seri

These *Graded Reading Sets* are designed for u *Learner's Course* (KLC), a step-by-step guide needed for genuine literacy in Japanese. KLC's self-guiding, self-reinforcing curriculum teaches non-native learners to read and write kanji, gain a native-like understanding of kanji meanings, and acquire a rich kanji-based vocabulary.

The Kanji Learner's Course Series also includes the *Kanji Learner's Course Green Book* (a writing practice workbook), the *Kanji Learner's Course Wall Chart*, and *The Ultimate Kana Wall Chart: A Visual Guide to Japanese Phonetic Writing*.

All nine volumes of this *Graded Reading Sets* series are available in ebook form at keystojapanese.com/klcgrs-volumes. Thank you very much for supporting this series.

The Kanji Learner's Course
Graded Reading Sets

漢

Volume 1: Kanji 1-100
Paperback version

Andrew Scott Conning

© 2017-2021 by Andrew Scott Conning. All rights reserved.

ISBN: 9798617869806

Except for sharing Volume 1 in its complete original form, no part of the *Kanji Learner's Course Graded Reading Sets* series may be reproduced in any form by any electronic or mechanical means (including photocopying, recording, or information storage and retrieval) without permission in writing from the author. Materials drawn from the "Original Works" list at the end of this book are freely available to the reader under the licenses listed therein. Please note, however, that the pages of these Graded Reading Sets have been edited and are protected by copyright. The author reserves all rights to the original content of this series, including the introductory text; selection, sequencing, and arrangement of items; cross-reference information; phonetic guides; glosses; and annotations; as well as the full text of all original items (i.e., those not displaying a citation number after the English translation).

The author donates to the public domain his original Japanese translations of items deriving from the following original works (as numbered in the "Original Works" section):
#21, 38, 56, 59, 63, 65, 66, 78, 80, and 94.

Acknowledgments

The author gratefully acknowledges the valuable work of the authors and institutions that have made available the source material used in this series, as well as the following organizations, without whom this project would not have been possible:

The Agency for Cultural Affairs

The Harvard Graduate School of Education

The Harvard University Libraries

The Harvard-Yenching Institute

The Okayama Prefectural Library

The University of Tokyo Libraries

I also wish to gratefully acknowledge the skilled support of Amy Mae Lee, who performed a very complex series of data processing tasks, as well as Kunisuke Hirano and Rina Zahlten, who checked the Japanese text and phonetic guides with meticulous care. Thank you very much for making this project possible.

This series honors the memory of Misako Takahashi
With gratitude for your warm friendship and hospitality
And blessings for the precious children you left behind
Bless Robert
Bless Sayaka
Bless Asami

Authors of source material

Aesop
Akutagawa, Ryunosuke
Andersen, Hans Christian
Bailey, Arthur Scott
Barrie, James Matthew
Baum, L. Frank
Benjamin, Walter
Bierce, Ambrose
Chesterton, Gilbert K.
Clinton, William J.
Conan Doyle, Arthur
Darwin, Charles
Descartes, Rene
Douglass, Frederick
DuBois, W.E.B.
Dumas, Alexandre
Dunbar, Paul Laurence
Fitzgerald, F. Scott
Gogol, Nikolai V.
Harper, Frances
Hearn, Lafcadio
Henry, O.
Hurston, Zora Neale
Jacobs, Joseph
Johnston, Ian
Joyce, James
Kajii, Motojiro
Kennedy, John F.
Lamb, Mary
Lang, Andrew
Lawrence, D.H.
LeBlanc, Maurice
Leonard, Sean
Lincoln, Abraham
London, Jack
Machiavelli, Nicolo
Marx, Karl & Engels, Friedrich
McKay, Claude
Mill, John Stuart
Miyazawa, Kenji
Natsume, Soseki
Northup, Solomon
Ouida
Plato
Poe, Edgar Allan
Raymond, Eric S.
Roe, Benjamin
Schlabach, Gerald W.
Seebach, Peter
Stallman, Richard M.
Stevenson, Robert Louis
Strindberg, August
Taylor, Fredrick Winslow
Veblen, Thorstein
Verne, Jules
Wells, H.G.
Wharton, Edith
Wheatley, Phillis
Wilde, Oscar
Wilson, Harriet E.
Woolf, Virginia
World Health Organization
Yeats, William Butler

Works of traditional or collective authorship:

Constitution of Japan
Constitution of the United States
Declaration of Independence
Genesis, The Book of
Isaiah, The Book of
Japanese Law Translation Database System
Status of Forces Agreement between Japan and the United States
Treaty of San Francisco
Treaty of Mutual Cooperation and Security between Japan and the United States
Universal Declaration of Human Rights

Contents

KLC-GRS Series Introduction 1
How to Use This Series 13
The Reading Sets 16
Volume 2 134
Companion Resources 135
Index of Grammar Glosses 139
Original Works 175
Sources 181
About the Author 183
Thank You 183

Stages (*dan*) attained in this volume

生

セイ

NEWBORN

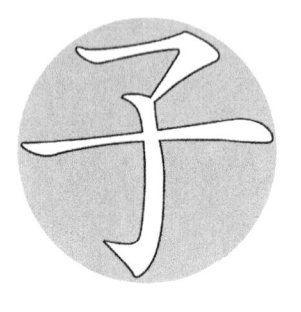

子

こ

LITTLE ONE

See full stage sequence at

keystojapanese.com/kanji-ranks

KLC-GRS Series Introduction

The *Kanji Learner's Course Graded Reading Sets* contain over 30,000 parallel text segments distributed as reading practice for all 2,300 kanji in the course. The exercises for each kanji contain only kanji previously introduced, and are designed to give you contextualized practice with reading the kanji-based vocabulary introduced in the course. The *Graded Reading Sets* allow you to immediately apply each kanji you learn, and continuously review what you have already studied.

Instant reading comprehension from the very first character

With the KLC Graded Reading Sets, there is no need to learn 1000 kanji or more before experiencing the pleasure of reading authentic written Japanese. **Each exercise contains only kanji you have already learned, and is supported by phonetic guides, an English equivalent, and, in ebook form, by easy-to-install dictionaries for looking up unfamiliar words**. Reading the exercises for each kanji after studying it in the KLC, you will never be stopped in your tracks by an unfamiliar character.

To further aid comprehension, **this series also introduces over 600 key grammatical structures** as they appear, with cross-references that allow you to quickly find in-depth information about any structure that may be unfamiliar to you. This contextualized grammar support allows you to master a wide range of sentence patterns through the natural process of reading and understanding.

Instant gratification = continuous motivation

The difficulty of understanding written Japanese has been a source of frustration and discouragement for generations of Japanese learners. This frustration contributes to a negative feedback cycle resulting in decreased motivation and decreased learning.

The KLC Graded Reading Sets are designed to reverse this discouraging cycle with the **energizing gratification of understanding one sentence after another – including an ever-expanding range of kanji, kanji-based words, and grammar patterns**. Each success will enhance your enthusiasm for further study, contributing to a positive feedback cycle of increased learning and motivation.

The power of "extensive reading"

"Extensive reading" – reading large amounts of comprehensible material – is widely regarded as one of the most effective methods of language learning. **By reading a large volume of material that you can understand, you will absorb grammar patterns, vocabulary words, and subtleties of usage in the most natural and enjoyable way.**

For extensive reading to be educational, it must meet two conditions. First, it must *challenge* you with new forms you have not yet mastered. Second, it must give you adequate *support* to understand what you are reading.

The KLC Graded Reading Sets fulfill these conditions by design. Because each exercise includes a word containing the kanji you have just studied, it necessarily presents a new *challenge*. And since no unfamiliar kanji are used, you are always ready to meet that challenge.

Moreover, because the exercises are supported by phonetic guides, English equivalents, and grammar glosses, you have all the *support* you need to completely understand each sentence and acquire new insights into how kanji, words, and grammatical structures are used in authentic Japanese.

Optimized practice of recently learned kanji and vocabulary

Various procedures have been used to ensure that the exercises give you **maximum practice with recently learned kanji and vocabulary** while fully illustrating the meaning and usage of the character you are studying in that set (the "target kanji").

First, items were selected by sorting a massive database of over 300,000 bilingual text pairs to prioritize items containing recently learned kanji and vocabulary.

Second, additional automated sorting and text conversion was used to replace many pronouns (かれ He, かのじょ She) and katakana names (トム Tom, メアリ Mary) in the source material with Japanese names (宮崎さん Miyazaki-san) and other personal nouns (記者 reporter, 教授 professor, 総理 Prime Minister, etc.) **selected to maximize your practice with recently learned kanji**. Because the "recently learned kanji" vary throughout the series, this procedure automatically ensures exposure to a constantly changing set of personal and proper nouns, helping you master a long list of Japanese names along the way, including both surnames and given names.

Quality and variety

Language learning resources typically use artificial texts to provide reading practice for beginning and low-intermediate learners. While such texts serve a useful purpose, they tend to be dry and unnatural. Moreover, they tend to repeat specific patterns and subject matter, and lack the range of usage of authentic writing.

The KLC Graded Reading Sets series does incorporate artificial items as needed for specific purposes (particularly in the first two volumes), but it primarily consists of **authentic writing drawn from distinguished authors and texts across a diverse range of fields**. Drawing on a rich corpus of over 100 original sources, this series assembles writing of the highest quality from literature, science, technology, history, law, ethnology, sociology, popular culture, government, business, public health, art, romance, philosophy, economics, and other fields.

This diversity of source material ensures that you are exposed to a range of vocabulary and usage similar to that which you will encounter in authentic Japanese texts. Indeed the extraordinary diversity of source material used in this series is perhaps unique among bilingual graded readers for Japanese.

A range of challenges to suit every level and every learner

To offer maximum value to the user, this series incorporates a prodigious volume of reading practice (the 290,000 words of the English translations are roughly equivalent to seventeen copies of *Macbeth*). While some users may wish to take advantage of all 30,000+ exercises in this series, others may find it more practical to read a smaller subset.

To make it easy for you to read as much or as little as you like, exercises are sorted by length, starting with short terms or phrases and building up to full sentences or even chains of sentences. At the intermediate and advanced levels, you will find an increasing number of long, complex sentences and multi-sentence exercises. Kanji sets at all levels begin with short, simple exercises to allow you to fully grasp the target kanji before tackling more complex structures.

Naturally, the exercises at the lower levels tend to be shorter and less interesting, since they must be constructed from a narrower range of characters. At these early stages, you may take encouragement from knowing that the reading will grow ever more interesting as you advance through the levels.

Grammar glosses

The exercises in this series incorporate thousands of glosses introducing grammatical phrases and other fixed expressions. These "grammar glosses" are designed to aid comprehension and help you master a wide range of sentence patterns in the course of your reading.

For example, the exercises below introduce the expressions 「〜ことがある」 ("__ has occurred") and 「いかに〜」 ("how __"):

以前に会ったことがある。

I've met him before.

「〜ことがある」 {〜事がある* 80} ["__ has occurred"]: DJG v1 p196; Genki ch11; Marx v1 day62; Tobira ch1 #6.

私たちはこれまで、君主が自分の基盤を固めることがいかに必要であり、そうしなければ必然的に破滅するのだということを見てきました。

We have seen above how necessary it is for a prince to have his foundations well laid; otherwise he will surely go to ruin.

「いかに〜」 {如何に〜** 2197; 815} ["how __"]: DJG v3 p135; Tobira ch14 #9.

3

In each case, the expression introduced is enclosed in Japanese quotation brackets 「」, followed in curved brackets {} by a kanji version, if one exists. Asterisks in the kanji version indicate that it is used less frequently (single asterisk) or much less frequently (double asterisk) than the kana-only version. Numerals indicate the kanji's KLC entry number(s). The end of the gloss contains references to popular grammar resources for more information on how the pattern is used:

- "**DJG**": *A Dictionary of Japanese Grammar*, by Seiichi Makino & Michio Tsutsui (a comprehensive reference series). References marked "v1" refer to *A Dictionary of Basic Japanese Grammar*, while those marked "v2" refer to *A Dictionary of Intermediate Japanese Grammar*; and those marked "v3" refer to *A Dictionary of Advanced Japanese Grammar*.

- "**Genki**": *Genki: An Integrated Course in Elementary Japanese, 2nd Edition*, by Eri Banno et al. (the most popular traditional textbook). References to chapters 1-12 refer to Volume 1, while those to chapters 13-23 refer to Volume 2.

- "**Marx**": *Speak Japanese in 90 Days*, by Kevin Marx (an inexpensive and easy-to-follow self-teaching guide). "Marx v1" refers to the first volume, and "v2" to the second volume.

- "**Tobira**": *Tobira: Gateway to Advanced Japanese*, by Mayumi Oka, et al. (a popular intermediate-level resource that picks up where Genki leaves off). The Tobira references point to numbered items in the 「文法ノート」 sections at the end of each chapter.

The resources above have been chosen for being the most popular in their categories. For information relevant to determining which of these resources is most suitable for you, visit keystojapanese.com/res.

Most grammar patterns are noted only the first several times they appear, unless they have a particularly challenging range of variants or applications. For this reason, the grammar glosses appear less frequently as this series progresses. The Index of Grammar Glosses at the back of this book lists every gloss in the series and the examples in which it appears.

With a few exceptions, no glosses are provided for individual words, which can generally be looked up, in ebook or PDF format, using a J-E dictionary installed on one's computer or mobile device.

Phonetic guides

Each exercise is followed by a phonetic guide displaying all kanji readings in parentheses:

著作権の制限に真っ向から逆らって、地下のアニメ流通は1980年代から1990年代初期に花開き、生まれくる国内産業の基盤を構築した。

著作権(ちょさくけん) の 制限(せいげん) に 真っ向(まっこう) から 逆らっ(さからっ)て、 地下(ちか) の アニメ 流通(りゅうつう) は

4

1980年代(ねんだい) から 1990年代(ねんだい) 初期(しょき) に 花開き(はなひらき)、 生まれ(うまれ)くる 国内(こくない) 産業(さんぎょう) の 基盤(きばん) を 構築(こうちく) した。

Quite against the restrictions of copyright, underground anime distribution flourished throughout the 1980s and early 1990s to build a base for a nascent domestic industry.

- Progress Against the Law: Fan Distribution, Copyright, and the Explosive Growth of Japanese Animation, by Sean Leonard (web.mit.edu/seantek/www/papers/progress-columns.pdf)

Phonetic guides are displayed in a contrastive format to make it easy for you to find the word you're looking for. Word division is provided as an additional learning aid.

How this series is organized

Differences between lower and higher levels

As noted above, the exercises tend to get longer and more advanced at the higher levels. Because they encompass more complex content, higher-level exercises are also more interesting to read. After the 300 mark, the average number of exercises also increases, while the proportion of artificial sentences decreases, giving way to authentic material.

The increasing volume of reading practice from level to level is well adapted to your needs as a learner. Early on, you should spend relatively little time trying to read, and focus instead on learning more kanji. After all, you will get plenty of practice with the basic kanji later on, and there are many important kanji still awaiting your attention. At this stage, you should just get a quick handle on each kanji and move on to the next one.

As you advance, your needs change. Reading practice becomes more important, as you have ever more kanji to hang onto, and ever fewer left to learn (not to mention that the remaining kanji are increasingly less important). **This series adapts to your developing needs by gradually increasing the volume of reading practice as you make your way through the course**.

Imbalance among sets

You will find that some kanji sets in this series have few exercises, while others have many. This is consistent with the purpose and organization of this series.

For one thing, some kanji only appear in a few words, or even one word, such that there are both fewer examples using these kanji and less need of practicing them.

Moreover, some kanji will have only a few exercises in their own set due to their location in the KLC sequence, but will appear with great frequency later on, once you have learned an important vocabulary word containing the kanji. For example, the kanji 犠 and 牲 are both used almost exclusively in the word 犠牲, so whichever of these appears first is bound to have few or no exercises.

What matters is not the amount of reading practice you get *in any given set*, but that you ultimately get an appropriate amount of practice for each character. To ensure this happens, I have deliberately included a large number of exercises in those sets where it was possible to do so. You will thus find that **each volume, taken as a whole, provides extensive practice across the full range of kanji and vocabulary you have learned to that point**, with special emphasis on recently learned kanji and vocabulary.

Combination of short and long exercises

As noted above, sets at all levels begin with short, simple exercises to allow you to practice the target kanji before tackling more complex structures. These short exercises (often just compound words or short phrases) give you repeated practice with the target kanji, before giving way to longer items in which the target kanji is mixed in with many others.

The short and long exercises thus serve complementary purposes: **short exercises give you relatively intensive practice with the target kanji, while long exercises give you more practice with sentence structure and review of kanji already studied**. The fact that the exercises are arranged by length thus allows you to tailor your reading selection to your own purposes.

While the longer exercises tend to be more interesting, I have done my best to include many short exercises that manage to say something interesting in just a few words or characters.

Selection and editing of exercises

The following principles were used in selecting and writing exercises for each set (in rough order of priority):

1) To illustrate the most important vocabulary and usages of the target kanji;
2) To illustrate a wide range of usages of the target kanji;
3) To illustrate usages of previously learned kanji;
4) To combine short and simple examples (focused on illustrating the target kanji) with longer and more substantive examples;
5) To use examples that are authentic and engaging, while still providing some plain vanilla examples for the sake of representing typical patterns;
6) To represent a range of source material (literature, natural sciences, social sciences, everyday speech, etc.).

As noted elsewhere, a great deal of effort has gone into selecting and editing the exercises to be easy to understand without context.

Personal names

Many pronouns and katakana names have been replaced with Japanese names (and other nouns) to provide additional kanji practice, particularly with recently introduced kanji. To distinguish surnames from given names, note that Japanese surnames will generally have a "-san", "-sensei", "Dr.", etc. **in the English equivalent**, while given names will not:

> 本田さんは舌がよく回る。
>
> *Honda-san is very talkative.*
>
> ("san" is included in the English equivalent, signaling that Honda is a surname)

> 明さんは舌がよく回る。
>
> *Akira is very talkative.*
>
> ("san" is not included in the English equivalent, signaling that Akira is a given name)

In the Japanese text, the suffix さん (or an alternative such as くん or any one of various titles like 先生, 社長, etc.) **is always included with Japanese names**, to help you avoid mistaking names for common nouns. This rule is not followed for foreign names, which are readily distinguished by virtue of being written in katakana.

These conventions in the presentation of personal names are intended to aid the learning process, and are internal to this series.

Long vowels in Japanese

In the English equivalents, Japanese words (usually names) are written in Hepburn romaji without macrons, which are omitted to avoid display issues across different devices and operating systems. Hence the English versions do not discriminate between, for example, the long "o" of Jiro and the short "o" of Hiroyuki. Similarly, the capital is transliterated as "Tokyo", without macrons. The correct pronunciation of all Japanese words will be apparent from the Japanese phonetic guides.

Unlisted kanji

The main KLC book includes a handful of vocabulary words, such as 石鹸 (soap), that contain a kanji not listed in the course. Such words appear together with a mixed kanji-kana form (石けん), and are allowed only because the word frequently appears in this mixed form. The same handful of words is also allowed in the reading sets. As in the main book, the unlisted kanji are marked with an ×. Unlike the main book, these reading sets do not show the mixed kanji-kana forms, which are obviated here by the phonetic guides.

When you encounter a kanji marked with an ×, just try to recognize the word it appears in, which will already be familiar to you from the course. It is not important to learn the marked kanji.

Use of optional kanji

As explained below, these reading sets sometimes use kanji where it would be more common to use Arabic numerals or hiragana.

<u>Kanji vs. numerals</u>
In horizontal writing in contemporary Japanese, numbers are usually written with Arabic numerals:

    1929 年 10 月 29 日: *29 October 1929*

    JIS X 0213: 1 面 40 区 32 点: *JIS X 0213: Plane 1, Subdivision 40, Point 32*

…though large numbers are usually shortened by the use of a kanji like 万 or 億, similar to the way we would use English words to refer to numbers of one million or more:

    800 万人: *8 million people*

    40 億円: *4 billion yen*

Despite the prevalence of Arabic numerals, it is still necessary for learners to become proficient in reading numbers in kanji. For this reason, this series (particularly the first part of Volume 1) includes exercises in which numbers typically written in numerals are expressed in kanji:

    三田の人口は九千五百五十人です。

    The population of Mita is nine thousand five hundred fifty.

    千代さんは宝くじで三千万円も手に入れた。

    Chiyo won thirty million yen in the lottery.

When you encounter items like these, keep in mind that one would more likely write them like this:

    三田の人口は 9550 人です。

    The population of Mita is 9,550.

    千代さんは宝くじで 3000 万円も手に入れた。

    Chiyo won thirty million yen in the lottery.

Kanji vs. hiragana

In these reading sets you will find the same words sometimes written with kanji and sometimes without:

> 分かり易い。
>
> 分かりやすい。
>
> わかりやすい。
>
> *Easy to understand.*

> 子供達。
>
> 子供たち。
>
> 子どもたち。
>
> *Children*

This reflects real-life usage and helps you learn to read different forms interchangeably. This remains an essential skill, as the use of optional kanji seems to have increased in recent years, likely due to the convenience of keyboard- and voice-based text input. Moreover, writers sometimes opt for kanji to clarify word division in a long string of hiragana, or for stylistic reasons, such as to express polite formality, to present a learned image, or simply to vary things up a bit!

Compared to real-life usage, **this series is moderately biased in favor of using optional kanji once you have learned them**. After all, the main purpose of this series is to help you master kanji and kanji-based vocabulary. This bias is especially pronounced for recently introduced kanji, which require frequent reinforcement. This pro-kanji bias is partly offset by the fact that only hiragana spellings are used until the kanji in question have been introduced. Just keep in mind that the series is biased 100% against using optional kanji before they have been introduced, and moderately in favor of using them thereafter.

Regardless of the usages you find in this series, a good rule to remember for your own writing is to **be sparing in the use of optional kanji when not necessary for eliminating ambiguity, punctuating a long string of hiragana, or otherwise improving clarity**. In the example below, the first version uses every possible kanji, the last version uses a minimal number of kanji, and the middle version strikes a judicious balance:

> 子供達は最も酷く苦しんだ。
>
> 子供たちは最もひどく苦しんだ。
>
> 子どもたちはもっともひどく苦しんだ。
>
> *The children suffered worst of all.*

Use of esoteric English

A few of the English translations include words that may not be familiar to some native speakers. While I provided glosses in some instances, I did not attempt to filter out examples that contained esoteric English vocabulary. For one thing, you can look up any word instantly just by tapping on it, and some users may appreciate the opportunity to learn some new words. Moreover, it is often easy to infer the meaning of these words based on the kanji of their Japanese equivalent. For example, it is easy to deduce the medical meaning of "indolent" from the example below:

無痛潰瘍 ("non-pain-broken-boil")。

An indolent ulcer.

- Wordnet

I personally learned from this example that the English word "indolent" (which I thought just meant "lazy") can also mean *"causing little or no pain"* (New Oxford). While I did know that "dol" means "pain" – from "dolor" (Spanish), "doleful", "condolences", etc. – I never connected this in my mind with "indolent" until I saw this example, where the kanji 痛 ("pain") make this connection hard to miss. Thanks to kanji, I now know both senses of "indolent", and have a more nuanced understanding of its usual sense "lazy", which suggests the idea of "avoiding suffering".

Indeed, one of the things I love most about kanji is the way they can help us better appreciate the Latin and Greek roots of our own native language, roots that we all too easily ignore. For example, I had no idea where the word "clinical" came from until I learned its equivalent in Japanese (臨床), whose kanji mean "attend" and "bed". In fact the word "clinical" itself derives from the Greek word for "bed", which makes it easy to remember its precise meaning: *"relating to the observation and treatment of actual patients rather than theoretical or laboratory studies* [from Greek *klinikē (tekhnē)* 'bedside (art),' from *klinē* 'bed']" (New Oxford American Dictionary).

As illustrated by these examples and countless others, an outstanding feature of kanji is their capacity to make words more transparent to us than they are in our native tongue. To permit just these sorts of insights, I have not attempted to filter out examples containing esoteric English terms.

Parallel definitions

Roughly a tenth of the exercises in this series are drawn from a set of parallel definitions released by Wordnet. These exercises will present definitions in Japanese and English of the same word, which is often not shown. For example:

四旬節の最後の日。

The last day of Lent.

This text is part of the definition of "Holy Saturday", segmented from the full definition ("*the Saturday before Easter; the last day of Lent*"). A few things to note about these exercises:

* The English translations for such items are definitions, or parts thereof, and

may often sound like crossword or Jeopardy clues. Yet they are not definitions of, or clues for, the Japanese examples. Rather, they are *equivalents* of the Japanese text, which is itself a definition of some term that is not shown.

* The identity of the terms being defined is irrelevant, as your purpose is to learn to comprehend Japanese text, not to fill out a crossword puzzle!

* While these exercises are not complete sentences, they are actually **quite useful for practicing kanji and kanji-based vocabulary**, which they contain in high density and without forcing you to read the same old kana and grammatical expressions over and over again.

* To make reading these parallel definitions a bit more interesting, I often took the trouble of inserting the defined term into the text in both English and Japanese, creating complete sentences along the following pattern:

「内陣」とは、牧師や聖歌隊が使う、教会の祭壇の周りの場所のことを指す。

The "chancel" is the area around the altar of a church used by the clergy and choir

Sometimes these exercises define terms for which a native speaker would require no definition, such as "death row":

「死刑囚独房棟」とは、死刑を宣告された者が執行を待つ刑務所の独房棟のことを指す。

"Death row" is the cellblock in a prison where those condemned to death await execution.

While the meaning of "death row" is obvious to any native speaker of English, the meaning of 死刑囚独房棟 is not, and such examples provide intensive and high-quality reading practice for the target kanji (akin to reading an entry in a Japanese-Japanese dictionary).

Style

Reflecting the wide variety of source texts from which they are drawn, the exercises follow a variety of conventions for style, punctuation, and spelling (labor & labour, fulfill & fulfil, behoove & behove, etc.). Almost no attempt has been made to make the text conform to a consistent style, other than to run a procedure to move quote marks from outside of commas and periods to inside them, which I have done to help legitimize this (far more rational!) practice.

In original items, I have also made a point of using plural pronouns in lieu of masculine pronouns for generic third-person singular subjects, e.g., the now legitimate "*Each plays their respective role*" in lieu of the needlessly gendered "*Each plays his respective role.*"

Outdated expressions

Largely due to the absurdly long duration of copyrights, the material used for these reading sets relies heavily on texts written prior to 1923. While I have attempted to exclude any item containing offensive language, the remaining items still inevitably reflect the language and ideas of their respective eras. If you come across anything you consider particularly objectionable, please report it to me at info@lexicaglobal.com, thank you.

Lack of diversity among source authors

This series draws most heavily on sources made available by Project Gutenberg and Aozora Bunko. Among the dozens of bilingual texts available from these projects at the time of writing, not a single source was written by an author of African, Hispanic, or Native American descent, to name just a few excluded categories. Female authors were underrepresented.

As a symbolic gesture, I personally translated a small quantity of public domain material written by Afro-American and Afro-European authors. But this material is far from adequate, and for future projects I seek suggestions from readers for sources of copyright-free bilingual material from a wider diversity of authors.

I was particularly disappointed not to be able to use Martin Luther King's historic "I Have a Dream Speech" of 1963. In this case the barrier was not the lack of a translation, but the control Dr. King's estate continues to exert over this copyrighted work.

I invite readers to share their opinions on the issue of author diversity in public domain texts (particularly bilingual texts), both with copyright owners and with the translation community. For more information, please consult the following websites:

weneeddiversebooks.tumblr.com

projectgutenbergproject.blogspot.com/2014/05/wishlist-black-writers-in-public-domain.html

How to Use This Series

Choose your platform

This series is available on both Kindle and Apple Books from keystojapanese.com/klcgrs-volumes. For instructions on using the electronic versions of this book, please download the "How to Use This Series" file from keystojapanese.com/klc-grs-files. The instructions below apply to all formats.

Incorporate this series into your study routine

Reading is likely to be the most enjoyable and important part of your kanji study regimen, especially once you have learned a few hundred kanji and begin seeing more substantial material. Read the exercises for each kanji as an integral part of studying that kanji. For information on how to incorporate the Graded Reading Sets into your kanji learning routine, visit keystojapanese.com/how-to-study (the instructions posted there supersede the "Step-by-Step Method" described on pages 24-25 of the Kanji Learner's Course book, which was published before these reading sets came into existence).

First try to pronounce and comprehend each exercise without referring to its phonetic and English glosses. Use a bookmark or your hand to cover the glosses.

With such a vast and diverse corpus of readings before you, you should not concern yourself with understanding every word of every exercise. Instead, **focus on familiarizing yourself with the meaning and function of the target kanji within each exercise**. If the KLC lists more than one meaning for the kanji, try to figure out which meaning the kanji conveys in that example. Also try to figure out the meaning the *other* kanji contribute to the compounds the target kanji appears in. Every appearance of an earlier studied kanji is an opportunity to deepen your knowledge of how it is used to convey meaning.

If you have forgotten any of the other kanji in the exercise, you can quickly find its KLC entry numbers using the cross-reference number file posted at keystojapanese.com/klc-grs-cross-refs.

Make your own book

I have deliberately included a large volume of material so that those who wish to read a great deal may do so. Even so, **my intention is not to suggest that you read all the exercises provided, but to give you the opportunity to determine what amount is optimal for you**. Read whatever amount gives you solid practice and positive reinforcement without reaching the point of tedium, which will only sap your enthusiasm for further study. To make it easy for you to customize your "workout" for each kanji, I have arranged the exercises by length.

Don't worry about every word; do be aware of loose translations

Again, you should not burden yourself with understanding every bit of every exercise. Unlike a typical textbook, **this series does not present carefully homogenized content** to prevent inconvenient questions from arising. Instead it uses authentic sentences and translations drawn from "the wild", including over 100 different sources written in different eras by different writers with distinct ways of using the language. With such a diverse variety of real-world sources and over 30,000 exercises, the range of questions that will arise is necessarily broader than can possibly be answered in the series directly, despite the support provided by the English translations, the grammar glosses, and the progressive introduction of kanji.

Moreover, even though most exercises in this series present a transparent correspondence between English and Japanese, many translations are relatively liberal or "loose" – especially those from literary sources. If you find a Japanese word that does not seem to correspond exactly to an English word, keep in mind that this may simply be a case of "translator's license" – not a case of your having incorrectly learned the word. Indeed, **many of the translations are written to convey an overall idea or impression, and may not provide a perfect one-to-one componential correspondence with the original**. In some cases, one or more parts of the Japanese version may not correspond to any part of the English version. In addition, some expressions may be translated in a variety of ways, given the wide range of sources, translators, and eras from which the material has been drawn.

In short, when you can't figure out the Japanese text word-for-word (even after looking up the words), just **focus on understanding the gist of each item, and how the target kanji is used within it**. Also, **be sure to...**

Use complementary resources

Needless to say, even with these Graded Reading Sets, the Kanji Learner's Course series is not adequate by itself for developing your reading comprehension. Be sure to use it in conjunction with similarly structured tools that – unlike this series – are designed to progressively introduce grammatical expressions, verb conjugations, politeness registers, and other aspects of the language. Keystojapanese.com/res lists a selection of tools that may be particularly helpful.

Skim key sources for background

The vast majority of exercises in this series are easy to understand despite having no context. A great deal of effort has gone into selecting items that met this criterion – or to edit them until they did.

Moreover, for literary sources, priority has been given to stories that many readers are likely to be familiar with from books or movies, such as *The Wizard of Oz*, *Around the World in 80 Days*, *Treasure Island*, and the *Book of Genesis*. For example, the following item will evoke a vivid image for anyone who has seen The Wizard of Oz:

> 家を支える大きな横材の角の下から、銀色の爪先が尖った靴を履いた足が二本、突き出ていました。
>
> *Just under the corner of the great beam the house rested on, two feet were sticking out, shod in silver shoes with pointed toes.*

…even if they changed the color of the slippers for the movie.

Still, while most exercises should be easy to understand without context, there are a few sources that contain unfamiliar references, or are otherwise highly context-dependent. In particular, it is worthwhile for you to skim the following two free sources, particularly if you have any interest in the subject matter:

Progress Against the Law: Fan Distribution, Copyright, and the Explosive Growth of Japanese Animation, by Sean Leonard:
web.mit.edu/seantek/www/papers/progress-columns.pdf

Homesteading the Noosphere, by Eric S. Raymond:
www.catb.org/esr/writings/cathedral-bazaar/homesteading/homesteading.ps

The text will refer you to these sources when they begin to be used heavily.

Understood subjects

One way in which Japanese differs sharply from English is that speakers often omit the subject when it can be understood from context:

> 全力で力んだ。
>
> *I tried with all my might.*

Many translations in this series reflect this distinction, so you won't always find a subject in the Japanese sentence to correspond to the one in the English equivalent.

Unfamiliar vocabulary and readings

In each set, pay special attention to any unfamiliar words using the target kanji. Look them up in a dictionary. Try to relate the meaning of these words to the core meaning(s) given in the KLC. For kanji with a wide range of meanings, look up their entries in a good J-E kanji dictionary like the Kodansha Kanji Dictionary or Kodansha Kanji Learner's Dictionary.

You will also encounter kanji readings (i.e, pronunciations) not listed in the KLC, which mostly restricts itself to the official readings published in the official Joyo Kanji List. The KLC avoids listing unofficial readings – other than some of the more commonly used ones – to avoid leading you down unorthodox paths with your own usage. But authentic Japanese texts are rife with unofficial usages, and this series makes no attempt to shelter you from them.

The Reading Sets

1：日

1-1. 1日ごとに。

1日(にち) ごと に。

(Once) every day.

「-ごとに」 {-毎に* 105} ["every __"]: DJG v1 p128. **[What's this? See Series Intro/Grammar glosses]**

Note: No phonetic guides are provided for Arabic numerals, unless they form part of a word whose reading is irregular, such as「1日(ついたち)」or「2日(ふつか)」. Hence「1日(にち)」signals that the reading of "1" is regular, forming the word「いちにち」.

1-2. 1日がすぎた。

1日(にち) が すぎた。

A day passed.

「が」 [subject marker]: DJG v1 p118; Genki ch8; Marx v1 day8. 「**Past tense verbs**」: DJG v1 p576; Genki ch4&9; Marx v1 day31.

1-3. 日々いそがしい。

日々(ひび) いそがしい。

Busy every day.

Note: Use a bookmark to hide the glosses as you read each exercise.

1-4. あと1日しかない。

あと 1日(にち) しか ない。

There's only one day left. (87)

「あと〜」 {後〜 114} ["__ left", "__ longer", "__ until"]. 「ない」 [informal negative of ある]: DJG v1 p576. 「しか〜ない」 ["no more than __/no other than __"]: DJG v1 p398; Genki ch14; Marx v2 day40.

Note: Parenthesized numerals after the English version indicate the source of the entire item (both Japanese and English). Items having no such numeral are original. To identify the source of any numbered item, look for the corresponding numbered work in the "Original works" section.

1-5. 1日コースがありますか。

1日(にち) コース が あります か。

Do you have one-day routes? (87)

「が」 [subject marker]: DJG v1 p118; Genki ch8; Marx v1 day8. 「か」 [question marker]: DJG v1 p166; Marx v1 day11. 「〜**ありますか**」 {〜有りますか* 400} ["is/are there any __?"; "do you have any __?"]: Genki ch4; Marx v1 day15.

Note: For anyone familiar with basic Japanese, many of the grammar glosses in this first volume will be unnecessary. Simply ignore them if you already understand the sentence. The glosses will become more useful to you later, when the sentence patterns become more advanced.

1-6. わたしは2、3日ニューヨークにいた。

わたし は 2、3日(にち) ニューヨーク に いた。

I was in New York for a few days. (87)

17

「〜に」 [time of occurrence]: DJG v1 p289 & 303. 「いる」 {居る* 255} ["exist"; "be present"]: DJG v1 p153. 「**Past tense verbs**」 : DJG v1 p576; Genki ch4&9.

1-7. クリスマスまであとなん日ありますか。

クリスマス　まで　あと　なん日(なんにち)　あります　か。

How many more days are there until Christmas? (87)

「〜まで」 {〜迄** 1806} ["until __"]: DJG v1 p225; Genki ch23. 「あと〜」 {後〜 114} ["__ left", "__ longer", "__ until"].

1-8. いよいよサイトが20日にオープンします。

いよいよ　サイト　が　20日(はつか)　に　オープン　します。

The site will open on the 20th. (10)

「が」 [subject marker]: DJG v1 p118; Genki ch8; Marx v1 day8. 「〜に」 [time of occurrence]: DJG v1 p289 & 303. 「**Irregular verb: する**」 : DJG v1 p578-79.

Note: Numerous exercises in these very early sets have multiple grammar glosses. This highlights the fact that this series is organized to introduce one kanji at a time, rather than one grammar point at a time. The glosses are intended only to offer a helpful reference when unfamiliar patterns arise, rather than to present an organized course of study in their own right.

The thicket of grammar glosses will soon start to clear, once you get the most common structures under your belt. Each gloss will stop repeating once it becomes superfluous (I apologize if I may have erred on the side of repetition in some cases).

A word about this series

Unsurprisingly, the set you have just completed is among the least useful in the entire series. After all, there's not much we can do with only one kanji! And of course reviewing earlier kanji is out of the question.

Rest assured that the exercises will grow ever more useful as you advance through this series. The best way to quantify this is to calculate the "kanji content" of each volume (i.e., the number of instances of kanji in the text). By this measure, the progressive development of the series is readily apparent:

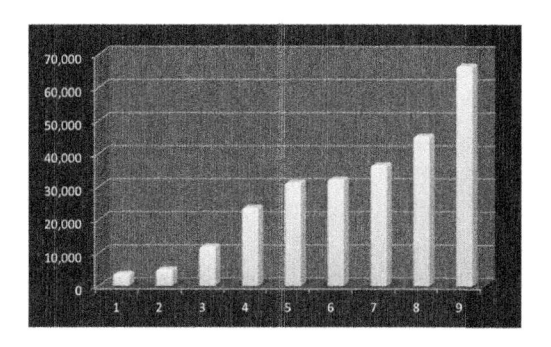

Kanji content for each volume

You will read about 4,000 kanji in this first volume — the first bar in the chart above. The set of exercises you just completed contains only 8 of those 4,000 kanji. The full series contains about 260,000.

Here are a few examples to give you a sense of how the content of this series develops (each example is relatively long for its level):

Set 95 (好), Exercise 14:
休日には好きなだけ月子さんと話すことができます。

Set 910 (舎), Exercise 17:
大丈夫だよ。きみを獄舎から出すのに大した金は要らないよ。告発者だって、大したお金を言ってこないよ。少し払えば満足してくれるさ。
   - Crito, by Plato (Benjamin Jowett, Transl.)

Set 1915 (項), Exercise 21:
第九条：日本国民は、正義と秩序を基調とする国際平和を誠実に希求し、国権の発動たる戦争と、武力による威嚇又は武力の行使は、国際紛争を解決する手段としては、永久にこれを放棄する。前項の目的を達するため、陸海空軍その他の戦力は、これを保持しない。国の交戦権は、これを認めない。
   - Constitution of Japan.

As noted in the Introduction, **the cumulative structure of this series adapts automatically to your evolving needs as a learner, providing relatively little practice at the early stages** (when your priority should be to learn more kanji and grammar patterns), **and increasing the volume of practice later on** (as your priority shifts toward applying and reinforcing the kanji and vocabulary you have already learned).

2：一

2-1. 一つになる。

一つ(ひとつ) に なる。

Unite into one. (100)

「**Counters**」：DJG v1 p604; Genki ch9; Marx v1 day81.

2-2. 一々うるさい。

一々(いちいち) うるさい。

Fussy about every little thing.

2-3. しみ一つもない。

しみ 一つ(ひとつ) も ない。

Without so much as a single stain.

「〜も」["even __"]: DJG v1 p250; Genki ch14. 「ない」 [informal negative of ある]: DJG v1 p576. 「ある」 {有る 400} ["exist"; "have"]: DJG v1 p73.

2-4. たのしい一日だった。

たのしい 一日(いちにち) だった。

It was a fun day.

「だった」 [past tense of copula だ]: DJG v1 p580 bottom; Genki ch9; Marx v1 day37. 「**Past tense verbs**」：DJG v1 p576; Genki ch4&9; Marx v1 day31.

2-5. いつもの一日だった。

いつも の 一日(いちにち) だった。

It was a routine day. (101)

「いつも」 {何時も** 815; 383} ["always"]: DJG v1 p253. 「の」 [marks end of modifying phrase]: DJG v1 p312; Genki ch10.

2-6. 一シリングもなかった。

一(いち) シリング も なかった。

He had nary a shilling. (7)

「〜も」["even __"]: DJG v1 p250; Genki ch14. 「なかった」 [negative past tense of ある]: DJG v1 p577; Genki ch9; Marx v1 day37.

Note: The word "He" in the English version is not present in the Japanese version, as understood subjects are normally omitted in Japanese. See the section on "Ellipsis" in Makino & Tsutsui's Dictionary of Basic Japanese Grammar (p. 23).

2-7. オフィスでのつらい一日。

オフィス で の つらい 一日(いちにち)。

A trying day at the office. (101)

「〜で」 [location]: DJG v1 p105. 「の」 [marks end of modifying phrase]: DJG v1 p312; Genki ch10.

2-8. これとこれを一つずつください。

これ と これ を 一つ(ひとつ)ずつ ください。

Please give me one each of this one and this one.

「こ/そ/あ/ど」 : DJG v1 p600; Genki ch2; Marx v1 day16-17. 「と」 ["and" within an exhaustive list; cf. や]: DJG v1 p473; Genki ch4; Marx v1 day57. 「～を」 [indicates direct object]: DJG v1 p347; Genki ch3; Marx v1 day9. 「-ずつ」 ["__ each"]: DJG v1 p572; Tobira ch11 #9.

2-9. リンゴをもう一ついかがですか。

リンゴ を もう 一つ(ひとつ) いかが です か。

Would you like another apple? (87)

「～を」 [indicates direct object]: DJG v1 p347; Genki ch3; Marx v1 day9. 「もう + (numeral) + (counter)」 ["__ more"]. 「いかが」 {如何** 2197; 815} ["how"; "would you like __"]: DJG v1 p114. 「か」 [question marker]: DJG v1 p166. 「**Ellipsis**」 : DJG v1 p23.

2-10. きみにもう一つのチャンスをあたえよう。

きみ に もう 一つ(ひとつ) の チャンス を あたえよう。

I'll give you another chance. (7)

「きみ」 {君 1407} [informal: "you"]: DJG v1 p28. 「～に」 [marks indirect object]: DJG v1 p291 & 303. 「もう + (numeral) + (counter)」 ["__ more"]. 「の」 [marks end of modifying phrase]: DJG v1 p312; Genki ch10. 「**Volitional**」 ["let's __"; "I'll __"]: DJG v1 p576 & 578 second column from right; Genki ch15; Marx v1 day29.

3 : 二

3-1. 二日ごとに。

二日(ふつか) ごと に。

Every other day.

「～に」 [time of occurrence]: DJG v1 p289 & 303.

3-2. これを二つあげます。

これ を 二つ(ふたつ) あげます。

I'll give you two of these.

「～を」 [indicates direct object]: DJG v1 p347; Genki ch3; Marx v1 day9. 「**Counters**」 : DJG v1 p604; Genki ch9; Marx v1 day81. 「あげる」 {上げる* 41} ["give (to someone)"]: DJG v1 p63; Genki ch14; Marx v2 day30.

3-3. みかんを二つください。

みかん を 二つ(ふたつ) ください。

Two tangerines please.

3-4. はなしが一つ二つあります。

はなし が 一つ(ひとつ) 二つ(ふたつ) あります。

I have a couple of things to speak with you about.

「ある」 {有る 400} ["exist"; "have"]: DJG v1 p73.

3-5. ジムとジョージはうり二つだ。

ジム と ジョージ は うり二つ(うりふたつ) だ。

Jim and George are exactly alike (うり二つ = a pair of melons).

「と」 ["and" within an exhaustive list; cf. や]: DJG v1 p473; Genki ch4; Marx v1 day57. 「**A は B だ**」 ["A is B"]: DJG v1 p521; Genki ch1; Marx v1 day8.

21

3-6. トムは一も二もなくひきうけた。

トム は 一(いち) も 二(に) も なく ひきうけた。

Tom readily [unhesitatingly] accepted.

「〜も〜も」 ["both __ and __"; "neither __ nor __"]: DJG v1 p255, v2 p185; Marx v2 day14; Tobira ch6 #3. 「**Past tense verbs**」: DJG v1 p576; Genki ch4&9; Marx v1 day31.

3-7. ラクダには一つか二つのこぶがある。

ラクダ に は 一つ(ひとつ) か 二つ(ふたつ) の こぶ が ある。

Camels have either one or two humps (こぶ). (87)

「〜に」 [location of existence]: DJG v1 p299 & 303. 「の」 [marks end of modifying phrase]: DJG v1 p312; Genki ch10. 「ある」 {有る 400} ["exist"; "have"]: DJG v1 p73.

Note: Animal species are generally written in katakana in scientific contexts, and frequently in non-scientific contexts as well. Given its specific purpose, this series preferentially uses kanji to refer to animal species, when such kanji exist and have already been learned.

4：三

4-1. まだ三日あります。

まだ 三日(みっか) あります。

We still have three days.

「まだ〜」 ["still __"; "not yet __"]: DJG v1 p224; Genki ch9; Marx v1 day87.

4-2. これを三つください。

これ を 三つ(みっつ) ください。

I'd like three of these please. (87)

4-3. 二、三日のあいだには、……

二、三日(に、さんにち) の あいだ に は、……

In just a few days, …

「の」 [marks end of modifying phrase]: DJG v1 p312; Genki ch10. 「〜あいだに」 {〜間に 448} ["while __"]: DJG v1 p67; Genki ch21; Marx v1 day88. 「〜に」 [time of occurrence]: DJG v1 p289 & 303.

4-4. まだ三グラムたりません。

まだ 三(さん) グラム たりません。

It's still three grams short.

「まだ〜」 ["still __"; "not yet __"]: DJG v1 p224; Genki ch9; Marx v1 day87.

4-5. ここ二、三日はあたたかいです。

ここ 二、三日(に、さんにち) は あたたかい です。

It's been warm the last few days. (87)

「**A は B だ**」 ["A is B"]: DJG v1 p521; Genki ch1; Marx v1 day8.

4-6. もう三日もログインしていません。

もう 三日(みっか) も ログイン して いません。

It's already three days since I've logged in.

「もう〜」 [changed state]: DJG v1 p254; Marx v1 day87. 「**Irregular verb:** する」: DJG v1 p578-79. 「-ている」 ["be __ing"; "have (done) __"]: DJG v1 p155; Genki ch7.

5：十

5-1. 十ぶんだ。
十ぶん(じゅうぶん)　だ。
That's plenty.

5-2. 二十キロやせた。
二十(にじゅっ)　キロ　やせた。
I lost twenty kilos.
「**Numerals**」: DJG v1 p602; Genki ch1-2; Marx v1 day78-80. 「**Past tense verbs**」: DJG v1 p576; Genki ch4&9; Marx v1 day31.

5-3. 二十になりました。
二十(はたち)　に　なりました。
I've turned twenty.
「**Past tense verbs**」: DJG v1 p576; Genki ch4&9; Marx v1 day31.

5-4. きょうは十日です。
きょう　は　十日(とおか)　です。
Today is the 10th.
「**A は B だ**」 ["A is B"]: DJG v1 p521; Genki ch1; Marx v1 day8.

5-5. 一から十までうるさい！
一(いち)　から　十(じゅう)　まで　うるさい！
I don't need all those details!
「〜から〜まで」 ["from __ to __"]: DJG v2 p99.

5-6. 一から十まで一々うるさい。
一(いち)　から　十(じゅう)　まで　一々(いちいち)　うるさい。
Fussy about every little thing.

5-7. トムは一をきいて十をしる。
トム　は　一(いち)　を　きいて　十(じゅう)　を　しる。
Tom can deduce a lot of information from the smallest clue.
「〜を」 [indicates direct object]: DJG v1 p347; Genki ch3; Marx v1 day9. 「-て / -で」 [connective form of verbs]: DJG v1 p464, v2 p64 of front matter; Genki ch6.

5-8. 一から十までいわないとわからないの？
一(いち)　から　十(じゅう)　まで　いわない　と　わからない　の？
Must I spell out every little thing?
「〜と」 ["if __"; "when __"]: DJG v1 p480; Genki ch18. 「わかる」 {分かる 88} ["understand"]: DJG v1 p529. 「の(?)」 [female: question marker]: DJG v1 p48.

5-9. かれはそれに十シリング十一ペンスついやした。

23

かれ は それ に 十(じゅう) シリング 十一(じゅういち) ペンス ついやした。

It had cost him ten and elevenpence. (51)

6：四

6-1. 四つんばい。
四つんばい(よつんばい)。
On all fours.

6-2. 四日ぶりです。
四日(よっか)ぶり です。
It's been four days.
「-ぶり」 {-振り * 903} ["for the first time in __"]: DJG v2 p343 (under -らい).

6-3. 四ミリながいです。
四(よん) ミリ ながい です。
It's four millimeters too long.

6-4. 四グラムにしてください。
四(よん) グラム に して ください。
Please make it four grams.
「**Irregular verb:** する」 : DJG v1 p578-79. 「〜にする」 ["opt for __"]: DJG v1 p310; Marx v2 day80. 「-てください」 {-て下さい 40} ["please __"]: DJG v1 p209; Genki ch6.

6-5. ドーナツを四つください。
ドーナツ を 四つ(よっつ) ください。
I'll have four doughnuts please.

6-6. 四かくいテーブルがほしい。
四かくい(しかくい) テーブル が ほしい。
I want a square table.
「〜がほしい」 {〜が欲しい 1035} ["want __"]: DJG v1 p144; Genki ch14.

6-7. 四ぶんの一がイギリスじん。
四(よん)ぶん の 一(いち) が イギリス じん。
A quarter are English.
「の」 [marks end of modifying phrase]: DJG v1 p312; Genki ch10.

7：五

7-1. バナナを五つください。
バナナ を 五つ(いつつ) ください。
Five bananas please.

7-2. 二十五リットルあります。
二十(にじゅう) 五(ご) リットル あります。

We've got 25 liters.

7-3. とうとう、十五になりました。
とうとう、 十五(じゅうご) に なりました。
At last her fifteenth birthday came. (55)
「とうとう〜」 ["finally __"]: DJG v2 p528; Tobira ch8 #17. 「**Past tense verbs**」: DJG v1 p576; Genki ch4&9; Marx v1 day31.

7-4. ハンバーガーを五つください。
ハンバーガー を 五つ(いつつ) ください。
Five hamburgers please.

7-5. ネロは十五で、アロアは十二だ。
ネロ は 十五(じゅうご) で、 アロア は 十二(じゅうに) だ。
Nello is fifteen now, and Alois is twelve. (29)
「**A** は **B** だ」 ["A is B"]: DJG v1 p521; Genki ch1; Marx v1 day8. 「-て/-で」 [connective form of verbs]: DJG v1 p464, v2 p64 of front matter; Genki ch6.

7-6. アントワープまでは五マイルありました。
アントワープ まで は 五(ご) マイル ありました。
Antwerp was a good five miles off. (29)
「〜まで」 {〜迄** 1806} ["until __"]: DJG v1 p225; Genki ch23.

8：六

8-1. 六ぶんの一。
六(ろく)ぶん の 一(いち)。
One-sixth.

8-2. 五、六日ある。
五(ご)、 六(ろく) 日(にち) ある。
We have five or six days.

8-3. むすめは十六です。
むすめ は 十六(じゅうろく) です。
My daughter is sixteen.
「**A** は **B** だ」 ["A is B"]: DJG v1 p521; Genki ch1; Marx v1 day8.

8-4. 六グラムふえました。
六(ろく) グラム ふえました。
It's increased by six grams.

8-5. 六メートルでいいですか。
六(ろく) メートル で いい です か。
Is six meters OK?
「〜で」 [instrument]: DJG v1 p106.

8-6. 六ページをみてください。

25

六(ろく) ページ を みて ください。
Please see page six.
「-てください」 {-て下さい 40} ["please __"]: DJG v1 p209; Genki ch6.

8-7. あれは四トントラックではありません。六トントラックです。
あれ は 四(よん) トン トラック で は ありません。 六(ろく) トン トラック です。
That is not a four-ton truck. It's a six-ton truck.
「こ / そ / あ / ど」: DJG v1 p600; Genki ch2; Marx v1 day16-17. 「**A** は **B** だ」 ["A is B"]: DJG v1 p521; Genki ch1; Marx v1 day8.

9 : 七

9-1. 七ぶんの一。
七(なな)ぶん の 一(いち)。
One-seventh.

9-2. 十七になりました。
十七(じゅうなな) に なりました。
I've turned seventeen.

9-3. きょうは七五三だ。
きょう は 七五三(しちごさん) だ。
Today is Shichi-go-san.

9-4. 十七日にあいましょう。
十七日(じゅうしちにち) に あいましょう。
Let's meet on the 17th.
「〜に」 [time of occurrence]: DJG v1 p289 & 303.

9-5. 二かける七は十四です。
二(に) かける 七(なな) は 十四(じゅうよん) です。
Two times seven is fourteen. (87)

9-6. 七十五メートルのロープ。
七十五(ななじゅうご) メートル の ロープ。
A seventy-five meter rope.
「の」 [marks end of modifying phrase]: DJG v1 p312; Genki ch10.

9-7. 七つのだいざいの一つだ。
七つ(ななつ) の だいざい の 一つ(ひとつ) だ。
It's one of the seven deadly sins.

9-8. このコンテナは七トンだ。
この コンテナ は 七(なな) トン だ。
This container is seven tons.
「こ / そ / あ / ど」: DJG v1 p600; Genki ch2; Marx v1 day16-17. 「**A** は **B** だ」 ["A is B"]: DJG v1 p521; Genki ch1; Marx v1 day8.

9-9. 七日にフリーマーケットがある。
　　七日(なのか)　に　フリー　マーケット　が　ある。
　　There's a flea market on the 7th.

10：八

10-1. 八十日でいける。
　　八十日(はちじゅうにち)　で　いける。
　　I can get there in eighty days.
　　「〜で」 [time]: DJG v1 p109. 「**Verbs of potential**」 ["can __"]: DJG v1 p370; Genki ch13; Marx v1 day50.

10-2. 八十日のあいだに。
　　八十日(はちじゅうにち)　の　あいだ　に。
　　In the space of eighty days.
　　「〜あいだに」 {〜間に 448} ["while __"]: DJG v1 p67; Genki ch21; Marx v1 day88. 「の」 [marks end of modifying phrase]: DJG v1 p312; Genki ch10.

10-3. 一か八かのチャンス。
　　一(いち)　か　八(ばち)　か　の　チャンス。
　　A sporting chance. (101)

10-4. 十八日、ひまですか。
　　十八日(じゅうはちにち)、　ひま　です　か。
　　Are you free on the eighteenth?

10-5. きょうは十八日です。
　　きょう　は　十八日(じゅうはちにち)　です。
　　Today is the eighteenth.

10-6. ネコはお八つがほしい。
　　ネコ　は　お八つ(おやつ)　が　ほしい。
　　The cat wants a snack.
　　「**A は B が C**」 [C describes something about B, as an attribute of subject A]: DJG v1 p525. 「**お-**」 [prefix expressing politeness]: DJG v1 p343. 「〜がほしい」 {〜が欲しい 1035} ["want __"]: DJG v1 p144; Genki ch14; Marx v1 day48.

10-7. のこりはもう二十八日しかなかった。
　　のこり　は　もう　二十八日(にじゅうはちにち)　しか　なかった。
　　There were only twenty-eight days left. (7)
　　「もう〜」 [changed state]: DJG v1 p254; Marx v1 day87. 「しか〜ない」 ["no more than __/no other than __"]: DJG v1 p398; Genki ch14; Marx v2 day40.

10-8. このケーキを八きれにきってください。
　　この　ケーキ　を　八(はち)　きれ　に　きって　ください。
　　Please cut this cake into eight slices.
　　「〜に」 ["to __", "toward __"]: DJG v1 p302 & 303.

27

11：九

11-1. 五十九です。
五十九(ごじゅうきゅう) です。
I am fifty-nine.

11-2. 十九せいき。
十九(じゅうきゅう) せいき。
The nineteenth century.

11-3. 九日めについた。
九日め(ここのかめ) に ついた。
We arrived on the ninth day.
「-め」{-目 21} ["__th"]: DJG v2 p174.

11-4. 九九をあんきする。
九九(くく) を あんき する。
Memorize the times table.

11-5. 九十ねんだいのヒット。
九十(きゅうじゅう) ねんだい の ヒット。
A hit from the nineties.

11-6. エリカは十九のむすめだ。
エリカ は 十九(じゅうきゅう) の むすめ だ。
Erika is a girl of nineteen.

11-7. ココナッツを九つください。
ココナッツ を 九(ここの)つ ください。
Nine coconuts, please.

12：丸

12-1. 丸くする。
丸く(まるく) する。
Make round. (100)

12-2. ポスターを丸める。
ポスター を 丸める(まるめる)。
Roll up a poster.
「**Transitive and intransitive verbs**」: DJG v1 p585; Genki ch18; Marx v1 day51.

12-3. 九九を丸あんきする。
九九(くく) を 丸(まる) あんき する。
Rotely memorize the times table.

12-4. これは丸くないです。
これ は 丸く(まるく)ない です。

This is not round.

12-5. 丸いテーブルがほしい。

丸い(まるい) テーブル が ほしい。

I want a round table.

「〜がほしい」 {〜が欲しい 1035} ["want __"]: DJG v1 p144; Genki ch14.

12-6. マットレスを丸めよう。

マットレス を 丸めよ(まるめよ)う。

Let's roll up the mattress.

「**Volitional**」 ["let's __"; "I'll __"]: DJG v1 p576 & 578 second column from right; Genki ch15; Marx v1 day29.

Note: Where a phonetic gloss displays text attached at the end of a parentheses with no intervening space [as with 丸めよ(まるめよ)う here], such text is being treated as part of the same word. This division of a single word on either side of a phonetic parenthesis most commonly occurs with conjugated verbs.

While I have implemented several procedures to make the word division as consistent as possible, the volume of manual adjustments required across the 30,000 exercises precluded me from attaining perfect consistency. Hence if you find 「二十一日(にじゅういちにち)」 in one place and 「二十(にじゅう) 一日(いちにち)」 in another, please take it in stride, as any such variations are completely without significance.

More generally, please note that the word division used in this series is meant only to be helpful, not authoritative. The artificial spacing of Japanese words is notoriously irregular and arbitrary. In lieu of analyzing too closely why the words in an exercise have been divided in a certain way, simply remember that any such word division is artificial and does not exist in real Japanese.

12-7. オポッサムが丸まっている。

オポッサム が 丸まっ(まるまっ)て いる。

The possum is all rolled up in a ball.

「**Transitive and intransitive verbs**」 : DJG v1 p585; Genki ch18; Marx v1 day51. 「-ている」 ["be __ing"; "have (done) __"]: DJG v1 p155; Genki ch7; Marx v1 day36.

12-8. チーム一丸となってたたかう。

チーム 一丸(いちがん) と なって たたかう。

We fight as a team.

「〜となる」 ["become __"]: DJG v2 p511. 「-て / -で」 [connective form of verbs]: DJG v1 p464, v2 p64 of front matter; Genki ch6; Marx v1 day30.

Note: Look for any differences between the appearance of the "chôonpu" (ー) in 「チーム」 and the "ichi" (一) in 「一丸」. In gothic (sans serif) fonts, the two may be identical.

12-9. この丸いくすりはなんですか。

この 丸い(まるい) くすり は なん です か。

What is this round medication?

13 : 円

13-1. 円をかく。

円(えん) を かく。

29

Draw a circle.

13-2. 円のかたち。
円(えん) の かたち。
A circular shape.

13-3. 円をつくる。
円(えん) を つくる。
Form a circle.

13-4. 円いクモのす。
円い(まるい) クモ の す。
A circular spider web (す = nest).

13-5. これは五十円です。
これ は 五十円(ごじゅうえん) です。
This costs fifty yen.

13-6. たったの九十円です。
たった の 九十円(きゅうじゅうえん) です。
It's only ninety yen.
「たった〜」 ["just __", "only __"]: DJG v2 p448 (under ただ〜); Tobira ch15 #7.

14：〇

14-1. アンケートに〇をつけた。
アンケート に 〇(まる) を つけた。
I marked "yes" (=circle mark) on the survey.
「〜に」 ["on __"]: DJG v1 p295 & 303.
Note: In this context, the circle mark conveys the same meaning as a check mark in English.

14-2. これは〇×のテストです。
これ は 〇×(まるバツ) の テスト です。
This is a true-false test.
Note: Elsewhere, × will be used to mark unlisted kanji (see "Unlisted kanji" in the Series Introduction). Here, it represents a "cross-out" mark (the opposite of the circle mark).

14-3. 九六〇円のオムライスをください。
九六〇円(きゅうひゃくろくじゅうえん) の オムライス を ください。
I'll have the 960-yen omuraisu (omelette-wrapped rice) please.

14-4. とりあえずかれを「〇〇さん」とよびましょう。
とりあえず かれ を 「〇〇(まるまる) さん」 と よびましょう。
Let's just call him "Mr. X" for now.
「とりあえず〜」 {取り敢えず〜* 59; 809} ["__ at once"; "__ for now"]. 「と」 [marks sound/manner or quoted speech]: DJG v1 p478. 「-ましょう」 ["I/we shall __"; "let's __"]: DJG v1 p240; Genki ch5; Marx v1 day29.

15：人

15-1.　一人につき十円。
　　　一人(ひとり)　につき　十円(じゅうえん)。
　　　Ten yen per person. (100)
　　　「～につき」 {～に付き* 64} ["per __"]: DJG v2 p283.

15-2.　七人のさむらい。
　　　七人(しちにん)　の　さむらい。
　　　The Seven Samurai.

15-3.　一人いくらですか？
　　　一人(ひとり)　いくら　です　か？
　　　How much does it cost for one person? (87)

15-4.　ヨーロッパの人々。
　　　ヨーロッパ　の　人々(ひとびと)。
　　　The people of Europe.

15-5.　あの人がきらいです。
　　　あの　人(ひと)　が　きらい　です。
　　　I don't like that person.
　　　「こ / そ / あ / ど」 : DJG v1 p600; Genki ch2; Marx v1 day16-17. 「～がきらいだ」{～が嫌いだ* 2058} ["dislike __"]: DJG v1 p190; Genki ch5; Marx v1 day41.

15-6.　一人ずつ、一人ずつ。
　　　一人(ひとり)ずつ、　一人(ひとり)ずつ。
　　　One at a time, one at a time. (90)
　　　「-ずつ」　["__ each"]: DJG v1 p572; Tobira ch11 #9.

15-7.　四人だけがのこります。
　　　四人(よにん)　だけ　が　のこります。
　　　Only four are left. (8)
　　　「～だけ」　["just __"]: DJG v1 p93; Marx v2 day39.

15-8.　やっと二人になれたね。
　　　やっと　二人(ふたり)　に　なれた　ね。
　　　The two of us are finally alone. (87)
　　　「やっと～」 ["finally __"]: DJG v2 p591. 「**Verbs of potential**」　["can __"]: DJG v1 p370; Genki ch13; Marx v1 day50. 「ね」 [speaker seeks confirmation or agreement]: DJG v1 p45 & 286; Genki ch2; Marx v2 day2.

15-9.　ロシア人のためのスパイ。
　　　ロシア人(じん)　の　ため　の　スパイ。
　　　A spy for the Russians. (101)
　　　「～ため(に)」 {～為に* 1236} ["for (the sake of) __"]: DJG v1 p447; Tobira ch2 #6.

15-10.　アダムはユダヤ人である。

アダム は ユダヤ人(じん) で ある。

Adam is Jewish. (101)

「である vs. だ」: DJG v2 p30, v3 p35 of front matter; Tobira ch7 #5.

15-11. わたしは、一人になりたい。

わたし は、 一人(ひとり) に なりたい。

I want to be alone. (101)

「-たい」 ["want to __"]: DJG v1 p441; Genki ch11; Marx v1 day48.

15-12. ジェーンはどんな人ですか。

ジェーン は どんな 人(ひと) です か。

What kind of person is Jane? (87)

「こ / そ / あ / ど」: DJG v1 p600; Genki ch2; Marx v1 day16-17.

15-13. チケットは、一人5ドルである。

チケット は、 一人(ひとり) 5 ドル で ある。

Tickets are $5 per head. (101)

15-14. 三人とも、すごくラッキーだね。

三人(さんにん) とも、 すごく ラッキー だ ね。

All three of you are very lucky. (87)

「〜とも」 ["both/all __"; "(n)either (of) __"]. 「ね」 [speaker seeks confirmation or agreement]: DJG v1 p45 & 286; Genki ch2; Marx v2 day2.

15-15. 五十人のメンバーのうちの一人。

五十人(ごじゅうにん) の メンバー の うち の 一人(ひとり)。

One of the fifty members. (100)

15-16. かれらも六人、われらも六人だ。

かれら も 六人(ろくにん)、 われら も 六人(ろくにん) だ。

Six they are, and six are we. (90)

「-ら」 {-等* 393} [plural personal pronoun suffix]: DJG v1 p28 bottom & 440, v3 p47 & 50-51 of front matter (under -たち); Tobira ch9 #12. 「〜も〜も」 ["both __ and __"; "neither __ nor __"]: DJG v1 p255, v2 p185; Marx v2 day14; Tobira ch6 #3.

15-17. ぼくたち、二人っきりなんだよ。

ぼくたち、 二人(ふたり)っきり なん だ よ。

We are all alone, you and I. (29)

「ぼく」 {僕 1358} [informal: "I"]: DJG v1 p28. 「-たち」 {-達 1475} [plural personal pronoun suffix]: DJG v1 p28 bottom & 440, v3 p47 & 50-51 of front matter. 「〜(っ)きり」 ["since __"; "only __"]: DJG v3 p219. 「〜よ」 [assertion]: DJG v1 p46-47 examples 12-13 and 15; Genki ch2; Marx v1 day11.

15-18. ここにはコドモは一人もいません。

ここ に は コドモ は 一人(ひとり) も いません。

There are no children here. (64)

「こ / そ / あ / ど」: DJG v1 p600; Genki ch2; Marx v1 day16-17. 「〜に」 [location of existence]: DJG v1 p299 & 303. 「〜も」 ["even __"]: DJG v1 p250; Genki ch14.

15-19. イギリス人はテレビをテリーとよぶ。

イギリス人(じん) は テレビ を テリー と よぶ。

The British call a TV set a telly. (101)

15-20. かれらはアメリカ人ではないらしい。

かれら は アメリカ人(じん) で は ない らしい。

They don't seem to be Americans. (87)

「ではない vs. じゃない」: DJG v3 p35 of front matter. 「〜らしい」 ["(it) seems (that) __", "I heard (that) __"; "__-like"]: DJG v1 p373; Marx v2 day70; Tobira ch5 #13.

15-21. あの二人はどうもできているらしい。

あの 二人(ふたり) は どうも できて いる らしい。

They seem to be in love with each other. (87)

「どうも」 ["somehow"; "no matter how"]: DJG v2 p36. 「-ている」 ["be __ing"; "have (done) __"]: DJG v1 p155; Genki ch7; Marx v1 day36.

15-22. ジョルダンはもう一人ではありません。

ジョルダン は もう 一人(ひとり) で は ありません。

Jordan isn't alone anymore. (87)

「もう〜」 [changed state]: DJG v1 p254; Marx v1 day87.

15-23. トムはうちのバンドのボーカルの一人です。

トム は うち の バンド の ボーカル の 一人(ひとり) です。

Tom is one of the singers in my band. (87)

15-24. エジプト人はかれらのファラオをミイラにした。

エジプト人(じん) は かれら の ファラオ を ミイラ に した。

The Egyptians mummified their pharaohs. (101)

「**Irregular verb:** する」: DJG v1 p578-79.

15-25. サッカーは十一人で一丸となってたたかうスポーツです。

サッカー は 十一人(じゅういちにん) で 一丸(いちがん) と なって たたかう スポーツ です。

In soccer, all eleven players compete as one unit.

「〜となる」 ["become __"]: DJG v2 p511.

15-26. ロシア人は astronaut を cosmonaut とよぶ。

ロシア人(じん) は astronaut を cosmonaut と よぶ。

The Russians call their astronauts cosmonauts. (101)

「と」 [marks sound/manner or quoted speech]: DJG v1 p478.

16：百

16-1. 九百トン。

九百(きゅうひゃく) トン。

Nine hundred tons.

16-2. 百日ぜき。
　　百日ぜき(ひゃくにちぜき)。
　　Whooping-cough.

16-3. 百人に一人。
　　百人(ひゃくにん) に 一人(ひとり)。
　　One person in a hundred.

16-4. 百人がきました。
　　百人(ひゃくにん) が きました。
　　A hundred people came.
　　「くる」 {来る 274} ["come"]: DJG v1 p219. 「**Irregular verb:** くる」 : DJG v1 p578-79.

16-5. このノートは百円です。
　　この ノート は 百円(ひゃくえん) です。
　　This notebook costs one hundred yen.

16-6. 三百円のケーキにしようか。
　　三百円(さんびゃくえん) の ケーキ に しよう か。
　　What do you say we just order the three hundred yen cake?
　　「〜にする」 ["opt for __"]: DJG v1 p310; Marx v2 day80. 「**Irregular verb:** する」 : DJG v1 p578-79. 「**Volitional**」 ["let's __"; "I'll __"]: DJG v1 p576 & 578 second column from right; Genki ch15; Marx v1 day29.

17：千

17-1. 八千円のワイン。
　　八千円(はっせんえん) の ワイン。
　　An eight thousand yen wine.

17-2. 一千ボルトのレール。
　　一千(いっせん) ボルト の レール。
　　A one thousand volt rail.

17-3. 千円でおねがいします。
　　千円(せんえん) で おねがい します。
　　Please take it out of one thousand yen.
　　「〜で」 [instrument]: DJG v1 p106; Genki ch10. 「お-〜する」 [polite description of action by oneself or another ingroup person]: DJG v1 p39 bottom; Genki ch20. 「ねがう/ねがいます」 {願う / 願います 214} [request]: DJG v3 p377.

17-4. ぼくは二千八百円をはらった！
　　ぼく は 二千(にせん) 八百円(はっぴゃくえん) を はらった！
　　I paid 2,800 yen!
　　「ぼく」 {僕 1358} [informal: "I"]: DJG v1 p28.

17-5. ホンコンから千六百六十マイルだ。

ホンコン　から　千(せん)　六百(ろっぴゃく)　六十(ろくじゅう)　マイル　だ。

It is sixteen hundred and sixty miles from Hong Kong. (7)

「〜から」　["from ＿"]: DJG v1 p176.

18：万

18-1. 一千万円。

一千万円(いっせんまんえん)。

Ten million yen. (100)

18-2. 百万ぶんの一。

百万(ひゃくまん)ぶん　の　一(いち)。

One millionth.

18-3. １万円でたりる？

１万円(まんえん)　で　たりる？

Is ten thousand yen enough? (87)

18-4. 六千万円のヨット。

六千万円(ろくせんまんえん)　の　ヨット。

A sixty million yen yacht.

18-5. 五万五千ポンドですよ！

五万(ごまん)　五千(ごせん)　ポンド　です　よ！

Fifty-five thousand pounds! (7)

「〜よ」　[assertion]: DJG v1 p46-47 examples 12-13 and 15; Genki ch2.

18-6. 一万円おあずかりします。

一万円(いちまんえん)　おあずかり　します。

[Cashier, when receiving cash from a customer] Out of ten thousand yen.

「お-〜する」　[polite description of action by oneself or another ingroup person]: DJG v1 p39 bottom; Genki ch20.

18-7. このアパートは三千万円かかる。

この　アパート　は　三千万円(さんぜんまんえん)　かかる。

This apartment costs thirty million yen.

「かかる」　{掛かる* 1117}　["hang"; "be caught"]: Marx v1 day52.

18-8. 万一いけなかったら、メールする。

万一(まんいち)　いけなかったら、　メール　する。

If by some chance I'm unable to go, I'll text you.

「**Verbs of potential**」　["can ＿"]: DJG v1 p370; Genki ch13; Marx v1 day50.　「-たら」　["if ＿"; "when ＿"]: DJG v1 p452; Genki ch17; Marx v2 day21.

19：口

19-1. 一口のエール。

一口(ひとくち)　の　エール。
A sup of ale. (101)

19-2. おいしい一口。
おいしい　一口(ひとくち)。
A tasty morsel. (101)

19-3. 一口ちょうだい。
一口(ひとくち)　ちょうだい。
Let me have a small piece.

19-4. 一口だけたべる。
一口(ひとくち)　だけ　たべる。
Take small bites of. (100)
「〜だけ」　["just __"]: DJG v1 p93; Marx v2 day39.

19-5. 人口六百九十五人。
人口(じんこう)　六百(ろっぴゃく)　九十(きゅうじゅう)　五人(ごにん)。
Population six hundred ninety-five.

19-6. そんなことは口にするなよ。
そんな　こと　は　口(くち)　に　する　な　よ。
Don't say such a thing.
「こ/そ/あ/ど」: DJG v1 p600; Genki ch2; Marx v1 day16-17. 「こと」{事 80} [intangible thing]: DJG v1 p191; Tobira ch7 (first page). 「**infinitive + な**」 [prohibitive: "don't __"]: DJG v1 p266; Marx v1 day40. 「〜よ」 [assertion]: DJG v1 p46-47 examples 12-13 and 15; Genki ch2; Marx v1 day11.

19-7. ジョージアのスラブ人の人口。
ジョージア　の　スラブ人(じん)　の　人口(じんこう)。
The Slav population of Georgia. (101)

19-8. フランスの人口はなん人ですか？
フランス　の　人口(じんこう)　は　なん人(にん)　です　か？
What is the population of France? (87)

20：田

20-1. 田んぼみち。
田んぼ(たんぼ)　みち。
A path passing between rice paddies.

20-2. ガス田をいかす。
ガス田(でん)　を　いかす。
Exploit a gas field.

20-3. あの人は田口さんです。
あの　人(ひと)　は　田口(たぐち)さん　です。

That's Taguchi-san.

Note: This series usually leaves untranslated the name suffix "-san" and the title "-sensei", as these terms often don't translate smoothly into English, and in any event are commonly understood. Leaving "-san" untranslated also prevents the awkwardness of gendering the translation (with "Mr." or "Ms.") when the original is ungendered.

20-4. 三田の人口は六百九十五万人です。

三田(みた) の 人口(じんこう) は 六百(ろっぴゃく) 九十(きゅうじゅう) 五万人(ごまんにん) です。

The population of Mita is six million nine hundred fifty thousand (6,950,000).

21：目

21-1. ラマダンの 10 日目。

ラマダン の 10 日目(とおかめ)。

The tenth day of Ramadan. (100)

21-2. 人目をひくポスター。

人目(ひとめ) を ひく ポスター。

Eye-catching posters. (101)

21-3. あなたで六人目です。

あなた で 六人目(ろくにんめ) です。

You're the sixth person.

「あなた」{貴方 1177; 173} [formal: "you"]: DJG v1 p28.

21-4. ひどい目にあいますよ。

ひどい 目(め) に あいます よ。

You'll have a rough time. (87)

「～に」["to __", "toward __"]: DJG v1 p302 & 303. 「～よ」 [assertion]: DJG v1 p46-47 examples 12-13 and 15; Genki ch2; Marx v1 day11.

21-5. 丸い田んぼがすぐ目についた。

丸い(まるい) 田んぼ(たんぼ) が すぐ 目(め) に ついた。

The round rice paddy caught my eye immediately. (10)

「すぐ」 ["immediately"; "directly"]: DJG v2 p439. 「～に」 ["to __", "toward __"]: DJG v1 p302 & 303.

21-6. わたしの目がヒリヒリしている。

わたし の 目(め) が ヒリヒリ して いる。

My eyes are burning. (101)

「-ている」 ["be __ing"; "have (done) __"]: DJG v1 p155; Genki ch7; Marx v1 day36.

21-7. またいつかお目にかかりましょう。

また いつか お目にかかり(おめにかかり)ましょう。

I hope to see you sometime. (87)

「いつか」{何時か** 815; 383} ["sometime"]: Marx v1 day18. 「～に」 [marks agent/source]: DJG v1 p292 & 303. 「かかる」 {掛かる* 1117} ["hang"; "be caught"]: Marx

37

v1 day52. 「-ましょう」 ["I/we shall __"; "let's __"]: DJG v1 p240; Genki ch5; Marx v1 day29. 「**Irregular humble polite forms**」 : DJG v1 p40; Genki ch20.

21-8. 人目につかないロマンチックなスポット。

    人目(ひとめ) に つかない ロマンチック な スポット。

  A secluded romantic spot. (101)

  「〜に」 [marks agent/source]: DJG v1 p292 & 303.

21-9. えらいオズにお目にかかりにきたのです。

    えらい オズ に お目(め)にかかり に きた の です。

  We came here to see the Great Oz. (99)

  「**Verb stem + に + verb of motion**」 ["(go) __ing"; "(go) to (do) __"]: DJG v1 p297; Genki ch7; Tobira ch3 #9. 「くる」 {来る 274} ["come"]: DJG v1 p219. 「**Irregular verb:** くる」 : DJG v1 p578-79. 「のである／のです／のだ／んだ」 [explanation or assertion]: DJG v1 p325; Genki ch12.

21-10. ここから一千の田んぼが一目でみえるのです。

    ここ から 一千(いっせん) の 田(た)んぼ が 一目(ひとめ) で みえる の です。

  From here you can look out on one thousand rice fields.

  「〜で」 [instrument]: DJG v1 p106; Genki ch10. 「〜みえる」 {〜見える 83} ["__ can be seen"; "looks __"]: DJG v1 p243; Marx v1 day50, v2 day69. 「のである／のです／のだ／んだ」 [explanation or assertion]: DJG v1 p325; Genki ch12.

22：川

22-1. あの川は千田川です。

    あの 川(かわ) は 千田川(せんだがわ) です。

  That's the Sendagawa (River).

22-2. 田川さんは川口にすんでいる。

    田川(たがわ)さん は 川口(かわぐち) に すんで いる。

  Tagawa-san lives in Kawaguchi (municipality).

  「〜に」 [location of existence]: DJG v1 p299 & 303. 「〜にすむ」 {〜に住む 366} ["live in (a particular place)" - generally conjugated in -ている form]. 「-ている」 ["be __ing"; "have (done) __"]: DJG v1 p155; Genki ch7; Marx v1 day36.

22-3. 田口さんは四川にすんでいる。

    田口(たぐち)さん は 四川(しせん) に すんで いる。

  Taguchi-san lives in Sichuan (Chinese province).

22-4. ここから川口が一目でみえるんだ。

    ここ から 川口(かわぐち) が 一目(ひとめ) で みえる ん だ。

  From here you can look out over the river mouth.

  「〜で」 [instrument]: DJG v1 p106; Genki ch10. 「〜みえる」 {〜見える 83} ["__ can be seen"; "looks __"]: DJG v1 p243; Marx v1 day50, v2 day69. 「のである／のです／のだ／んだ」 [explanation or assertion]: DJG v1 p325; Genki ch12.

23：月

23-1. 三日月。

三日月(みかづき)。

A falcate [crescent] moon. (101)

23-2. きょうは3月8日です。

きょう は 3月(がつ) 8日(ようか) です。

Today is March 8.

23-3. きょうは十月一日です。

きょう は 十月(じゅうがつ) 一日(ついたち) です。

Today is October 1.

23-4. お日さまも、お月さまも。

お日(ひ)さま も、 お月(つき)さま も。

Both the sun and the moon. (98)

「お-」 [prefix expressing politeness]: DJG v1 p343.「〜も〜も」 ["both __ and __"; "neither __ nor __"]: DJG v1 p255, v2 p185; Marx v2 day14; Tobira ch6 #3.

23-5. 1月9日、4日まえのことだ。

1月(がつ) 9日(ここのか)、 4日(よっか) まえ の こと だ。

On the ninth of January, now four days ago. (84)

「こと」{事 80} [intangible thing]: DJG v1 p191; Tobira ch7 (first page).

23-6. クリスマスは12月25日です。

クリスマス は 12月(がつ) 25日(にち) です。

Christmas is December 25th. (87)

24：明

24-1. 明るくなる。

明るく(あかるく) なる。

Become light. (100)

24-2. 明らかになる。

明(あき)らか に なる。

Become manifest. (100)

24-3. 目に明らかな。

目(め) に 明(あき)らか な。

Obvious to the eye. (100)

「〜に」 ["to __", "toward __"]: DJG v1 p302 & 303.

24-4. 明月の明かり。

明月(めいげつ) の 明(あ)かり。

A bright moon's light.

24-5. このミスは明らかだ。

39

この　ミス　は　明(あき)らか　だ。
This error is obvious.

24-6. 明日は七五三ですよ。
明日(あした)　は　七五三(しちごさん)　です　よ。
Tomorrow is *Shichi-go-san*.
「〜よ」 [assertion]: DJG v1 p46-47 examples 12-13 and 15; Genki ch2.

24-7. ランプからの明かり。
ランプ　から　の　明かり(あかり)。
Light from a lamp. (100)
「〜から」 ["from __"]: DJG v1 p176.

24-8. 明日はテストがあります。
明日(あした)　は　テスト　が　あります。
We have a test tomorrow. (87)

24-9. 川口さんは明るい人ですね。
川口(かわぐち)さん　は　明るい(あかるい)　人(ひと)　です　ね。
Kawaguchi-san sure is cheerful.
「ね」 [speaker seeks confirmation or agreement]: DJG v1 p45 & 286; Genki ch2.

24-10. 月明かりがとてもきれいです。
月明かり(つきあかり)　が　とても　きれい　です。
The moonlight is lovely.
「とても〜」 ["quite __"]: DJG v2 p210 (under なかなか〜); Marx v2 day47.

25：曜

25-1. きょうは月曜です。
きょう　は　月曜(げつよう)　です。
Today is Monday.

25-2. 明日は日曜日です。
明日(あした)　は　日曜日(にちようび)　です。
Tomorrow is Sunday.

25-3. はい、明日の月曜に。
はい、　明日(あした)　の　月曜(げつよう)　に。
Yes, for tomorrow, Monday. (7)
「〜に」 [time of occurrence]: DJG v1 p289 & 303.

25-4. 明日はなん曜日ですか。
明日(あした)　は　なん曜日(ようび)　です　か。
What day is tomorrow?

25-5. きょうはなん曜日ですか。
きょう　は　なん曜日(ようび)　です　か。

What's the date today?

25-6. 明日の月曜でいいですか。
明日(あした) の 月曜(げつよう) で いい です か。
Would tomorrow Monday be all right?

25-7. 田川さん、日曜日になにをしましたか。
田川(たがわ)さん、 日曜日(にちようび) に なに を しました か。
Tagawa-san, what did you do on Sunday?

Note: If you wish to review the KLC entry of any kanji appearing in these examples, you can quickly find its entry number using the cross-reference number file posted at keystojapanese.com/klc-grs-cross-refs.

26：火

26-1. 火口をつける。
火口(ひぐち) を つける。
Light a fuse [pilot burner]. (101)

26-2. この火はあつい。
この 火(ひ) は あつい。
This fire is hot.

26-3. タバコに火をつける。
タバコ に 火(ひ) を つける。
Light a cigarette. (101)
「〜に」 ["to __", "toward __"]: DJG v1 p302 & 303.

26-4. 明日の火曜でいいかい。
明日(あした) の 火曜(かよう) で いい かい。
Is tomorrow Tuesday OK?
「かい」 [male alternative to か]: DJG v1 p48 middle & 170.

26-5. 田川さんは口火をきった。
田川(たがわ)さん は 口火(くちび) を きった。
Tagawa-san started in (on all he had to say).

27：水

27-1. 水はなかった。
水(みず) は なかった。
We had no water.

27-2. お水をください。
お水(みず) を ください。
Can I have some water, please? (87)
「お-」 [prefix expressing politeness]: DJG v1 p343.

27-3. 水を火にかける。
　　　水(みず) を 火(ひ) に かける。
　　　Heat some water.
　　　「〜に」 ["on __"]: DJG v1 p295 & 303.

27-4. ソーダ水ください。
　　　ソーダ水(すい) ください。
　　　Sparkling water please.

27-5. バケツに水がない。
　　　バケツ に 水(みず) が ない。
　　　There's no water in the bucket. (87)
　　　「〜に」 [location of existence]: DJG v1 p299 & 303.

27-6. 水っぽいコーヒー。
　　　水っぽい(みずっぽい) コーヒー。
　　　Watery coffee. (101)
　　　「-っぽい」 [" __like"]: DJG v2 p337; Marx v2 day68.

27-7. 川口さんは月水しごとです。
　　　川口(かわぐち)さん は 月水(げっすい) しごと です。
　　　Kawaguchi-san works on Mondays and Wednesdays.

27-8. この川の水はとてもきれいだ。
　　　この 川(かわ) の 水(みず) は とても きれい だ。
　　　The water in this river is very clean. (87)
　　　「とても〜」 ["quite __"]: DJG v2 p210 (under なかなか〜); Marx v2 day47.

27-9. 川田さんは月曜日と水曜日しごとです。
　　　川田(かわだ)さん は 月曜日(げつようび) と 水曜日(すいようび) しごと です。
　　　Kawada-san works on Mondays and Wednesdays.

27-10. 田口さんは水曜日にアルバイトをします。
　　　田口(たぐち)さん は 水曜日(すいようび) に アルバイト を します。
　　　Taguchi-san works a part-time job on Wednesdays.

27-11. 「田」は、「田んぼ」や「水田」ともいう。
　　　「田(た)」 は、 「田(た)んぼ」 や 「水田(すいでん)」 と も いう。
　　　"Ta" (rice fields) are also called "tanbo" or "suiden".
　　　「や」 ["and" within a non-exhaustive list; cf. と]: DJG v1 p536; Genki ch11; Marx v1 day57. 「と」 [marks sound/manner or quoted speech]: DJG v1 p478. 「も」 ["also __"]: DJG v1 p247; Genki ch2&4.

28：木

28-1. 木目にそって。
    木目(もくめ) に そって。
    With the grain.
    「〜に」 ["to __", "toward __"]: DJG v1 p302 & 303. 「-て/-で」 [connective form of verbs]: DJG v1 p464, v2 p64 of front matter; Genki ch6; Marx v1 day30.

28-2. 木々のカーテン。
    木々(きぎ) の カーテン。
    A curtain of trees. (101)

28-3. レモンの木に水をやる。
    レモン の 木(き) に 水(みず) を やる。
    Water the lemon tree. (100)
    「〜に」 [marks indirect object]: DJG v1 p291 & 303.

28-4. 8月4日は木曜日ですか。
    8月(がつ) 4日(よっか) は 木曜日(もくようび) です か。
    Is August 4 a Thursday?

28-5. 月曜から木曜までここにいます。
    月曜(げつよう) から 木曜(もくよう) まで ここ に います。
    I will be here from Monday to Thursday. (87)
    「〜から〜まで」 ["from __ to __"]: DJG v2 p99.

28-6. わたしは木こりで、ブリキでできています。
    わたし は 木こり(きこり) で、 ブリキ で できて います。
    I am a woodman, and made of tin. (99)
    「-て/-で」 [connective form of verbs]: DJG v1 p464, v2 p64 of front matter; Genki ch6; Marx v1 d30. 「〜でできる」 {〜で出来る 38; 274} ["be made of __"]: Tobira ch1 #1.

29：金

29-1. お金がかかる。
    お金(おかね) が かかる。
    It costs money.
    「お-」 [prefix expressing politeness]: DJG v1 p343.

29-2. 金曜日のことでした。
    金曜日(きんようび) の こと でした。
    It was on a Friday.
    「〜のこと」 {〜の事* 80} ["about __"]: DJG v2 p304.

29-3. これは田川さんのお金です。
    これ は 田川(たがわ)さん の お金(おかね) です。
    This money belongs to Tagawa-san.

29-4. 18カラット金は75%が金。

18 カラット　金(きん)　は　75%(パーセント)　が　金(きん)。
18-karat gold is 75% gold. (100)
「AはBがC」 [C describes something about B, as an attribute of subject A]: DJG v1 p525.

29-5. 八木さんはまったくお金がない。
八木(やぎ)さん　は　まったく　お金(おかね)　が　ない。
Yagi-san hasn't any money whatsoever.
「AはBがC」 [C describes something about B, as an attribute of subject A]: DJG v1 p525.

29-6. 金田さんはお金にとてもケチである。
金田(かねだ)さん　は　お金(おかね)　に　とても　ケチ　で　ある。
Kaneda-san is very tight with money. (101)
「〜に」 ["to __", "toward __"]: DJG v1 p302 & 303.

29-7. 三木さんは田口さんにたくさんのお金をあげた。
三木(みき)さん　は　田口(たぐち)さん　に　たくさん　の　お金(おかね)　を　あげた。
Miki-san gave Taguchi-san a lot of money.
「〜に」 [marks indirect object]: DJG v1 p291 & 303. 「たくさん」 {沢山* 1504; 37} ["a lot of"]: DJG v1 p356 (under おおい); Genki ch4. 「あげる」 {上げる* 41} ["give (to someone)"]: DJG v1 p63; Genki ch14; Marx v2 day30.

29-8. 金丸さんのカバンは金の口金が二つついている。
金丸(かなまる)さん　の　カバン　は　金(きん)　の　口金(くちがね)　が　二(ふた)つ　ついて　いる。
Kanamaru-san's bag has two gold clasps.
「AはBがC」 [C describes sth. about B, as an attribute of subject A]: DJG v1 p525. 「-ている」 ["be __ing"; "have (done) __"]: DJG v1 p155; Genki ch7; Marx v1 day36.

30：土

30-1. 土となる。
土(つち)　と　なる。
Die; be laid to rest.
「〜となる」 ["become __"]: DJG v2 p511.

30-2. 土がつく。
土(つち)　が　つく。
Hit the dirt; be defeated.

30-3. 水田の土木。
水田(すいでん)　の　土木(どぼく)。
The engineering of rice paddies.

30-4. 土日に土いじりする。
土日(どにち)　に　土(つち)いじり　する。

44

On weekends I putter around in the garden.
「〜に」 [time of occurrence]: DJG v1 p289 & 303.

30-5. 土日は人がすくない。
土日(どにち) は 人(ひと) が すくない。
It's not crowded on weekends.
「A は B が C」 [C describes sth. about B, as an attribute of subject A]: DJG v1 p525. 「すくない」 {少ない 677} ["few"; "little"]: DJG v1 p427.

30-6. 土曜日にお金をもらう。
土曜日(どようび) に お金(おかね) を もらう。
I will get paid on Saturday.
「〜に」 [time of occurrence]: DJG v1 p289 & 303. 「もらう」 {貰う* 1160} ["receive"]: DJG v1 p261; Genki ch14; Marx v2 day30.

30-7. 三木さんは土曜日にパーティにいく。
三木(みき)さん は 土曜日(どようび) に パーティ に いく。
Miki-san's going to the party on Saturday.
「〜に」 [time of occurrence]: DJG v1 p289 & 303. 「〜に」 ["to __", "toward __"]: DJG v1 p302 & 303.

30-8. 土田さんはたくさんお金をもっている。
土田(つちだ)さん は たくさん お金(おかね) を もって いる。
Tsuchida-san has a lot of money.
「たくさん」 {沢山* 1504; 37} ["a lot of"]: DJG v1 p356 (under おおい); Genki ch4.

31 : 本

31-1. 二本のパイプ。
二本(にほん) の パイプ。
Two pipes. (101)

31-2. ヨーロッパ本土。
ヨーロッパ 本土(ほんど)。
The European mainland. (100)

31-3. 一本のダイナマイト。
一本(いっぽん) の ダイナマイト。
A stick of dynamite. (101)

31-4. ロゼを一本ください。
ロゼ を 一本(いっぽん) ください。
We'd like a bottle of rosé. (87)

31-5. 金田さんは日本人です。
金田(かねだ)さん は 日本人(にほんじん) です。
Kaneda-san is Japanese.

31-6. 水川さんは日本からきた。

45

水川(みずかわ)さん　は　日本(にほん)　から　きた。
Mizukawa-san has come from Japan.
「くる」 {来る 274} ["come"]: DJG v1 p219.

31-7. 本田さんの本がなくなった。
本田(ほんだ)さん　の　本(ほん)　が　なくなった。
Honda-san lost his book.

31-8. 本人は本日、日本にいません。
本人(ほんにん)　は　本日(ほんじつ)、　日本(にほん)　に　いません。
The person in question is not in Japan today.
「〜に」 [location of existence]: DJG v1 p299 & 303.

31-9. 本日は木曜日、12月15日です。
本日(ほんじつ)　は　木曜日(もくようび)、　12月(がつ)　15日(にち)　です。
Today is Thursday, December 15.

31-10. 川本さんは三本のリボンをきった。
川本(かわもと)さん　は　三本(さんぼん)　の　リボン　を　きった。
Kawamoto-san cut three ribbons.

31-11. 土田さんは二本目の木でとまった。
土田(つちだ)さん　は　二本目(にほんめ)　の　木(き)　で　とまった。
Tsuchida-san stopped at the second tree.

31-12. 明くんは木が一本ある田んぼをかった。
明(あきら)くん　は　木(き)　が　一本(いっぽん)　ある　田んぼ(たんぼ)　を　かった。
Akira bought a rice paddy containing one tree.

31-13. 日本の人口はアメリカのよりもすくない。
日本(にほん)　の　人口(じんこう)　は　アメリカ　の　より　も　すくない。
The population of Japan is less than that of America. (87)
「すくない」 {少ない 677} ["few"; "little"]: DJG v1 p427.

32：東

32-1. 東インドの木。
東(ひがし)　インド　の　木(き)。
An East Indian tree. (100)

32-2. 東口であおう。
東口(ひがしぐち)　で　あおう。
Let's meet at the East Exit.
「**Volitional**」 ["let's __"; "I'll __"]: DJG v1 p576 & 578 second column from right; Genki ch15; Marx v1 day29.

32-3. 日は東からのぼる。
　　　日(ひ)　は　東(ひがし)　から　のぼる。
　　　The sun rises in the east.
　　　「〜から」　["from __"]: DJG v1 p176.

32-4. 東日本の人口は五千九百万人です。
　　　東日本(ひがしにほん)　の　人口(じんこう)　は　五千(ごせん)　九百(きゅうひゃく)　万人(まんにん)　です。
　　　The population of Eastern Japan is fifty-nine million.

33：大

33-1. 大したことがない。
　　　大した(たいした)　こと　が　ない。
　　　It's no big deal. (100)
　　　「こと」　{事 80}　[intangible thing]: DJG v1 p191; Tobira ch7 (first page).

33-2. 目がかなり大きい！
　　　目(め)　が　かなり　大(おお)きい！
　　　Your eyes are so big!

33-3. このジャーは口が大きい。
　　　この　ジャー　は　口(くち)　が　大(おお)きい。
　　　This jar has a wide mouth.

33-4. テキサスは日本より大きい。
　　　テキサス　は　日本(にほん)　より　大(おお)きい。
　　　Texas is larger than Japan.

33-5. 東口に大きな木が四本ある。
　　　東口(ひがしぐち)　に　大(おお)きな　木(き)　が　四本(よんほん)　ある。
　　　There are four large trees by the east exit.
　　　「〜に」　[location of existence]: DJG v1 p299 & 303.

33-6. 大川さんは大人になりたくない。
　　　大川(おおかわ)さん　は　大人(おとな)　に　なりたくない。
　　　Okawa-san does not want to grow up.
　　　「-たくない」　[negative form of -たい ("want to __"): "do not want to __"]: DJG v1 p441; Genki ch11; Marx v1 day48.

33-7. 大木さんにとって八百万円は大金です。
　　　大木(おおき)さん　に　とって　八百(はっぴゃく)　万円(まんえん)　は　大金(たいきん)　です。
　　　To Oki-san eight million yen is a large sum of money.
　　　「〜にとって」　["as far as __ is concerned", "for/to __"]: DJG v2 p278; Marx v2 day82; Tobira ch2 #4.

47

33-8. 目の大きい川本さんは東口でまっていた。
　　　目(め) の 大(おお)きい 川本(かわもと)さん は 東口(ひがしぐち) で まって いた。
　　　Big-eyed Kawamoto-san waited at the east exit.
　　　「～で」 [location]: DJG v1 p105. 「-ている」 ["be __ing"; "have (done) __"]: DJG v1 p155; Genki ch7; Marx v1 day36.

33-9. 日本とイギリスではどちらが大きいのですか。
　　　日本(にほん) と イギリス で は どちら が 大(おお)きい の です か。
　　　Which is larger, Japan or Britain? (87)
　　　「のである / のです / のだ / んだ」 [explanation or assertion]: DJG v1 p325; Genki ch12.

33-10. むかしは六本木に六本の大きな木がありました。
　　　むかし は 六本木(ろっぽんぎ) に 六本(ろっぽん) の 大(おお)きな 木(き) が ありました。
　　　In the old days there were six large trees in Roppongi [a Tokyo neighborhood].

33-11. 丸くて、サッカーボールくらいの大きさだった。
　　　丸く(まるく)て、 サッカー ボール くらい の 大き(おおき)さ だった。
　　　It was a round thing, the size of a football [soccer ball]. (89)
　　　「-て / -で」 [connective form of adjectives]: DJG v1 p464; Marx v1 day66. 「～くらい」 {～位* 577} ["about __"]: DJG v1 p212; Marx v2 day78. 「-さ」 ["__ness"]: DJG v1 p381; Marx v1 day67; Tobira ch1 #2. 「だった」 [past tense of copula だ]: DJG v1 p580 bottom; Genki ch9; Marx v1 day37.

33-12. 土曜日に大田さんとあえるチャンスが大いにある。
　　　土曜日(どようび) に 大田(おおた)さん と あえる チャンス が 大(おお)いに ある。
　　　There's a great chance I'll be able to get together with Ota-san on Saturday.
　　　「～と」 ["with __"]: DJG v1 p476; Genki ch4. **「Verbs of potential」** ["can __"]: DJG v1 p370; Genki ch13.

34：小

34-1. 日本は小さいが、人口がおおい。
　　　日本(にほん) は 小(ちい)さい が、 人口(じんこう) が おおい。
　　　Japan is small, but its population is large.

34-2. 田んぼによくいる小さいフィンチ。
　　　田んぼ(たんぼ) に よく いる 小(ちい)さい フィンチ。
　　　A small finch that frequents rice fields. (100)
　　　「～に」 [location of existence]: DJG v1 p299 & 303.

34-3. 小川さんは明るいかみ、小さな口をしていた。

小川(おがわ)さん は 明るい(あかるい) かみ、 小(ちい)さな 口(くち)
を して いた。
　　Ogawa-san had light-colored hair and a small mouth.
　　　「-ている」 ["be __ing"; "have (done) __"]: DJG v1 p155; Genki ch7; Marx v1 day36.

34-4. 八木さんのボートは三本の小さな木からできている。
　　　八木(やぎ)さん の ボート は 三本(さんぼん) の 小(ちい)さな 木
(き) から できて いる。
　　Yagi-san's boat was made from three small trees.
　　　「～からできる」 {～から出来る 38; 274} ["be made from __"]: Tobira ch1 #1.

34-5. ティースプーンより大きくテーブルスプーンより小さいスプーン。
　　　ティースプーン より 大(おお)きく テーブルスプーン より 小(ちい)
さい スプーン。
　　A spoon larger than a teaspoon and smaller than a tablespoon. (100)

35：中

35-1. 水中ポンプ。
　　　水中(すいちゅう) ポンプ。
　　A submersible pump. (101)

35-2. 8月の中ごろ。
　　　8月(がつ) の 中ごろ(なかごろ)。
　　The middle part of August. (100)
　　　「～ごろ」 {～頃* 1916} ["around __"]: DJG v1 p126.

35-3. 明くんは丸一日中たっていた。
　　　明(あきら)くん は 丸(まる) 一日中(いちにちじゅう) たって いた。
　　Akira was standing all day long. (100)

35-4. 十中八九これは明くんの本だ。
　　　十中八九(じゅっちゅうはっく) これ は 明(あきら)くん の 本(ほん)
だ。
　　I bet you anything this is Akira's book.

35-5. 田んぼの中に六人がたっていた。
　　　田んぼ(たんぼ) の 中(なか) に 六人(ろくにん) が たって いた。
　　Six people were standing amid the rice field.

35-6. 大きな木、小さな木、中くらいの木。
　　　大(おお)きな 木(き)、 小(ちい)さな 木(き)、 中(ちゅう) くらい の
木(き)。
　　Big trees and little trees and middle-sized trees. (99)
　　　「～くらい」 {～位* 577} ["about __"]: DJG v1 p212; Marx v2 day78.

35-7. わたしは中田です。どうぞよろしく。

49

わたし は 中田(なかた) です。 どうぞ よろしく。
I'm Nakata. Pleased to meet you.
「どうぞ」 ["please"]: DJG v3 p84 (under どうか〜).

35-8. 土田さんは一日中ベッドの中にいた。
土田(つちだ)さん は 一日中(いちにちじゅう) ベッド の 中(なか) に いた。
Tsuchida-san was in bed all day.
「〜に」 [location of existence]: DJG v1 p299 & 303. 「いる」 {居る* 255} ["exist"; "be present"]: DJG v1 p153.

35-9. 田中さんはギターをひいている人です。
田中(たなか)さん は ギター を ひいて いる 人(ひと) です。
Tanaka-san is the person playing guitar.
「-ているひと」 {-ている人 15} ["person (who is) __ing"]: Genki ch9.

35-10. 田中さんのおかあさんはアメリカ人です。
田中(たなか)さん の おかあさん は アメリカ人(じん) です。
Tanaka-san's mother is American.
「お-」 [prefix expressing politeness]: DJG v1 p343.

35-11. 小田さんのポケットの中に小さな本がある。
小田(おだ)さん の ポケット の 中(なか) に 小(ちい)さな 本(ほん) が ある。
There's a small book in Oda-san's pocket.

35-12. 大田さんは中東のガス田で大金をつかんだ。
大田(おおた)さん は 中東(ちゅうとう) の ガス田(でん) で 大金(たいきん) を つかんだ。
Ota-san made a bundle on Middle Eastern gas fields.
「〜で」 [instrument]: DJG v1 p106; Genki ch10.

35-13. この中は、日中でさえまったく明るくないのです。
この 中(なか) は、 日中(にっちゅう) で さえ まったく 明(あか)るく ない の です。
In here it's not bright at all, even during the day.
「〜で」 [time]: DJG v1 p109. 「〜さえ」 ["even __"; "(if) just __"]: DJG v2 p363; Marx v2 day60-61; Tobira ch5 #6. 「のである / のです / のだ / んだ」 [explanation or assertion]: DJG v1 p325; Genki ch12.

36：生

36-1. 一生のパートナー。
一生(いっしょう) の パートナー。
Lifelong partner.

36-2. 日本で生まれた人々。

日本(にほん) で 生まれ(うまれ)た 人々(ひとびと)。
Those born in Japan.

「〜で」 [location]: DJG v1 p105. 「**Transitive and intransitive verbs**」: DJG v1 p585; Genki ch18; Marx v1 day51.

36-3. パワープレーを生かす。
パワー プレー を 生かす(いかす)。
[Ice hockey] Capitalize on a power play. (101)

36-4. 生き生きとしてはなす。
生き生き(いきいき) と して はなす。
Talk in a vivid manner. (100)

「〜とする」 [follows description of an impression or sensation]: DJG v2 p523.

36-5. どこから生じたのだろう？
どこ から 生じ(しょうじ)た の だろう？
From what had it proceeded? (25)

「こ/そ/あ/ど」: DJG v1 p600; Genki ch2; Marx v1 day16-17. 「〜から」 ["from ＿"]: DJG v1 p176. 「のである/のです/のだ/んだ」 [explanation or assertion]: DJG v1 p325; Genki ch12. 「〜だろう/〜でしょう」 ["probably ＿"]: DJG v1 p100; Genki ch12; Tobira ch2 #9.

Note: 「しょうじる」 *(conjugated as* 「しょうじた」 *above) is not listed as a reading for* 生 *in the KLC book, as it is not given in the official Joyo Kanji List. As noted in the Introduction, this series makes no attempt to shelter you from such unofficial kanji usages. Familiarize yourself with these as you go along, by tapping on them to look them up in your J-E dictionary.*

36-6. ボールはまだ生きている。
ボール は まだ 生き(いき)て いる。
The ball is still in play. (101)

「まだ〜」 ["still ＿"; "not yet ＿"]: DJG v1 p224; Genki ch9; Marx v1 day87.

36-7. わたしは日曜日に生まれた。
わたし は 日曜日(にちようび) に 生まれ(うまれ)た。
I was born on a Sunday.

「**Transitive and intransitive verbs**」: DJG v1 p585; Genki ch18; Marx v1 day51.

36-8. 大木さんはまだ生きています。
大木(おおき)さん は まだ 生き(いき)て います。
Oki-san is still alive.

36-9. 人は水なしでは生きられない。
人(ひと) は 水(みず) なし で は 生き(いき)られない。
One can't live without water. (87)

「〜なしでは」 ["without ＿"]: DJG v2 p230. 「**Verbs of potential**」 ["can ＿"]: DJG v1 p370; Genki ch13; Marx v1 day50.

36-10. 小田さんのいない人生はむなしい。
小田(おだ)さん の いない 人生(じんせい) は むなしい。

51

My life is empty without Oda-san.
「いる」 {居る* 255} ["exist"; "be present"]: DJG v1 p153.

36-11. 中本さんはブラジル生まれの人だ。
中本(なかもと)さん は ブラジル 生まれ(うまれ) の 人(ひと) だ。
Nakamoto-san is a native of Brazil.

36-12. これは人生であるのか、それとも人生ではないのか？
これ は 人生(じんせい) で ある の か、 それとも 人生(じんせい) で は ない の か？
Is this life, or not life? (70)
「〜か〜か」 ["whether __ or __"]: DJG v2 p87; Tobira ch2 #8. 「それとも〜」 {其れとも** 1757} ["or __"]: DJG v1 p421; Marx v2 day14.

36-13. 中川さんとであうまで、わたしの人生はつまらなかった。
中川(なかがわ)さん と であう まで、 わたし の 人生(じんせい) は つまらなかった。
My life was dull until I met Nakagawa-san.
「〜と」 ["with __"]: DJG v1 p476; Genki ch4. 「〜まで」 {〜迄** 1806} ["until __"]: DJG v1 p225; Genki ch23. 「**Past tense adjectives**」 : DJG v1 p580; Genki ch5&9.

37：山

37-1. あの山は火山です。
あの 山(やま) は 火山(かざん) です。
That mountain is a volcano.

37-2. 円山から東山まであるく。
円山(まるやま) から 東山(ひがしやま) まで あるく。
Walk from Maruyama (district) to Higashiyama (district).
「〜から〜まで」 ["from __ to __"]: DJG v2 p99.

37-3. はじめまして、わたしは中山です。
はじめまして、 わたし は 中山(なかやま) です。
How do you do, I'm Nakayama.

37-4. こんな山の中で人が生きられるの？
こんな 山(やま) の 中(なか) で 人(ひと) が 生き(いき)られる の？
People can survive all the way up here in the mountains?
「〜で」 [location]: DJG v1 p105. 「**Verbs of potential**」 ["can __"]: DJG v1 p370; Genki ch13. 「の(?)」 [female: question marker]: DJG v1 p48; Marx v1 day11.

37-5. 山東の人口は9900万人です。日本の人口よりもちょっとすくない。
山東(さんとう) の 人口(じんこう) は 9900万(まん) 人(にん) です。 日本(にほん) の 人口(じんこう) より も ちょっと すくない。
The population of Shandong is 99 million—a bit less than the population of Japan.

「すくない」 {少ない 677} ["few"; "little"]: DJG v1 p427.

38：出

38-1. 明るみに出る。
　　明るみ(あかるみ) に 出る(でる)。
　　Come to light. (100)
　　「〜に」 ["to __", "toward __"]: DJG v1 p302 & 303.

38-2. 明るみに出す。
　　明るみ(あかるみ) に 出す(だす)。
　　Bring to light. (100)

38-3. もう月が出ている。
　　もう 月(つき) が 出(で)て いる。
　　The moon is already out. (87)
　　「もう〜」 [changed state]: DJG v1 p254; Marx v1 day87.

38-4. ここを出るところです。
　　ここ を 出る(でる) ところ です。
　　We're about to leave here. (87)
　　「〜を」 [indicates place from which one exits]: DJG v1 p351.

38-5. ちょっと出かけてきます。
　　ちょっと 出かけ(でかけ)て きます。
　　I'm going out for a while. (87)
　　「-て / -で」 [connective form of verbs]: DJG v1 p464, v2 p64 of front matter; Genki ch6; Marx v1 day30.

38-6. 一日につき百ポンド出します。
　　一日(いちにち) につき 百(ひゃく) ポンド 出し(だし)ます。
　　I offer you a hundred pounds per day. (7)
　　「〜につき」 {〜に付き* 64} ["per __"]: DJG v2 p283.

38-7. すみません、出口はどこですか？
　　すみません、 出口(でぐち) は どこ です か？
　　Excuse me, where's the exit? (87)

38-8. お金なしには丸山さんは出ません。
　　お金(おかね) なし に は 丸山(まるやま)さん は 出(で)ません。
　　Maruyama-san won't go out without her money.
　　「〜なしには」 ["without __"]: DJG v2 p231.

38-9. 中山さんの本はいつ出るのですか？
　　中山(なかやま)さん の 本(ほん) は いつ 出る(でる) の です か？
　　When is Nakayama-san's book coming out?

53

「のである / のです / のだ / んだ」 [explanation or assertion]: DJG v1 p325; Genki ch12.

38-10. それがスキャンダルを明るみに出した。
それ が スキャンダル を 明るみ(あかるみ) に 出し(だし)た。
It brought the scandal to light. (101)

38-11. 田中さんは金ボタンを川の水から出した。
田中(たなか)さん は 金(きん) ボタン を 川(かわ) の 水(みず) から 出し(だし)た。
Tanaka-san pulled a gold button from the water of the river.

38-12. 山本さんはショッピングセンターに出かけた。
山本(やまもと)さん は ショッピング センター に 出(で)かけた。
Yamamoto-san headed out to the shopping center. (101)
「〜に」 ["to __", "toward __"]: DJG v1 p302 & 303.

38-13. パーティーのため、山川さんはワインを出した。
パーティー の ため、 山川(やまかわ)さん は ワイン を 出し(だし)た。
Yamakawa-san served wine for the party.
「〜ため(に)」 {〜為に* 1236} ["for (the sake of) __"]: DJG v1 p447; Tobira ch2 #6.

38-14. エープリルさんと日の出をみにちょっと出かけてくるわ。
エープリルさん と 日の出(ひので) を み に ちょっと 出(で)かけて くる わ。
I'm heading out for a bit with April to watch the sunrise.
「〜と」 ["with __"]: DJG v1 p476; Genki ch4. 「**Verb stem + に + verb of motion**」 ["(go) __ing"; "(go) to (do) __"]: DJG v1 p297; Genki ch7; Tobira ch3 #9. 「わ」 [female speech marker]: DJG v1 p47 & 520; Marx v2 day1.

39 : 入

39-1. 入ってください。
入っ(はいっ)て ください。
Please come in. (101)

39-2. 目になにか入った。
目(め) に なに か 入っ(はいっ)た。
There's something in my eye. (87)
「なにか」 {何か* 815} ["something"; "anything"]: Genki ch8; Marx v1 day18.

39-3. 火山がすぐ目に入る。
火山(かざん) が すぐ 目(め) に 入る(はいる)。
The volcano will soon come into view.
「すぐ」 ["immediately"; "directly"]: DJG v2 p439.

39-4. 六万五千円を入金した。

六万(ろくまん)　五千(ごせん)　円(えん)　を　入金(にゅうきん)　した。
I deposited 65,000 yen.

39-5. 中本さんは水に入った。
中本(なかもと)さん　は　水(みず)　に　入っ(はいっ)た。
Nakamoto-san went into the water.

39-6. アンチョビー入りのピザ。
アンチョビー　入り(いり)　の　ピザ。
Pizza with anchovies. (100)

39-7. つりばりを川の水に入れる。
つりばり　を　川(かわ)　の　水(みず)　に　入れる(いれる)。
Put a fishhook into the water of the river.

39-8. 54の中に18がいくつ入るか。
54　の　中(なか)　に　18　が　いくつ　入る(はいる)　か。
How many times does 18 go into 54? (101)

39-9. その中には二百万円入っている。
その　中(なか)　に　は　二百(にひゃく)　万円(まんえん)　入っ(はいっ)ている。
There are two million yen inside.

39-10. ねぇ、明くん、入れてちょうだい。
ねぇ、　明(あきら)　くん、　入れ(いれ)て　ちょうだい。
Hey Akira, let me in.
「ねえ / ねぇ」 [exclamation]: DJG v1 p47 bottom.

39-11. 大山さんと金田さん中に入りました。
大山(おおやま)さん　と　金田(かねだ)さん　中(なか)　に　入り(はいり)ました。
In went Oyama-san and Kaneda-san.

39-12. 入口でコートをチェックしてください。
入口(いりぐち)　で　コート　を　チェック　して　ください。
Please check your coat at the door. (101)

39-13. 「フルーツポンチ」とは、フルーツジュースに水かソーダ水を入れたポンチのことをいう。
「フルーツ　ポンチ」　と　は、　フルーツ　ジュース　に　水(みず)　か　ソーダ水(すい)　を　入れ(いれ)た　ポンチ　の　こと　を　いう。
"Fruit punch" is a punch made of fruit juices mixed with water or soda water. (100)
「と」 [marks sound/manner or quoted speech]: DJG v1 p478. 「か」 ["or"]: DJG v1 p164.

40：下

40-1. タラップを下げる。
　　　タラップ　を　下げ(さげ)る。
　　　Lower the gang-plank. (8)

40-2. ぼくは目を下ろした。
　　　ぼく　は　目(め)　を　下ろし(おろし)た。
　　　I looked down. (84)
　　　「ぼく」 {僕 1358} [informal: "I"]: DJG v1 p28.

40-3. りんごを三つ下さい。
　　　りんご　を　三つ(みっつ)　下さい(ください)。
　　　Three apples please.

40-4. 明るい月の下の木々。
　　　明るい(あかるい)　月(つき)　の　下(もと)　の　木々(きぎ)。
　　　Trees beneath the nitid moon. (101)

40-5. チョークを一本下さい。
　　　チョーク　を　一本(いっぽん)　下さい(ください)。
　　　Please give me a piece of chalk. (87)

40-6. あの大きな本を下さい。
　　　あの　大(おお)きな　本(ほん)　を　下さい(ください)。
　　　Please give me that large book.

40-7. すみません。水を下さい。
　　　すみません。　水(みず)　を　下さい(ください)。
　　　Excuse me, water please.

40-8. あの木の下のほうにいる。
　　　あの　木(き)　の　下(した)　の　ほう　に　いる。
　　　He's under that tree.
　　　「いる」 {居る* 255} ["exist"; "be present"]: DJG v1 p153.

40-9. 川下りでびしょびしょになった。
　　　川下り(かわくだり)　で　びしょびしょ　に　なった。
　　　I got soaked boating down river. (87)

40-10. 木下さんは川をカヤックで下った。
　　　木下(きのした)さん　は　川(かわ)　を　カヤック　で　下っ(くだっ)た。
　　　Kinoshita-san kayaked down the river. (101)
　　　「〜で」 [instrument]: DJG v1 p106; Genki ch10.

40-11. 木下さん、ちょっとまって下さい。
　　　木下(きのした)さん、　ちょっと　まって　下さい(ください)。
　　　Kinoshita-san, please wait a moment.

40-12. テレビのリモコンがソファーの下にある。
　　　テレビ　の　リモコン　が　ソファー　の　下(した)　に　ある。

The TV remote control is under the couch. (87)

40-13. 目下のところ、八百七十万円が入金されています。
　　　目下(もっか) の ところ、八百(はっぴゃく) 七十(ななじゅう) 万(まん) 円(えん) が 入金(にゅうきん) されて います。
　　　As of now, 8,700,000 yen has been deposited.
　　　「-られる」 [passive]: DJG v1 p364; Genki ch21.

41：上

41-1. 上へどうぞ。
　　　上(うえ) へ どうぞ。
　　　Go on up. (25)
　　　「へ」 [indicates direction]: DJG v1 p116. 「どうぞ」 ["please"]: DJG v3 p84 (under どうか〜).

41-2. 目上の人々。
　　　目上(めうえ) の 人々(ひとびと)。
　　　One's seniors.

41-3. 目を上下する。
　　　目(め) を 上下(じょうげ) する。
　　　Move one's eyes up and down.

41-4. ボートで川を上った。
　　　ボート で 川(かわ) を 上っ(のぼっ)た。
　　　We ascended the river by boat.

41-5. 四人がステージに上がった。
　　　四人(よにん) が ステージ に 上がっ(あがっ)た。
　　　Four people appeared on stage.

41-6. テーブルの上に本があります。
　　　テーブル の 上(うえ) に 本(ほん) が あります。
　　　There is a book on the table.

41-7. 山中さんは小川さんより三つ上です。
　　　山中(やまなか)さん は 小川(おがわ)さん より 三つ(みっつ) 上(うえ) です。
　　　Yamanaka-san is three years older than Ogawa-san.

41-8. つくえの上にえんぴつ三本があります。
　　　つくえ の 上(うえ) に えんぴつ 三本(さんぼん) が あります。
　　　There are three pencils on the desk.

42：止

42-1. エンジンを止める。

エンジン を 止める(とめる)。
Kill the engine. (101)

42-2. ガスを止めて下さい。
ガス を 止め(とめ)て 下さい(ください)。
Please turn off the gas. (87)

42-3. プロジェクトを止める。
プロジェクト を 止める(とめる)。
Stop the project. (101)

42-4. メディアは口止めされた。
メディア は 口止め(くちどめ) された。
The media was gagged.
「-られる」 [passive]: DJG v1 p364; Genki ch21.

42-5. ハイキングは中止にしたほうがいい。
ハイキング は 中止(ちゅうし) に した ほう が いい。
We'd better cancel the hike. (87)
「〜にする」 ["opt for __"]: DJG v1 p310; Marx v2 day80. 「〜ほうがいい」 {〜方がいい / 〜方が良い* 173} ["had better __"]: DJG v1 p138; Genki ch12.

42-6. 川上さんはタバコを止めようとしている。
川上(かわかみ)さん は タバコ を 止め(やめ)よう と して いる。
Kawakami-san is trying to quit smoking. (87)
「-ようとする」 ["try to __"]: DJG v1 p246 (under みる).

43：正

43-1. それは正しくない。
それ は 正しく(ただしく)ない。
That's incorrect.

43-2. 十中八九きみが正しい。
十中八九(じゅっちゅうはっく) きみ が 正しい(ただしい)。
No doubt you are right. (49)
「きみ」 {君 1407} [informal: "you"]: DJG v1 p28.

43-3. 上田さんは正しかった。
上田(うえだ)さん は 正しかっ(ただしかっ)た。
Ueda-san was right.

43-4. それが正しいことだから。
それ が 正しい(ただしい) こと だ から。
Because it is right. (45)

「こと」 {事 80} [intangible thing]: DJG v1 p191; Marx v1 day34; Tobira ch7 (first page). 「〜から」 ["because __"]: DJG v1 p179; Genki ch6&9; Marx v1 day60. 「だから」 ["so", "that's why"; "since", "because"]: DJG v1 p413; Marx v2 day11.

Note: The structure 「〜から」 is glossed here by itself and also as part of the structure 「だから」. Such nested glosses will be presented whenever the nested item has not been introduced previously by itself.

43-5. 正に出かけるところだった。

正(まさ)に 出(で)かける ところ だった。

I was just about to leave.

「〜ところだ」 ["be just about to __", "be just now __ing", "have just now __ed"]: DJG v1 p496; Tobira ch5 #18. 「だった」 [past tense of copula だ]: DJG v1 p580 bottom; Genki ch9; Marx v1 day37.

43-6. 丸山さんが正しいのは明らかだ。

丸山(まるやま)さん が 正しい(ただしい) の は 明(あき)らか だ。

It is obvious that Maruyama-san is right.

「の」 [nominalizer]: DJG v1 p318; Genki ch8.

43-7. 一生のあやまりを正すつもりだ。

一生(いっしょう) の あやまり を 正(ただ)す つもり だ。

I intend to rectify my life's errors.

「〜つもり」 {〜積もり*832} [intention/conviction]: DJG v1 p503; Genki ch10.

44 : 足

44-1. 小さな足。

小(ちい)さな 足(あし)。

Tiny feet. (101)

44-2. 足一本になる。

足(あし) 一本(いっぽん) に なる。

Be left with one leg.

44-3. 4足す4は8になる。

4 足す(たす) 4 は 8 に なる。

Four and four make eight. (101)

44-4. 生ビールが足りません。

生(なま) ビール が 足り(たり)ません。

There's not enough draft beer.

「**Transitive and intransitive verbs**」: DJG v1 p585; Genki ch18; Marx v1 day51.

44-5. 三に二を足すと五になる。

三(さん) に 二(に) を 足す(たす) と 五(ご) に なる。

Add two to three, and you get five. (87)

「**Transitive and intransitive verbs**」: DJG v1 p585; Genki ch18; Marx v1 day51. 「〜と」 ["if __"; "when __"]: DJG v1 p480; Genki ch18; Marx v2 day24.

44-6. まだ三グラム足りません。

まだ 三(さん) グラム 足り(たり)ません。

59

It's still three grams short.

44-7. これでは四シリング足りません。
これ で は 四(よん) シリング 足り(たり)ません。
This is four shillings short. (58)

44-8. 小金丸さんは土足で中に入った。
小金丸(こがねまる)さん は 土足(どそく) で 中(なか) に 入(はい)った。
Koganemaru-san went inside with her shoes on.
「〜で」 [instrument]: DJG v1 p106; Genki ch10.

44-9. 三木さんはやかんに水を足した。
三木(みき)さん は やかん に 水(みず) を 足(た)した。
Miki-san added water to the kettle.

44-10. 丸山さんはブーツ一足が足りない。
丸山(まるやま)さん は ブーツ 一足(いっそく) が 足り(たり)ない。
Maruyama-san is missing a pair of boots.

44-11. 上田さんの本は六ページ足りない。
上田(うえだ)さん の 本(ほん) は 六(ろく) ページ 足り(たり)ない。
There are six pages missing from Ueda-san's book. (87)

44-12. 水が土にしみたので、足下がわるい。
水(みず) が 土(つち) に しみた ので、 足下(あしもと) が わるい。
The ground is soaked, so the footing is poor.
「〜ので」 ["because __"]: DJG v1 p328; Genki ch12; Marx v1 day60.

45：定

45-1. 一定のパターン。
一定(いってい) の パターン。
A defined pattern. (100)

45-2. 一定の金の出入りを定める。
一定(いってい) の 金(かね) の 出入り(でいり) を 定(さだ)める。
Set a fixed pattern of income and expenditure.

45-3. 山本さんはねらいを定めた。
山本(やまもと)さん は ねらい を 定め(さだめ)た。
Yamamoto-san took aim at her target. (100)

45-4. 出金の日をあらかじめ定める。
出金(しゅっきん) の 日(ひ) を あらかじめ 定める(さだめる)。
Determine the date of payment in advance.

45-5. 中止の日にちは定かではない。

中止(ちゅうし) の 日にち(ひにち) は 定か(さだか) では ない。
The cancellation date is not certain.

45-6. それはお金の出入りによって定められる。
それ は お金(おかね) の 出入り(でいり) に よって 定め(さだめ)られる。
That's determined by our income and expenditures.
「〜によって/〜により」 {〜に依って* / 〜に依り* 701} ["based on/depending on __"; "due to __"]: DJG v2 p292; Marx v2 day43; Tobira ch8 #2.

45-7. 木曜日は入金のために定められた日です。
木曜日(もくようび) は 入金(にゅうきん) の ため に 定め(さだめ)られた 日(ひ) です。
Thursday is the day designated for deposits.
「〜ため(に)」 {〜為に* 1236} ["for (the sake of) __"]: DJG v1 p447; Marx v2 day41; Tobira ch2 #6. 「-られる」 [passive]: DJG v1 p364; Genki ch21.

46：手

46-1. 手足がいたい。
手足(てあし) が いたい。
My hands and legs hurt.

46-2. 小さな手足の人。
小(ちい)さな 手足(てあし) の 人(ひと)。
A fellow with small hands and feet. (101)

46-3. 手を上げて下さい。
手(て) を 上げ(あげ)て 下さい(ください)。
Please raise your hands. (101)

46-4. 手を口の中に入れる。
手(て) を 口(くち) の 中(なか) に 入れる(いれる)。
Put one's hand in one's mouth.

46-5. 中川さんはテニスが上手い。
中川(なかがわ)さん は テニス が 上手い(うまい)。
Nakagawa-san is very good at tennis.

46-6. 木下さんは下手なダンサーだ。
木下(きのした)さん は 下手(へた) な ダンサー だ。
Kinoshita-san is an awkward dancer. (101)

46-7. 小山さんは大金を手に入れた。
小山(おやま)さん は 大金(たいきん) を 手(て) に 入れ(いれ)た。
Oyama-san acquired a large fortune.

46-8. あなたは手も足も出ないんだぞ。

あなた は 手(て) も 足(あし) も 出(で)ない ん だ ぞ。
There's nothing you can do to me now! (72)
「あなた」 {貴方 1177; 173} [formal: "you"]: DJG v1 p28. 「のである / のです / のだ / んだ」 [explanation or assertion]: DJG v1 p325; Genki ch12. 「～ぞ」 ["＿, I'm telling you"]: DJG v1 p47, v2 p609; Marx v2 day1.

46-9. タクシーを止めるため手を上げた。
タクシー を 止める(とめる) ため 手(て) を 上げ(あげ)た。
I held up my hand to stop a taxi. (87)
「～ため(に)」 {～為に* 1236} ["for (the sake of) ＿"]: DJG v1 p447; Tobira ch2 #6.

46-10. 川上さんはスノーボードが上手です。
川上(かわかみ)さん は スノーボード が 上手(じょうず) です。
Kawakami-san is good at snowboarding.

46-11. あの本を手に入れるのがむずかしい。
あの 本(ほん) を 手(て) に 入れる(いれる) の が むずかしい。
That book is hard to come by.

46-12. このメーカーの水は手に入れにくい。
この メーカー の 水(みず) は 手(て) に 入れ(いれ)にくい。
This brand of water is hard to come by.
「-にくい」 {-難い* 712} ["hard to ＿"]: DJG v1 p307, v2 p52 & 96; Genki ch20.

46-13. 上田さんは上手にお金を手に入れた。
上田(うえだ)さん は 上手(じょうず) に お金(おかね) を 手(て) に 入れ(いれ)た。
Ueda-san adeptly took the money into his hands.

46-14. 明くんは五万円を手に入れて出かけた。
明(あきら)くん は 五万円(ごまんえん) を 手(て) に 入れ(いれ)て 出かけ(でかけ)た。
Akira took 50,000 yen in his hand and went out.
「-て / -で」 [connective form of verbs]: DJG v1 p464, v2 p64 of front matter; Genki ch6; Marx v1 day30.

46-15. 山本さんの本は日本では手に入らない。
山本(やまもと)さん の 本(ほん) は 日本(にほん) では 手(て) に 入ら(はいら)ない。
Yamamoto-san's book is not available in Japan. (87)

46-16. 八木さんはあの本には中々手が出ません。
八木(やぎ)さん は あの 本(ほん) には 中々(なかなか) 手(て) が 出(で)ません。
Yagi-san just can't afford that book.
「なかなか～」 {中々～* 35} ["quite ＿"; "not readily/quickly ＿"]: DJG v2 p206; Marx v2 day47; Tobira ch6 #14.

46-17. 金田さんがやっとその本を手に入れました。

金田(かねだ)さん が やっと その 本(ほん) を 手(て) に 入れ(い
れ)ました。
Kaneda-san finally got that book.
「やっと〜」 ["finally __"]: DJG v2 p591.

47：用

47-1. 土木に用いる。
土木(どぼく) に 用いる(もちいる)。
Used for civil engineering.

47-2. ネコが用を足した。
ネコ が 用(よう) を 足(た)した。
The cat did his business [went potty].

47-3. 定木を用いて、……
定木(じょうぎ) を 用い(もちい)て、……
By using a ruler, …
「-て / -で」 [connective verb form]: DJG v1 p464, v2 p64 of front matter; Genki ch6.

47-4. 上手な人を用いる。
上手(じょうず) な 人(ひと) を 用いる(もちいる)。
Use a talented person.

47-5. 二人用のボードゲーム。
二人用(ふたりよう) の ボード ゲーム。
A board game for two players. (100)

47-6. 木下さんがそれを用いる。
木下(きのした)さん が それ を 用いる(もちいる)。
Kinoshita-san uses it.

47-7. バックスペース用のキー。
バックスペース用(よう) の キー。
The typewriter key used for back spacing. (100)

47-8. なんの用だね、小さいの。
なん の 用(よう) だ ね、 小(ちい)さい の。
What do you want, child? (99)
「の」 [nominalizer]: DJG v1 p318; Genki ch8.

47-9. ご用むきはわかっているよ。
ご用(ごよう)むき は わかって いる よ。
I know very well what you have come here for. (55)
「わかる」 {分かる 88} ["understand"]: DJG v1 p529. 「〜よ」 [assertion]: DJG v1 p46-47 examples 12-13 and 15; Genki ch2; Marx v1 day11.

47-10. だれも上田さんに用はないんだ。

63

だれ　も　上田(うえだ)さん　に　用(よう)　は　ない　ん　だ。
No one has any need of Ueda-san.

「だれも」{誰も 2155} ["no one"; "anyone"]: DJG v1 p250; Marx v1 day18. 「～に」 [marks agent/source]: DJG v1 p292 & 303.

47-11. おもちゃとして用いられるレーザー。

おもちゃ　として　用い(もちい)られる　レーザー。

A laser used as a toy.

「～として」 ["in the capacity of __"]: DJG v1 p501; Tobira ch3 #6. 「-られる」 [passive]: DJG v1 p364; Genki ch21.

47-12. 日々に用いるものは「日用」とよばれる。

日々(ひび)　に　用いる(もちいる)　もの　は　「日用(にちよう)」　とよばれる。

Things we use every day are called "daily-use" things.

「もの」 {物 172} [tangible thing]: DJG v1 p193 (under こと); Marx v1 day34; Tobira ch7 (first page). 「-られる」 [passive]: DJG v1 p364; Genki ch21.

47-13. 上田さんは水をくみ上げて用水ミゾにうつしている。

上田(うえだ)さん　は　水(みず)　を　くみ上げ(くみあげ)て　用水(ようすい)　ミゾ　に　うつして　いる。

Ueda-san is drawing the water to transfer it to an irrigation ditch.

47-14. 小さなフォークはサラダ用、大きなフォークはメインディッシュ用だ。

小(ちい)さな　フォーク　は　サラダ用(よう)、　大(おお)きな　フォーク　は　メイン　ディッシュ用(よう)　だ。

The small fork is for your salad, and the large one is for the main course. (87)

48：無

48-1. 無水アルコール。

無水(むすい)　アルコール。

Absolute alcohol. (101)

48-2. あれは無になった。

あれ　は　無(む)　に　なった。

That was reduced to nothing.

48-3. 東口は無人だった。

東口(ひがしぐち)　は　無人(むじん)　だった。

The east exit was empty.

「だった」 [past tense of copula だ]: DJG v1 p580 bottom; Genki ch9.

48-4. ウナギは無足である。

ウナギ　は　無足(むそく)　で　ある。

Eels are apodal. (101)

48-5. ここは下手な人は無用だ。

64

ここ は 下手(へた) な 人(ひと) は 無用(むよう) だ。
A unskillful person is useless in this situation. (10)

48-6. 山口さんは金がもう無い。
山口(やまぐち)さん は 金(かね) が もう 無い(ない)。
Yamaguchi-san is out of money.
「もう〜」 [changed state]: DJG v1 p254; Marx v1 day87.

48-7. 中木さんは無口でまっていた。
中木(なかぎ)さん は 無口(むくち) で まって いた。
Nakagi-san waited reticently.
「-て/-で」 [connective form of adjectives]: DJG v1 p464; Marx v1 day66.

49：不

49-1. 不明な出金。
不明(ふめい) な 出金(しゅっきん)。
An unexplained expenditure.

49-2. 不定の入金。
不定(ふてい) の 入金(にゅうきん)。
Irregular receipt of payments.

49-3. 目下のところ不明。
目下(もっか) の ところ 不明(ふめい)。
Currently unknown.

49-4. 人手が不足している。
人手(ひとで) が 不足(ふそく) して いる。
We're lacking manpower.

49-5. 金が不足しています。
金(かね) が 不足(ふそく) して います。
Money is short. (101)

49-6. この土は水不足です。
この 土(つち) は 水不足(みずぶそく) です。
This soil lacks water.

49-7. 不ぞろいな木目の木。
不ぞろい(ふぞろい) な 木目(もくめ) の 木(き)。
Wood with an uneven grain. (101)

49-8. 不正にこのお金を入手した。
不正(ふせい) に この お金(おかね) を 入手(にゅうしゅ) した。
This money was fraudulently obtained. (101)

50：回

50-1. 土をかき回す。
　　　土(つち) を かき回す(かきまわす)。
　　　Stir the soil. (101)

50-2. ハンドルを回す。
　　　ハンドル を 回す(まわす)。
　　　Rotate a handle. (101)

50-3. カメラは回っていた。
　　　カメラ は 回っ(まわっ)て いた。
　　　The cameras were rolling. (101)

50-4. ダイアルを10に回す。
　　　ダイアル を 10 に 回す(まわす)。
　　　Turn the dial to 10. (101)

50-5. そこまで手が回らない。
　　　そこ まで 手(て) が 回ら(まわら)ない。
　　　I can't possibly manage it. (87)
　　　「こ／そ／あ／ど」: DJG v1 p600; Genki ch2; Marx v1 day16-17.

50-6. 木下さんは一日で三回も入金する。
　　　木下(きのした)さん は 一日(いちにち) で 三回(さんかい) も 入金(にゅうきん) する。
　　　Kinoshita-san makes a deposit even three times in a day.
　　　「～で」 [time]: DJG v1 p109. 「～も」 ["even __"]: DJG v1 p250; Genki ch14.

50-7. 小田さんがずっとカメラを回した。
　　　小田(おだ)さん が ずっと カメラ を 回し(まわし)た。
　　　Oda-san kept on filming.

50-8. 川田さんは月に二、三回ゴルフをする。
　　　川田(かわだ)さん は 月(つき) に 二(に)、 三回(さんかい) ゴルフ を する。
　　　Kawada-san plays golf two or three times a month.

50-9. 東山さんはいつも回りくどいことをいう。
　　　東山(ひがしやま)さん は いつも 回(まわ)りくどい こと を いう。
　　　Higashiyama-san always speaks in a roundabout way.
　　　「いつも」 {何時も** 815; 383} ["always"]: DJG v1 p253. 「こと」 {事 80} [intangible thing]: DJG v1 p191; Marx v1 day34; Tobira ch7 (first page).

50-10. 小金丸さんが六万五千円を上回るお金を入手した。
　　　小金丸(こがねまる)さん が 六万(ろくまん) 五千(ごせん) 円(えん) を 上回(うわまわ)る お金(おかね) を 入手(にゅうしゅ) した。
　　　Koganemaru-san obtained more than 65,000 yen.

66

祝 **Congratulations!** 祝

You have now attained the first *dan*:

生

セイ

NEWBORN

See the full list of KLC kanji ranks at keystojapanese.com/kanji-ranks

Color badges & custom mounting sheet available at
keystojapanese.com/stickers

51：言

51-1. 上手い言い回し。
　　　上手い(うまい)　言い回し(いいまわし)。
　　　A clever turn of phrase. (101)

51-2. 不明な言い回し。
　　　不明(ふめい)　な　言い回し(いいまわし)。
　　　An unclear turn of phrase.

51-3. だれにも言うなよ。
　　　だれ　に　も　言う(いう)　な　よ。
　　　You mustn't tell anyone. (87)
　　　「だれも」 {誰も 2155} ["no one"; "anyone"]: DJG v1 p250; Marx v1 day18. 「～に」 [marks indirect object]: DJG v1 p291 & 303. **infinitive + な** [prohibitive: "don't __"]: DJG v1 p266; Marx v1 day40.

51-4. 一言を言い足します。
　　　一言(ひとこと)　を　言い(いい)足し(たし)ます。
　　　I'll just add one more thing.

51-5. はっきり言って下さい。
　　　はっきり　言っ(いっ)て　下さい(ください)。
　　　Give it to me straight please. (87)

51-6. もう一言だけ言わせてくれ。
　　　もう　一言(ひとこと)　だけ　言わ(いわ)せて　くれ。
　　　Now let me say one word more. (84)
　　　「もう + (numeral) + (counter)」 ["__ more"]. 「～だけ」 ["just __"]: DJG v1 p93; Marx v2 day39. 「～くれ」 {～呉れ** 1478} [impolite request]: DJG v1 p210.

51-7. わたしの口からは言えません。
　　　わたし　の　口(くち)　から　は　言え(いえ)ません。
　　　I daren't say. (84)

51-8. 川上さんはさよならを言った。
　　　川上(かわかみ)さん　は　さよなら　を　言っ(いっ)た。
　　　Kawakami-san said her good-byes.

51-9. 三木さんに言わないで下さい。
　　　三木(みき)さん　に　言わ(いわ)ないで　下さい(ください)。
　　　Please don't tell Miki-san.
　　　「～に」 [marks indirect object]: DJG v1 p291 & 303. 「-ないで」 ["do not __"; "without __ing"]: DJG v1 p271; Genki ch8&20; Marx v1 day39.

51-10. あなたが言うのは正しいです。
　　　あなた　が　言う(いう)　の　は　正しい(ただしい)　です。
　　　What you say is correct.
　　　「の」 [nominalizer]: DJG v1 p318; Genki ch8.

51-11. ……と、川上さんが言い足した。
　　　……と、　川上(かわかみ)さん　が　言い(いい)足し(たし)た。
　　　..., added Kawakami-san.

51-12. まだ一言二言しか言ってません。
　　　まだ　一言(ひとこと)　二言(ふたこと)　しか　言っ(いっ)てません。
　　　I've only said a few words.
　　　「しか〜ない」 ["no more than __/no other than __"]: DJG v1 p398; Genki ch14.

51-13. わたしに一回だけ言わせてくれ。
　　　わたし　に　一回(いっかい)　だけ　言わ(いわ)せて　くれ。
　　　Let me say this just once. (87)
　　　「〜に」 [marks indirect object]: DJG v1 p291 & 303.

51-14. 正に丸田さんの言うとおりです。
　　　正(まさ)に　丸田(まるた)さん　の　言う(いう)　とおり　です。
　　　Maruta-san is quite correct.
　　　「〜とおり(に)/〜どおり(に)」 {〜通りに 159} ["just as __"]: DJG v2 p514; Marx v2 day3; Tobira ch8 #4.

51-15. 土田さんは生きたくないと言った。
　　　土田(つちだ)さん　は　生き(いき)たくない　と　言っ(いっ)た。
　　　Tsuchida-san said he did not want to live.
　　　「-たくない」 [negative form of -たい ("want to __"): "do not want to __"]: DJG v1 p441; Genki ch11. 「と」 [marks sound/manner or quoted speech]: DJG v1 p478.

51-16. 小山さんはなにも言いたくなかった。
　　　小山(こやま)さん　は　なに　も　言い(いい)たくなかった。
　　　Oyama-san did not like to say anything.
　　　「なにも」 {何も* 815} ["nothing"]: DJG v1 p250; Genki ch8; Marx v1 day18.

51-17. 山川さんの言ったことは正しかった。
　　　山川(やまかわ)さん　の　言っ(いっ)た　こと　は　正(ただ)しかった。
　　　Yamakawa-san had said the truth.
　　　「こと」 {事 80} [intangible thing]: DJG v1 p191; Tobira ch7 (first page).

51-18. そのことは一言も口には出さなかった。
　　　その　こと　は　一言(ひとこと)　も　口(くち)　に　は　出さ(ださ)なかった。
　　　I said nothing about the matter. (87)

51-19. これはお月さまがわたしに言ったことです。
　　　これ　は　お月(つき)さま　が　わたし　に　言っ(いっ)た　こと　です。
　　　These are the words the Moon told me. (98)

51-20. 金田さんの言明によるとその日東日本にいた。
　　　金田(かねだ)さん　の　言明(げんめい)　に　よる　と　その　日(ひ)　東日本(ひがしにほん)　に　いた。

According to Kaneda-san's statement he was in East Japan on that day.

「～によると」 {～に依ると* 701} ["according to __"]: DJG v3 p459; Marx v2 day43. 「いる」 {居る* 255} ["exist"; "be present"]: DJG v1 p153.

51-21. わたしはここのサービスについて一言言いたい。

わたし は ここ の サービス について 一言(ひとこと) 言い(いい)たい。

I have a gripe about the service here. (101)

「～について」 {～に就いて** 1283} ["about __"]: DJG v2 p280; Marx v2 day42. 「-たい」 ["want to __"]: DJG v1 p441; Genki ch11; Marx v1 day48.

51-22. 田口さんは水上スキーをしたことがないと言った。

田口(たぐち)さん は 水上(すいじょう) スキー を した こと が ない と 言っ(いっ)た。

Taguchi-san said he'd never tried water skiing. (87)

「～ことがある」 {～事がある* 80} ["__ has occurred"]: DJG v1 p196; Genki ch11; Tobira ch1 #6. 「と」 [marks sound/manner or quoted speech]: DJG v1 p478.

51-23. なぜプログラマー不足なんてことが言われるのか？

なぜ プログラマー 不足(ふそく) なんて こと が 言(い)われる のか？

Why does everyone say there's a programmer shortage? (72)

「～なんて」 ["such (things)/such (a thing)"]: DJG v3 p339; Tobira ch4 #3. 「こと」 {事 80} [intangible thing]: DJG v1 p191; Tobira ch7 (first page). 「-られる」 [passive]: DJG v1 p364; Genki ch21.

51-24. 本田さんが無言で用を足して、一言も言わないでオフィスを出た。

本田(ほんだ)さん が 無言(むごん) で 用(よう) を 足(た)して、 一言(ひとこと) も 言(い)わないで オフィス を 出(で)た。

Honda-san finished his work silently, then left the office without saying a word.

「-て / -で」 [connective form of verbs]: DJG v1 p464, v2 p64 of front matter; Genki ch6; Marx v1 day30. 「～も」 ["even __"]: DJG v1 p250; Genki ch14. 「-ないで」 ["do not __"; "without __ing"]: DJG v1 p271; Genki ch8&20; Marx v1 day39. 「～を」 [indicates place from which one exits]: DJG v1 p351.

52：舌

52-1. 舌を出して下さい。

舌(した) を 出し(だし)て 下さい(ください)。

Please stick out your tongue. (87)

52-2. 本田さんは舌がよく回る。

本田(ほんだ)さん は 舌(した) が よく 回る(まわる)。

Honda-san is very talkative.

52-3. 明日は舌を止めておいて下さい。

明日(あした) は 舌(した) を 止め(とめ)て おいて 下(くだ)さい。

Please hold your tongue tomorrow.

「-ておく」 {-て置く 843} [indicates act of prudence/getting something done]: DJG v1 p357; Genki ch15; Marx v2 day34.

52-4. 明くんは舌を出して「ベー」と言った。
明(あきら)くん は 舌(した) を 出(だ)して 「ベー」 と 言(い)った。
Akira stuck out his tongue and said "Behhh".

53：話

53-1. タブーの話。
タブー の 話(はなし)。
A taboo subject. (101)

53-2. 手話で話す。
手話(しゅわ) で 話す(はなす)。
Communicate in sign language. (100)

53-3. よくある話だ。
よく ある 話(はなし) だ。
One often hears that [such talk].

53-4. 明日お話します。
明日(あした) お話(おはなし) します。
I will speak with you tomorrow. (87)
「お-～する」 [polite description of action by oneself or another ingroup person]: DJG v1 p39 bottom; Genki ch20. 「**Humble expressions**」 : DJG v1 p36; Genki ch20.

53-5. 舌足らずに話す。
舌足らず(したたらず) に 話す(はなす)。
Speak with a lisp. (100)

53-6. 舌もつれで話す人。
舌(した) もつれ で 話す(はなす) 人(ひと)。
A speaker who lisps. (100)

53-7. あんな話は無用だ。
あんな 話(はなし) は 無用(むよう) だ。
Such talk is useless. (7)

53-8. お話し中すみません。
お話し中(おはなしちゅう) すみません。
I'm sorry to disturb you while you're talking. (87)
「お-」 [prefix expressing politeness]: DJG v1 p343.

53-9. 本人は生き生きと話した。
本人(ほんにん) は 生き生き(いきいき) と 話し(はなし)た。
He [the person in question] spoke animatedly.
「と」 [marks sound/manner or quoted speech]: DJG v1 p478.

71

53-10. その話は明日にしましょう。

その　話(はなし)　は　明日(あした)　に　しましょう。

Let's talk about that tomorrow. (7)

「～にする」 ["opt for __"]: DJG v1 p310; Marx v2 day80.

53-11. 一人が大木さんに話しかけました。

一人(ひとり)　が　大木(おおき)さん　に　話しかけ(はなしかけ)ました。

One of them addressed Oki-san.

「～に」 [marks indirect object]: DJG v1 p291 & 303.

53-12. みなさん、そんな話は止めて下さい。

みなさん、　そんな　話(はなし)　は　止め(やめ)て　下さい(ください)。

Everyone, please stop that talk. (90)

53-13. 丸山さん、ちょっとお話があるんです。

丸山(まるやま)さん、　ちょっと　お話(おはなし)　が　ある　ん　です。

Maruyama-san, I want to speak to you for a moment.

53-14. 上田さんがあなた本人に話したいと言いました。

上田(うえだ)さん　が　あなた　本人(ほんにん)　に　話(はな)したい　と　言(い)いました。

Ueda-san said she wants to speak with you personally.

「-たい」 ["want to __"]: DJG v1 p441; Genki ch11; Marx v1 day48.「と」 [marks sound/manner or quoted speech]: DJG v1 p478.

53-15. 「無口」とは、ほとんど話をしない人のことを言う。

「無口(むくち)」　と　は、　ほとんど　話(はなし)　を　しない　人(ひと)　の　こと　を　言う(いう)。

"Mukuchi" refers to a person who seldom talks.

「ほとんど～ない」 {殆ど～ない* 2192} ["almost no(t) __"; "almost never __"]: DJG v3 p252; Tobira ch5 #16.「～のこと」 {～の事* 80} ["about __"]: DJG v2 p304.

53-16. 「手話ニュース」は一日一回ほうそうされています。

「手話(しゅわ)　ニュース」　は　一日(いちにち)　一回(いっかい)　ほうそう　されて　います。

The "Sign Language News" is broadcast once a day.

「-られる」 [passive]: DJG v1 p364; Genki ch21.　**Irregular verb: する**　: DJG v1 p578-79.

53-17. 「話し手」とは、話す人のこと、もしくは話し上手な人のこと、を言う。

「話し手(はなして)」　と　は、　話(はな)す　人(ひと)　の　こと　もしくは　話(はな)し　上手(じょうず)　な　人(ひと)　の　こと　を　言(い)う。

"Hanashite" refers either to a speaker or to someone who is good at speaking.

「～のこと」 {～の事* 80} ["about __"]: DJG v2 p304.

54：活

54-1. 下水の活用。
　　　下水(げすい)　の　活用(かつよう)。
　　　The use of waste water.

54-2. 上手なところを活かす。
　　　上手(じょうず)　な　ところ　を　活かす(いかす)。
　　　Make use of one's area of skill.

54-3. 水なしで生活できない。
　　　水(みず)　なし　で　生活(せいかつ)　できない。
　　　We cannot live without water.
　　　「**Irregular verb:** する」：DJG v1 p578-79.

54-4. 日々の生活に活かせるタレント。
　　　日々(ひび)　の　生活(せいかつ)　に　活か(いか)せる　タレント。
　　　A talent one can put to use in everyday life.

54-5. 金山さんはぜいたくに生活する。
　　　金山(かねやま)さん　は　ぜいたく　に　生活(せいかつ)　する。
　　　Kaneyama-san lives large.

54-6. フラッキングでガス田を活用する。
　　　フラッキング　で　ガス田(でん)　を　活用(かつよう)　する。
　　　Exploit a gas field by fracking.
　　　「〜で」　[instrument]: DJG v1 p106; Genki ch10.

54-7. 中木さんは木の中で生活している。
　　　中木(なかぎ)さん　は　木(き)　の　中(なか)　で　生活(せいかつ)　している。
　　　Nakagi-san lives inside a tree.

54-8. 日本で、1カ月二十万円で生活できる？
　　　日本(にほん)　で、　1カ月(かげつ)　二十(にじゅう)　万円(まんえん)　で　生活(せいかつ)　できる？
　　　Can one live on 200,000 yen a month in Japan?

54-9. 日本のいちばん大きな活火山はあそ山である。
　　　日本(にほん)　の　いちばん　大(おお)きな　活火山(かっかざん)　は　あそ山(さん)　で　ある。
　　　Mt. Aso is Japan's largest active volcano.
　　　「いちばん」　{一番 2; 299} [superlative]: DJG v1 p148; Genki ch10; Marx v1 day70.

55：行

55-1. 月曜には行く。
　　　月曜(げつよう)　に　は　行く(いく)。
　　　I'll go on Monday.

「いく」 {行く 55} ["go"]: DJG v1 p149.

55-2. どこへ行くの？
  どこ へ 行く(いく) の？
  Where are you going?
  「へ」 [indicates direction]: DJG v1 p116. 「の(?)」 [female question]: DJG v1 p48.

55-3. もし行ったら、......
  もし 行っ(いっ)たら、......
  If I go, ... (6)
  「もし(も)〜」 ["if __"]: DJG v3 p205 bottom (under かりに〜); Marx v2 day21. 「-たら」 ["if __"; "when __"]: DJG v1 p452; Genki ch17; Marx v2 day21.

55-4. 日本に行けるだろうか。
  日本(にほん) に 行ける(いける) だろう か。
  I wonder if I could go to Japan.
  「**Verbs of potential**」 ["can __"]: DJG v1 p370; Genki ch13; Marx v1 day50. 「〜だろうか／〜でしょうか」 ["I wonder __"]: DJG v3 p715; Tobira ch6 #4.

55-5. 川口さんはすぐ出て行った。
  川口(かわぐち)さん は すぐ 出(で)て 行っ(いっ)た。
  Kawaguchi-san went out at once.
  「すぐ」 ["immediately"; "directly"]: DJG v2 p439. 「-て／-で」 [connective form of verbs]: DJG v1 p464, v2 p64 of front matter; Genki ch6; Marx v1 day30.

55-6. 金田さんは明日山東に行く。
  金田(かねだ)さん は 明日(あした) 山東(さんとう) に 行く(いく)。
  Tomorrow Kaneda-san is going to Shandong.

55-7. 10ページの5行目をみなさい。
  10ページ の 5行目(ぎょうめ) を み なさい。
  Let's begin with the fifth line on page 10. (87)
  「-なさい」 [imperative]: DJG v1 p284; Genki ch22; Marx v1 day40.

55-8. 土曜日行かなくてもいいですか。
  土曜日(どようび) 行か(いか)なくて も いい です か。
  Is it all right if I don't go on Saturday?
  「-なくても」 ["even without __"]: DJG v1 p280; Genki ch17; Marx v1 day39. 「-てもいい」 ["all right if __"]: DJG v1 p471; Marx v1 day56.

55-9. 三田さんは日本行きを中止した。
  三田(みた)さん は 日本(にほん) 行(い)き を 中止(ちゅうし) した。
  Mita-san called off her visit to Japan.

55-10. 四人でコンサートを行いました。
  四人(よにん) で コンサート を 行い(おこない)ました。
  The four of them held a concert.

55-11. 日本へ四回行ったことがあります。

日本(にほん) へ 四回(よんかい) 行っ(いっ)た こと が あります。
I've been to Japan four times.
「～ことがある」 {～事がある* 80} ["__ has occurred"]: DJG v1 p196; Genki ch11; Marx v1 day62; Tobira ch1 #6.

55-12. 上田さんはいつも正しいことを行う。
上田(うえだ)さん は いつも 正(ただ)しい こと を 行(おこな)う。
Ueda-san always does the right thing.
「いつも」 {何時も** 815; 383} ["always"]: DJG v1 p253. 「こと」 {事 80} [intangible thing]: DJG v1 p191; Tobira ch7 (first page).

55-13. 丸田さんが行くなら、わたしも行く。
丸田(まるた)さん が 行(い)く なら、 わたし も 行く(いく)。
If Maruta-san goes, I'll go too.
「～なら(ば)」 ["if __"]: DJG v1 p281; Genki ch13; Marx v2 day23; Tobira ch3 #5.

55-14. ちょうど出口まで行ったところに、……
ちょうど 出口(でぐち) まで 行っ(いっ)た ところ に、……
Just as I reached the exit, ...
「～に」 [time of occurrence]: DJG v1 p289 & 303.

55-15. 三川さんは五日ごとにスーパーへ行く。
三川(みかわ)さん は 五日(いつか) ごと に スーパー へ 行(い)く。
Mikawa-san goes to the supermarket every five days.
「-ごとに」 {-毎に* 105} ["every __"]: DJG v1 p128.

55-16. この川上さんの行いは明らかに不正だ。
この 川上(かわかみ)さん の 行い(おこない) は 明(あき)らか に 不正(ふせい) だ。
This conduct by Kawakami-san is plainly unjust.

55-17. 小金丸さんは東山行のバスで円山に行った。
小金丸(こがねまる)さん は 東山行(ひがしやまゆき) の バス で 円山(まるやま) に 行(い)った。
Koganemaru-san went to Maruyama on the Higashiyama-bound bus.
「～で」 [instrument]: DJG v1 p106; Genki ch10.

55-18. 火曜日に上田さんとヨガへ行くつもりです。
火曜日(かようび) に 上田(うえだ)さん と ヨガ へ 行く(いく) つもり です。
I'm planning to go to yoga on Tuesday with Ueda-san.
「～と」 ["with __"]: DJG v1 p476; Genki ch4. 「～つもり」 {～積もり* 832} [intention/conviction]: DJG v1 p503; Genki ch10; Marx v1 day63.

55-19. 山口さんと川田さんは上手く行かなかった。
山口(やまぐち)さん と 川田(かわだ)さん は 上手く(うまく) 行か(いか)なかった。
Things didn't work out between Yamaguchi-san and Kawada-san.

「と」 ["and" within an exhaustive list; cf. や]: DJG v1 p473; Genki ch4.

55-20. 金田さんは土曜日のパーティに行きましたか。
　　　金田(かねだ)さん　は　土曜日(どようび)　の　パーティ　に　行き(いき)ました　か。
　　　Did Kaneda-san attend the party on Saturday?

55-21. コンサートは水曜日、木曜日、金曜日、土曜日に行われることになった。
　　　コンサート　は　水曜日(すいようび)、　木曜日(もくようび)、　金曜日(きんようび)、　土曜日(どようび)　に　行わ(おこなわ)れる　こと　に　なった。
　　　The concerts were to be on Wednesday, Thursday, Friday and Saturday. (58)
　　　「-られる」 [passive]: DJG v1 p364; Genki ch21. 「〜ことになる」 {〜事になる* 80} ["be decided that __"]: DJG v1 p202; Marx v2 day80; Tobira ch3 #7&10.

56：心

56-1. 小心な人。
　　　小心(しょうしん)　な　人(ひと)。
　　　A timid person.

56-2. 用心して話した。
　　　用心(ようじん)　して　話し(はなし)た。
　　　She spoke warily.
　　　「-て / -で」 [connective verb form]: DJG v1 p464, v2 p64 of front matter; Genki ch6.

56-3. 火の用心をして下さい。
　　　火(ひ)　の　用心(ようじん)　を　して　下さい(ください)。
　　　Please be careful with flame.

56-4. 田中さんの心の中に入れた。
　　　田中(たなか)さん　の　心(こころ)　の　中(なか)　に　入れ(いれ)た。
　　　I put it in Tanaka-san's mind.

56-5. 明くんはおかあさんにお金を無心した。
　　　明(あきら)くん　は　おかあさん　に　お金(おかね)　を　無心(むしん)した。
　　　Akira asked mother for some money.
　　　「〜に」 [marks agent/source]: DJG v1 p292 & 303.

56-6. 一心に生活しようとしている、一人で。
　　　一心に(いっしんに)　生活(せいかつ)　しよう　と　して　いる、　一人(ひとり)　で。
　　　I'm trying earnestly to make a living, by myself.
　　　「-ようとする」 ["try to __"]: DJG v1 p246 (under みる).

56-7. あの無用な出金は心にのこっています。
　　　あの　無用(むよう)　な　出金(しゅっきん)　は　心(こころ)　に　のこって　います。

That useless expenditure remains in my mind.

56-8. 中山さんはどんなグループにいても、中心にいる。
中山(なかやま)さん は どんな グループ に いて も、 中心(ちゅうしん) に いる。
Nakayama-san takes the lead in any group. (101)

56-9. それを言ったとき、川本さんは心から話していた。
それ を 言(いっ)た とき、 川本(かわもと)さん は 心(こころ) から 話(はな)して いた。
When he said that, Kawamoto-san was speaking from the heart.
「～とき」 {～時* 383} ["when __"]: DJG v1 p490; Genki ch16.

56-10. 心から話したいんだ。あなたに本心をうち明けよう。
心(こころ) から 話(はな)したい ん だ。 あなた に 本心(ほんしん) を うち明(あ)けよう。
I really want to speak from the heart. I will confide my real intention to you.
「-たい」 ["want to __"]: DJG v1 p441; Genki ch11; Marx v1 d48. 「のである / のです / のだ / んだ」 [explanation/assertion]: DJG v1 p325; Genki ch12. 「**Volitional**」 ["let's __"; "I'll __"]: DJG v1 p576 & 578 second col. from right; Genki ch15; Marx v1 d29.

57：耳

57-1. 耳だけが出ている！
耳(みみ) だけ が 出(で)て いる！
Only your ears are sticking out!

57-2. 耳にしたことがありますか。
耳(みみ) に した こと が あります か。
Have you ever heard of it? (87)
「～ことがある」 {～事がある* 80} ["__ has occurred"]: DJG v1 p196; Genki ch11; Marx v1 day62; Tobira ch1 #6.

57-3. 三川さんは耳たぶにピアスをした。
三川(みかわ)さん は 耳たぶ(みみたぶ) に ピアス を した。
Mikawa-san pierced his ears.

57-4. 明くんは目と耳をそっちにむけた。
明(あきら)くん は 目(め) と 耳(みみ) を そっち に むけた。
Akira was all eyes and ears.
「と」 ["and" within an exhaustive list; cf. や]: DJG v1 p473; Genki ch4.

57-5. 耳かきを中耳まで入れないで下さい。
耳(みみ)かき を 中耳(ちゅうじ) まで 入(い)れないで 下(くだ)さい。
Please do not insert the ear pick as far as your middle ear.
「-ないで」 ["do not __"; "without __ing"]: DJG v1 p271; Genki ch8&20.

57-6. アフリカゾウの耳はアジアゾウの耳よりも大きい。

アフリカ ゾウ の 耳(みみ) は アジア ゾウ の 耳(みみ) よりも 大(おお)きい。
The African elephant has bigger ears than the Asian elephant. (87)

58：又

58-1. 耳又は目を用いる。

耳(みみ) 又は(または) 目(め) を 用いる(もちいる)。
Use your ears or your eyes.

「または」 {又は* 58} ["or"]: DJG v2 p171.

58-2. 又メガネを無くした。

又(また) メガネ を 無くし(なくし)た。
I've lost my glasses again! (101)

58-3. 土曜日は行きたくない。又の日に行きましょう。

土曜日(どようび) は 行き(いき)たくない。 又の日(またのひ) に 行き(いき)ましょう。
I don't feel like going on Saturday. Let's go another day.

「-たくない」 [negative form of -たい ("want to __"): "do not want to __"]: DJG v1 p441; Genki ch11; Marx v1 day48.

58-4. 「手に入れる」又は「入手する」と言えば、「obtain」と言うことをつたえる。

「手(て) に 入れる(いれる)」 又は(または) 「入手(にゅうしゅ) する」 と 言え(いえ)ば、「obtain」 と 言う(いう) こと を つたえる。
If you say either *te ni ireru* or *nyushu suru* you will convey the idea "obtain".

「-ば」 ["if __"]: DJG v1 p81; Genki ch22. 「～という」 {～と言う* 51} [links identifier with identified]: DJG v1 p486; Genki ch20; Tobira ch10 (first page). 「こと」 {事 80} [intangible thing]: DJG v1 p191; Tobira ch7 (first page).

58-5. 「活かす」又は「活用する」と言えば、「put to use」と言うことをつたえる。

「活かす(いかす)」 又は(または) 「活用(かつよう) する」 と 言え(いえ)ば、「put to use」 と 言う(いう) こと を つたえる。
If you say either *ikasu* or *katsuyo suru* you will convey the idea "put to use".

58-6. 「が足りない」又は「不足だ」と言えば、「It's not enough」と言うことをつたえる。

「が 足り(たり)ない」 又は(または) 「不足(ふそく) だ」 と 言え(いえ)ば、「It's not enough」 と 言う(いう) こと を つたえる。
If you say either *ga tarinai* or *fusoku da* you will communicate the idea that "It's not enough".

59：取

59-1. 取るに足らない人。

取る(とる) に 足ら(たら)ない 人(ひと)。
A person of no significance. (100)

59-2. 人の目を取り出す。
人(ひと) の 目(め) を 取り出す(とりだす)。
Pluck out a person's eye.
「-だす」 {-出す 38} ["__ out"; "start to __"]: DJG v1 p102; Tobira ch7 #6.
「**Compound verbs**」 : DJG v1 p610, v2 p626; Marx v1 day33.

59-3. 手で耳あかを取り出した。
手(て) で 耳(みみ)あか を 取り出し(とりだし)た。
She removed the earwax with her hand.

59-4. 丸い取っ手を用いて下さい。
丸い(まるい) 取っ手(とって) を 用い(もちい)て 下さい(ください)。
Please use the round handle.

59-5. 小さいバッグを取って下さい。
小(ちい)さい バッグ を 取っ(とっ)て 下さい(ください)。
Please take the small bag.

59-6. そのコップを三つ取って下さい。
その コップ を 三つ(みっつ) 取っ(とっ)て 下さい(ください)。
Please take three of those glasses.

59-7. 田口さんは中のものを取り出した。
田口(たぐち)さん は 中(なか) の もの を 取り出し(とりだし)た。
Taguchi-san removed the contents from inside.
「もの」 {物 172} [tangible thing]: DJG v1 p193 (under こと); Tobira ch7 (first page).

59-8. カップの取っ手が無くなっていた。
カップ の 取っ手(とって) が 無くなっ(なくなっ)て いた。
The handle of the cup was missing. (101)

59-9. 中本さんの手を取った、しっかりと。
中本(なかもと)さん の 手(て) を 取っ(とっ)た、 しっかり と。
I took Nakamoto-san by the hand, firmly.
「と」 [marks sound/manner or quoted speech]: DJG v1 p478.

59-10. そのシロップはカエデの木から取り出す。
その シロップ は カエデ の 木(き) から 取り出す(とりだす)。
We tap that syrup from maple trees. (101)

59-11. 木下さんはポケットから百円を取り出した。
木下(きのした)さん は ポケット から 百円(ひゃくえん) を 取り出し(とりだし)た。
Kinoshita-san took a hundred yen from his pocket.

59-12. みなさん、取るに足らない話は止めて下さい。

79

みなさん、 取る(とる) に 足ら(たら)ない 話(はなし) は 止め(やめ)て 下さい(ください)。
Everyone, please stop with the frivolous talk.

59-13. 無用なものを入れると、無用なものしか取り出せない。
無用(むよう) な もの を 入れる(いれる) と、 無用(むよう) な もの しか 取り出せない(とりだせない)。
If you put useless stuff in, you can only get useless stuff out.
「もの」 {物 172} [tangible thing]: DJG v1 p193 (under こと); Marx v1 day34; Tobira ch7 (first page). 「～と」 ["if __"; "when __"]: DJG v1 p480; Genki ch18; Marx v2 day24.

59-14. 三人の心中の話を、わたしの本で取り上げるつもりです。
三人(さんにん) の 心中(しんじゅう) の 話(はなし) を、 わたし の 本(ほん) で 取り上げる(とりあげる) つもり です。
I intend to take up the story of the triple-suicide in my book.
「～つもり」 {～積もり* 832} [intention/conviction]: DJG v1 p503; Genki ch10.

60 : 身

60-1. 身なりのよくない人。
身なり(みなり) の よくない 人(ひと)。
A person who is not well dressed. (100)

60-2. コートを身につける。
コート を 身(み) に つける。
Put a coat on. (100)
「～に」 ["on __"]: DJG v1 p295 & 303.

60-3. 中身のない人は無用だ。
中身(なかみ) の ない 人(ひと) は 無用(むよう) だ。
A person of no substance is useless.

60-4. ご出身はどちらですか。
ご出身(ごしゅっしん) は どちら です か。
Where do you come from? (87)

60-5. 一日一ぱい心身を活用する。
一日(いちにち) 一ぱい(いっぱい) 心身(しんしん) を 活用(かつよう) する。
Put one's body and mind to use the whole day.

60-6. わしの身の上話をしてあげよう。
わし の 身の上話(みのうえばなし) を して あげよう。
I will tell you my story. (99)
「-てあげる」 {-て上げる* 41} ["do __ (for someone)"]: DJG v1 p65; Genki ch16; Marx v2 day31. 「**Volitional**」 ["let's __"; "I'll __"]: DJG v1 p576 & 578 second column from right; Genki ch15; Marx v1 day29.

60-7. 小田さんはまだ小身ものである。

小田(おだ)さん は まだ 小身(しょうしん) もの で ある。

Oda-san still occupies a humble position.

「〜もの(だ)」 ["(is) something that __"]: DJG v2 p189.

60-8. 中田さんは山口出身の日本人である。

中田(なかた)さん は 山口(やまぐち) 出身(しゅっしん) の 日本人(にほんじん) で ある。

Nakata-san is a Japanese from Yamaguchi.

60-9. 無口に身の回りのものを取りにかけ出した。

無口(むくち) に 身の回り(みのまわり) の もの を 取り(とり) に かけ出し(だし)た。

He rushed to get his things without uttering a word.

60-10. 東ヨーロッパの、又は、ドイツ出身のユダヤ人。

東(ひがし) ヨーロッパ の、 又(また)は、 ドイツ 出身(しゅっしん) の ユダヤ人(じん)。

A Jew of eastern European or German descent. (100)

「または」 {又は* 58} ["or"]: DJG v2 p171.

60-11. 川上さん、身の回りのものをじゅんびして下さい。

川上(かわかみ)さん、 身の回り(みのまわり) の もの を じゅんび して 下さい(ください)。

Kawakami-san, please get your things ready.

61 : 休

61-1. 小休止を取る。

小(しょう) 休止(きゅうし) を 取る(とる)。

Catch one's breath. (101)

61-2. 明日は休日です。

明日(あした) は 休日(きゅうじつ) です。

It is a holiday tomorrow. (87)

61-3. 一休みしませんか。

一休み(ひとやすみ) しません か。

How about taking a rest? (87)

「-ませんか」 ["won't you __"]: Genki ch3; Marx v1 day49.

61-4. 火曜日は休みます。

火曜日(かようび) は 休み(やすみ)ます。

I'll be absent Tuesday.

61-5. 二十日も休みました。

二十日(はつか) も 休み(やすみ)ました。

81

I took off work for twenty whole days.

61-6. 話し手は休止しました。
　　話し手(はなして)　は　休止(きゅうし)　しました。
　　The speaker paused.

61-7. 二日ほど休みを取ります。
　　二日(ふつか)　ほど　休み(やすみ)　を　取り(とり)ます。
　　I am taking a couple of days off. (87)
　　「〜ほど」{〜程* 588} ["to __ extent"]: DJG v1 p135, v2 p57; Tobira ch10 #1.

61-8. お正月休みはどうするの？
　　お正月(おしょうがつ)　休み(やすみ)　は　どう　する　の？
　　What are you planning to do for the New Year vacation? (87)

61-9. 木曜日が小山さんの休日だ。
　　木曜日(もくようび)　が　小山(こやま)さん　の　休日(きゅうじつ)　だ。
　　Thursday is Koyama-san's day off. (101)

61-10. それからお休みを言い、出て行った。
　　それから　お休み(やすみ)　を　言い(いい)、　出(で)て　行っ(いっ)た。
　　Then he said good-night and went out. (25)
　　「それから〜」{其れから〜** 1757} ["and then __"]: DJG v1 p416.

61-11. 川上さんは一休みしたいと言っている。
　　川上(かわかみ)さん　は　一休み(ひとやすみ)　したい　と　言っ(いっ)ている。
　　Kawakami-san is saying he'd like to take a short break.
　　「-たい」["want to __"]: DJG v1 p441; Genki ch11; Marx v1 day48. 「と」 [marks sound/manner or quoted speech]: DJG v1 p478.

61-12. あそ山は休火山ではなく、活火山である。
　　あそ山(さん)　は　休火山(きゅうかざん)　で　は　なく、　活火山(かっかざん)　で　ある。
　　Mt. Aso is not a dormant volcano, but an active volcano.
　　「-なく」["not __, so __"; "not __, but __"]: DJG v2 p211; Tobira ch2 #15.

61-13. 大丸の定休日は月曜日ですか？／いいえ、大丸は無休です。
　　大丸(だいまる)　の　定休日(ていきゅうび)　は　月曜日(げつようび)　ですか？　／　いいえ、　大丸(だいまる)　は　無休(むきゅう)　です。
　　Is Monday the day Daimaru is closed? / No, Daimaru opens every day.

62：体

62-1. 六百円、大体。
　　六百円(ろっぴゃくえん)、　大体(だいたい)。
　　Six hundred yen, roughly speaking.

62-2. それは一体なんだろう？
　　　それ　は　一体(いったい)　なん　だろう？
　　　What the heck could that be?
　　　「〜だろう/〜でしょう」 ["probably __"]: DJG v1 p100; Genki ch12; Tobira ch2 #9.

62-3. この生活は体にやさしい。
　　　この　生活(せいかつ)　は　体(からだ)　に　やさしい。
　　　This lifestyle is good for your health.

62-4. ほぼ人体くらいの大きさだ。
　　　ほぼ　人体(じんたい)　くらい　の　大き(おおき)さ　だ。
　　　It's about the size of the human body.
　　　「〜くらい」 {〜位* 577} ["about __"]: DJG v1 p212; Marx v2 day78. 「-さ」 ["__ness"]: DJG v1 p381; Marx v1 day67; Tobira ch1 #2.

62-5. ついに正体をあらわしたな。
　　　ついに　正体(しょうたい)　を　あらわした　な。
　　　At last you've given yourself away. (87)
　　　「ついに〜」 {遂に〜* 2210} ["at last __", "at length __"]: DJG v2 p531 (under とうとう〜); Tobira ch5 #7. 「な」 [male alternative to ね]: DJG v1 p46 examples 9-11.

62-6. 体が木からぶら下がっていた。
　　　体(からだ)　が　木(き)　から　ぶら下がっ(ぶらさがっ)て　いた。
　　　The body was hanging from the tree. (101)

62-7. 一体だれがドクを入れたのか？
　　　一体(いったい)　だれ　が　ドク　を　入れ(いれ)た　の　か？
　　　Who on earth put the poison in?

62-8. 手で身体に耳あかをつけている。
　　　手(て)　で　身体(からだ)　に　耳(みみ)あか　を　つけて　いる。
　　　He's rubbing earwax on his body with his hand.
　　　「〜に」 ["on __"]: DJG v1 p295 & 303.

62-9. 身体中だるいから、ねるね。お休み。
　　　身体中(からだじゅう)　だるい　から、　ねる　ね。　お休(やす)み。
　　　I think I'll go to bed, since my whole body is wiped out. Good night.
　　　「〜から」 ["because __"]: DJG v1 p179; Genki ch6&9; Marx v1 day60. 「ね」 [speaker seeks confirmation/agreement]: DJG v1 p45 & 286; Genki ch2; Marx v2 day2.

62-10. 山本さんは体中がいたいと言っている。
　　　山本(やまもと)さん　は　体中(からだじゅう)　が　いたい　と　言っ(いっ)て　いる。
　　　Yamamoto-san says he's aching from head to foot.

62-11. 田本さんは一体なにをしているんですか。
　　　田本(たもと)さん　は　一体(いったい)　なに　を　して　いる　ん　です　か。

What on earth is Tamoto-san doing?

63：信

63-1. もう信じて下さい。
もう　信じ(しんじ)て　下さい(ください)。
Please believe me now.
「もう〜」 [changed state]: DJG v1 p254; Marx v1 day87.

63-2. 丸で信じられない！
丸(まる)　で　信じ(しんじ)られない！
This is utterly incredible! (89)
「**Verbs of potential**」 ["can __"]: DJG v1 p370; Genki ch13; Marx v1 day50.
Note: 「まるで〜」 *("as if ___"; "completely ___") is usually written in hiragana. In keeping with its special purposes, this series is moderately biased in favor of using optional kanji once you have learned them. This bias is especially pronounced for recently learned kanji, which require frequent reinforcement. Over the course of the Series,* 「まるで〜」 *will mostly appear in hiragana.*

63-3. 二人とも信用ならない。
二人(ふたり)　とも　信用(しんよう)　ならない。
I don't believe in either of them. (90)
「〜とも」 ["both/all __"; "(n)either (of) __"].

63-4. 人は目にしたものを信じる。
人(ひと)　は　目(め)　に　した　もの　を　信じる(しんじる)。
People believe what they see. (87)

63-5. この人々は休日を信じない。
この　人々(ひとびと)　は　休日(きゅうじつ)　を　信じ(しんじ)ない。
These people do not believe in holidays. (100)

63-6. 中本さんの話は心から信じている。
中本(なかもと)さん　の　話(はなし)　は　心(こころ)　から　信じ(しんじ)て　いる。
I believe Nakamoto-san's story from the bottom of my heart.

63-7. これはほとんど信用できない話だ。
これ　は　ほとんど　信用(しんよう)　できない　話(はなし)　だ。
This is a barely credible story.
「ほとんど〜ない」 {殆ど〜ない* 2192} ["almost no(t) __"; "almost never __"]: DJG v3 p252; Tobira ch5 #16.

63-8. 本山さんの言うことが正しいと信じています。
本山(もとやま)さん　の　言う(いう)　こと　が　正しい(ただしい)　と　信じ(しんじ)て　います。
I believe what Motoyama-san says is right.

63-9. あなたはわたしが信用できるたった一人の人です。

あなた は わたし が 信用(しんよう) できる たった 一人(ひとり) の 人(ひと) です。
You're the only person that I can trust. (87)
「たった〜」 ["just __", "only __"]: DJG v2 p448 (under ただ〜); Tobira ch15 #7.

63-10. 川上さんが木下さんのことを信用する。だからかのじょに心中をうち明ける。
川上(かわかみ)さん が 木下(きのした)さん の こと を 信用(しんよう) する。 だから かのじょ に 心中(しんちゅう) を うち明(あ)ける。
Kawakami-san trusts Kinoshita-san, so he confides in her.
「〜のこと」 {〜の事* 80} ["about __"]: DJG v2 p304. 「だから」 ["so", "that's why"; "since", "because"]: DJG v1 p413; Marx v2 day11.

63-11. ぼくは大体、話し上手な人を不信の目でみるが、山口さんが言うことを大いに信用する。
ぼく は 大体(だいたい)、 話(はな)し 上手(じょうず) な 人(ひと) を 不信(ふしん) の 目(め) で みる が、 山口(やまぐち)さん が 言(い)う こと を 大(おお)いに 信用(しんよう) する。
I generally distrust smooth talkers, but I have great trust in what Yamaguchi-san says.
「が」 ["but"]: DJG v1 p120, v2 p18; Marx v1 day59.

64：付

64-1. 体に火を付ける。
体(からだ) に 火(ひ) を 付ける(つける)。
Set fire to one's body.

64-2. ビルに火を付ける。
ビル に 火(ひ) を 付ける(つける)。
Set fire to a building. (101)

64-3. ベルト付きのドレス。
ベルト付き(つき) の ドレス。
A belted dress. (101)

64-4. 手にペンキが付いた。
手(て) に ペンキ が 付い(つい)た。
My hands are stained with paint. (87)
「〜に」 ["on __"]: DJG v1 p295 & 303.

64-5. ランプが付いていない。
ランプ が 付い(つい)て いない。
The lamp is switched off. (101)

64-6. 火の付いているタバコ。
火(ひ) の 付い(つい)て いる タバコ。
A lighted cigarette. (101)

85

64-7. 木にラベルを取り付けた。

木(き) に ラベル を 取り付け(とりつけ)た。

I attached a label to the tree.

「〜に」 ["on __"]: DJG v1 p295 & 303. 「**Compound verbs**」 : DJG v1 p610, v2 p626; Marx v1 day33.

64-8. 木下さん、明かりを付けて下さい。

木下(きのした)さん、 明かり(あかり) を 付け(つけ)て 下さい(ください)。

Kinoshita-san, please turn the lights on.

64-9. 中川さんはジーンズを身に付けた。

中川(なかがわ)さん は ジーンズ を 身(み) に 付け(つけ)た。

Nakagawa-san put her jeans on. (101)

「〜に」 ["on __"]: DJG v1 p295 & 303.

64-10. 田口さんはうそを付く人ではない。

田口(たぐち)さん は うそ を 付く(つく) 人(ひと) で は ない。

Taguchi-san is not one to tell lies.

64-11. ここから火山がすぐに目に付きます。

ここ から 火山(かざん) が すぐ に 目(め) に 付き(つき)ます。

From here you can easily see the volcano.

「すぐ」 ["immediately"; "directly"]: DJG v2 p439.

64-12. そのシステムを一回でしっかり身に付けた。

その システム を 一回(いっかい) で しっかり 身(み) に 付け(つけ)た。

He mastered that system from the very first time.

64-13. パッケージには、11月24日の日付がある。

パッケージ に は、 11月(がつ) 24日(にじゅうよっか) の 日付(ひづけ) が ある。

The package is dated November 24. (101)

Note: As noted above, no phonetic guides are provided for Arabic numerals, unless they form part of a word whose reading is irregular. In this example, "11" has a regular reading 「じゅういち」 *, whereas "24" forms part of the irregular* 「にじゅうよっか」 *.*

64-14. 話し手は、三回も「付言できれば、…」と言いました。

話し手(はなして) は、 三回(さんかい) も 「付言(ふげん) できれば、 …」 と 言(い)いました。

Three times the speaker said, "If I could add one more thing, …".

「-ば」 ["if __"]: DJG v1 p81; Genki ch22.

65：受

65-1. 受信メール。

受信(じゅしん)　メール。
Incoming mail. (101)

65-2. 心に受け止める。
心(こころ)　に　受け止める(うけとめる)。
Receive into one's mind. (100)

65-3. ぼくのメールを受信した？
ぼく　の　メール　を　受信(じゅしん)　した？
Did you receive my email [text]?

65-4. 水曜日にテストを受ける。
水曜日(すいようび)　に　テスト　を　受ける(うける)。
I have a test on Wednesday.

65-5. これを受け入れましょう。
これ　を　受け入れ(うけいれ)ましょう。
Let us embrace this. (32)

65-6. 受け身人生をあゆむ人々。
受け身(うけみ)　人生(じんせい)　を　あゆむ　人々(ひとびと)。
People who lead passive lives.

65-7. ホテルの受付であいましょう。
ホテル　の　受付(うけつけ)　で　あいましょう。
Let's meet at the hotel reception.

65-8. このお金を受け取って下さい。
この　お金(おかね)　を　受け取っ(うけとっ)て　下さい(ください)。
Please accept this money.

65-9. 山本さんを受け入れて下さい。
山本(やまもと)さん　を　受け入れ(うけいれ)て　下さい(ください)。
Please take in Yamamoto-san.

65-10. 土田さんは一生受け身に回った人だった。
土田(つちだ)さん　は　一生(いっしょう)　受け身(うけみ)　に　回っ(まわっ)た　人(ひと)　だった。
Tsuchida-san maintained a passive attitude throughout her life.

65-11. 上田さんは手に入るだけの金は受け取る。
上田(うえだ)さん　は　手(て)　に　入る(はいる)　だけ　の　金(かね)　は　受け取る(うけとる)。
Ueda-san will accept any money he can get. (87)
「〜だけ」　["just __"]: DJG v1 p93; Marx v2 day39.

65-12. 東大生のみなは、それぞれ三万五千円を受け取った。
東大生(とうだいせい)　の　みな　は、　それぞれ　三万(さんまん)　五千(ごせん)　円(えん)　を　受け取っ(うけとっ)た。

87

All Tokyo University students received 35,000 yen each.
「それぞれ」 {其々** 1757} ["each"; "respectively"]: DJG v2 p436; Tobira ch6 #6.

66：以

66-1. 十ぶん以上に。
十(じゅう)ぶん 以上(いじょう) に。
More than adequately. (100)

66-2. 十八以下の人。
十八(じゅうはち) 以下(いか) の 人(ひと)。
People eighteen and under.

66-3. 三つ以上はない。
三つ(みっつ) 以上(いじょう) は ない。
Not more than three.

66-4. それ以上は信じない。
それ 以上(いじょう) は 信じ(しんじ)ない。
More than that I will not believe.

66-5. 九月二十日を以て……
九月(くがつ) 二十日(はつか) を 以て(もって)……
. . . as of September 20th.

66-6. それ以上は言えません。
それ 以上(いじょう) は 言え(いえ)ません。
More I can't say. (90)

66-7. 一ヶ月に六百万円以下。
一ヶ月(いっかげつ) に 六百万(ろっぴゃくまん) 円(えん) 以下(いか)。
Six million yen a month or under.

66-8. いいえ、十人以上でした。
いいえ、 十人(じゅうにん) 以上(いじょう) でした。
No, it was more than ten persons. (4)

66-9. だれもそれ以上言わなかった。
だれ も それ 以上(いじょう) 言わ(いわ)なかった。
No one had anything more to say. (87)
「だれも」 {誰も 2155} ["no one"; "anyone"]: DJG v1 p250; Marx v1 day18.

67：立

67-1. 立体レンズ。
立体(りったい) レンズ。
Stereoscopic lenses. (101)

67-2. 四本の足で立つ体。

　　四本(よんほん)　の　足(あし)　で　立つ(たつ)　体(からだ)。

　　A body that stands on four feet.

67-3. ほとんど目立たない山。

　　ほとんど　目立た(めだた)ない　山(やま)。

　　A barely noticeable mountain.

　　「ほとんど～ない」 {殆ど～ない* 2192} ["almost no(t) __"; "almost never __"]: DJG v3 p252; Tobira ch5 #16.

67-4. 一からビジネスを立ち上げた。

　　一(いち)　から　ビジネス　を　立ち(たち)上げ(あげ)た。

　　She built her business up from scratch. (101)

67-5. ここから火山がすごく目立つ。

　　ここ　から　火山(かざん)　が　すごく　目立つ(めだつ)。

　　The volcano is really conspicuous from here.

67-6. 足立さんはゆらゆらと立ち上がった。

　　足立(あだち)さん　は　ゆらゆら　と　立ち上がっ(たちあがっ)た。

　　Adachi-san slowly got up.

　　「Compound verbs」 : DJG v1 p610, v2 p626; Marx v1 day33.

67-7. 立川さんはいつも中立だと言っている。

　　立川(たちかわ)さん　は　いつも　中立(ちゅうりつ)　だ　と　言っ(いっ)て　いる。

　　Tachikawa-san is always saying he's neutral.

　　「いつも」 {何時も** 815; 383} ["always"]: DJG v1 p253.

67-8. 足立さんは足がしびれて立ち上がれなかった。

　　足立(あだち)さん　は　足(あし)　が　しびれて　立ち上がれ(たちあがれ)なかった。

　　Adachi-san's leg had fallen asleep so he couldn't stand up. (87)

　　「Verbs of potential」 ["can __"]: DJG v1 p370; Genki ch13; Marx v1 day50.

67-9. 小田さんはポケットに手を入れて立っていた。

　　小田(おだ)さん　は　ポケット　に　手(て)　を　入れ(いれ)て　立っ(たっ)て　いた。

　　Oda-san was standing with his hands in his pockets. (87)

67-10. いつコンピュータは立ち上がるんでしょうか？

　　いつ　コンピュータ　は　立ち上がる(たちあがる)　ん　でしょう　か？

　　When will the computers be up? (101)

　　「～だろうか / ～でしょうか」 ["I wonder __"]: DJG v3 p715; Tobira ch6 #4.

67-11. 一日中立ちっぱなしだったので一休みをしたい。

　　一日中(いちにちじゅう)　立ち(たち)っぱなし　だった　ので　一休み(ひとやすみ)　を　したい。

I've been standing all day so I'd like to rest for a bit.
「-っぱなし」 {-放し* 574} [leave in an improper state]: DJG v2 p333; Marx v2 day49; Tobira ch15 #15. 「〜ので」 ["because __"]: DJG v1 p328; Genki ch12; Marx v1 day60. 「-たい」 ["want to __"]: DJG v1 p441; Genki ch11; Marx v1 day48.

67-12. 一行はそこで立ち止まり、ひそひそと話をした。
一行(いっこう) は そこ で 立ち止まり(たちどまり)、 ひそひそ と 話(はなし) を した。
The party [group] stopped there, and engaged in a whispered colloquy. (7)
「**Verbal connectives akin to -て**」 : DJG v1 p464, v2 p64 of front matter; Tobira ch1 #5.

67-13. このネコは大体、休んでいる人の体の上に立つ。
この ネコ は 大体(だいたい)、 休ん(やすん)で いる 人(ひと) の 体(からだ) の 上(うえ) に 立つ(たつ)。
This cat usually stands on top of people's bodies when they're resting.
「-ている」 ["be __ing"; "have (done) __"]: DJG v1 p155; Genki ch7; Marx v1 day36. 「-ているひと」 {-ている人 15} ["person who is) __ing"]: Genki ch9.

67-14. 一人が丸木の上で、もう一人が下のくぼみに立つ。
一人(ひとり) が 丸木(まるき) の 上(うえ) で、 もう 一人(ひとり) が 下(した) の くぼみ に 立つ(たつ)。
One man stood above the log and the other in a pit below. (100)
「もう + (numeral) + (counter)」 ["__ more"].

67-15. 川本さんは休んでいる一行に話しかけようと立ち止まった。
川本(かわもと)さん は 休ん(やすん)で いる 一行(いっこう) に 話しかけよ(はなしかけよ)う と 立ち止まっ(たちどまっ)た。
Kawamoto-san stopped to speak to the resting party. (87)
「-ようとする」 ["try to __"]: DJG v1 p246 (under みる).

68：部

68-1. 舌の下部。
舌(した) の 下部(かぶ)。
Under the tongue. (100)

68-2. 日本中部の山々。
日本(にほん) 中部(ちゅうぶ) の 山々(やまやま)。
The mountains of Central Japan.

68-3. コピー三部の一つ。
コピー 三部(さんぶ) の 一つ(ひとつ)。
One of three copies. (100)

68-4. コンゴ東部の活火山。
コンゴ 東部(とうぶ) の 活火山(かっかざん)。
An active volcano in eastern Congo. (100)

68-5. オーストラリア中部と東部。

オーストラリア　中部(ちゅうぶ)　と　東部(とうぶ)。

Central and eastern Australia. (100)

68-6. そこから一行の一部になった。

そこ　から　一行(いっこう)　の　一部(いちぶ)　に　なった。

From there I became part of the group. (100)

68-7. ホールの上部はとても明るい。

ホール　の　上部(じょうぶ)　は　とても　明るい(あかるい)。

The upper part of the hall is very bright.

「とても〜」　["quite __"]: DJG v2 p210 (under なかなか〜); Marx v2 day47.

68-8. 土曜日にシカゴの中心部に行こう。

土曜日(どようび)　に　シカゴ　の　中心部(ちゅうしんぶ)　に　行こ(いこ)う。

Saturday let's go to downtown Chicago.

68-9. 一部はおちて、一部はまだ立っている。

一部(いちぶ)　は　おちて、　一部(いちぶ)　は　まだ　立(た)って　いる。

Part of it has fallen and another part is still standing.

68-10. ネコがダンボールの上部を取りさった。

ネコ　が　ダンボール　の　上部(じょうぶ)　を　取り(とり)さった。

The cat removed the upper part of the cardboard.

68-11. 月曜までずっと取るに足らない部下だった。

月曜(げつよう)　まで　ずっと　取る(とる)　に　足ら(たら)ない　部下(ぶか)　だった。

Until Monday I had always been an insignificant assistant.

68-12. あのバンドの一部になりたい人はたくさんいる。

あの　バンド　の　一部(いちぶ)　に　なりたい　人(ひと)　は　たくさん　いる。

There are many people who would like to become part of that band.

「-たい」　["want to __"]: DJG v1 p441; Genki ch11; Marx v1 day48.　「たくさん」 {沢山* 1504; 37} ["a lot of"]: DJG v1 p356 (under おおい); Genki ch4.

69：倍

69-1. 百万倍に上げる。

百万倍(ひゃくまんばい)　に　上げる(あげる)。

Increase by a factor of a million. (100)

69-2. 三の倍は六である。

三(さん)　の　倍(ばい)　は　六(ろく)　で　ある。

Twice three is six.

91

69-3. 三十六は十八の倍である。
　　　三十(さんじゅう)　六(ろく)　は　十八(じゅうはち)　の　倍(ばい)　である。
　　　36 is double 18. (101)

69-4. 日本の人口は倍になった。
　　　日本(にほん)　の　人口(じんこう)　は　倍(ばい)　に　なった。
　　　Japan's population doubled.

69-5. かれらは金を百倍に上げた。
　　　かれら　は　金(かね)　を　百倍(ひゃくばい)　に　上げ(あげ)た。
　　　They increased their money a hundred fold. (101)

69-6. 十セントの十倍は一ドルである。
　　　十(じゅっ)　セント　の　十倍(じゅうばい)　は　一(いち)　ドル　である。
　　　Ten dimes are equal to one dollar. (87)

69-7. イスタンブールの人口はアテネの三倍である。
　　　イスタンブール　の　人口(じんこう)　は　アテネ　の　三倍(さんばい)　である。
　　　The population of Istanbul is three times that of Athens.

69-8. 足立さんの足は小山さんの足の二倍の大きさだ。
　　　足立(あだち)さん　の　足(あし)　は　小山(こやま)さん　の　足(あし)　の　二倍(にばい)　の　大き(おおき)さ　だ。
　　　Adachi-san's feet are twice the size of Koyama-san's.

70：成

70-1. 金日成。
　　　金日成(キム・イルソン)。
　　　Kim Il Sung.

70-2. 成立月日。
　　　成立(せいりつ)　月日(がっぴ)。
　　　Month and date of establishment.

70-3. 成り行きをみる。
　　　成り行き(なりゆき)　を　みる。
　　　(Wait and) see how things develop.

70-4. この成金やろう！
　　　この　成金(なりきん)　やろう！
　　　You no-good parvenu! (90)

70-5. やっと成立した。
　　　やっと　成立(せいりつ)　した。

At last it was established [came into being].
「やっと〜」 ["finally __"]: DJG v2 p591.

70-6. 成田さんは大成する人だ。
成田(なりた)さん は 大成(たいせい) する 人(ひと) だ。
Narita-san is sure to become a great success.

70-7. 二部から成るドキュメント。
二部(にぶ) から 成る(なる) ドキュメント。
A document composed of two parts. (101)

70-8. 成立月日は十二月一日だった。
成立(せいりつ) 月日(がっぴ) は 十二月(じゅうにがつ) 一日(ついたち) だった。
The month and date of establishment was December 1.

70-9. 成人には一日三百ミリグラムだ。
成人(せいじん) に は 一日(いちにち) 三百(さんびゃく) ミリグラム だ。
300 milligrams a day for adults.

70-10. 山川さんはガス田でざいを成した。
山川(やまかわ)さん は ガス田(でん) で ざい を 成し(なし)た。
Yamakawa-san made a fortune from gas fields.

70-11. 明くんは成人するのをたのしみにしている。
明(あきら)くん は 成人(せいじん) する の を たのしみ に して いる。
Akira is looking forward to being an adult.
「の」 [nominalizer]: DJG v1 p318; Genki ch8.

70-12. 明くんは大人に成るのをたのしみにしている。
明(あきら)くん は 大人(おとな) に 成る(なる) の を たのしみ に して いる。
Akira is looking forward to being an adult.

70-13. ぼくはこれ以上の金不足では生活も成り立たない。
ぼく は これ 以上(いじょう) の 金不足(かねぶそく) で は 生活(せいかつ) も 成り立た(なりたた)ない。
If my money gets any tighter I won't be able to sustain myself.

70-14. 「活」は「三水」と「舌」とから成り立っている。
「活(かつ)」 は 「三水(さんずい)」 と 「舌(した)」 と から 成り立(なりた)っている。
Katsu (活) is composed of sanzui (氵) and shita (舌).
「と」 ["and" within an exhaustive list; cf. や]: DJG v1 p473; Genki ch4.

70-15. ヨードの1部、カリウムヨードの2部と水の300部から成る。

ヨード の 1部(ぶ)、 カリウム ヨード の 2部(ぶ) と 水(みず) の 300部(ぶ) から 成る(なる)。

It consists of one part iodine, two parts potassium iodide, and 300 parts water. (100)

「と」 ["and" within an exhaustive list; cf. や]: DJG v1 p473; Genki ch4.

71：代

71-1. 取って代わる。

取っ(とっ)て 代わる(かわる)。

Take the place of. (100)

71-2. 水のお代わりを下さい。

水(みず) の お代わり(かわり) を 下さい(ください)。

I would like some more water please. (87)

71-3. 成田さん、代わってくれる？

成田(なりた)さん、 代わっ(かわっ)て くれる？

Narita-san, can you take over?

「-てくれる」 {-て呉れる** 1478} ["do __ for (me)"]: DJG v1 p216; Genki ch16; Marx v2 day31; Tobira ch3 #12.

71-4. 10代のころ、LSDをやった。

10代(だい) の ころ、 LSD を やった。

He dropped acid as a teenager. (101)

71-5. 足立さんの代わりに行けますか？

足立(あだち)さん の 代わり(かわり) に 行け(いけ)ます か？

Can you go in place of Adachi-san? (101)

「〜(の)かわりに」 {〜(の)代わりに 71} ["in place of __"; "in compensation for __"]: DJG v1 p184, v2 p116; Marx v2 day26; Tobira ch2 #5.

71-6. この本を代えてほしいのですが。

この 本(ほん) を 代え(かえ)て ほしい の です が。

I would like to receive a replacement book.

「-てほしい」 {-て欲しい 1035} ["want(s) (someone) to __"]: DJG v1 p146; Genki ch21; Marx v1 day48. 「のである / のです / のだ / んだ」 [explanation or assertion]: DJG v1 p325; Genki ch12.

71-7. 一月のガス代はイチバンたかい。

一月(いちがつ) の ガス代(だい) は イチバン たかい。

The January gas bill is the highest.

「いちばん」 {一番 2; 299} [superlative]: DJG v1 p148; Genki ch10; Marx v1 day70.

71-8. 成田さんたちは身代金を出した。

成田(なりた)さんたち は 身代金(みのしろきん) を 出(だ)した。

The Naritas paid the ransom.

「-たち」 {-達 1475} [plural personal pronoun suffix]: DJG v1 p28 bottom & 440, v3 p47 & 50-51 of front matter.

71-9. このお金の代わりに休みがほしい。
　　　この　お金(おかね)　の　代わ(かわ)り　に　休(やす)み　が　ほしい。
　　Instead of this money I'd rather have time to rest.
　　「～(の)かわりに」 {～(の)代わりに 71} ["in place of __"; "in compensation for __"]: DJG v1 p184, v2 p116; Marx v2 day26; Tobira ch2 #5.

71-10. 大木さんの代わりにわたしが行きます。
　　　大木(おおき)さん　の　代わり(かわり)　に　わたし　が　行き(いき)ます。
　　I'm going in place of Oki-san.

71-11. 田口さんは本の代わりにパソコンをつかう。
　　　田口(たぐち)さん　は　本(ほん)　の　代わり(かわり)　に　パソコン　を　つかう。
　　Taguchi-san uses her personal computer in place of books.

71-12. 木曜日に丸山さんは川田さんの代わりにはたらいた。
　　　木曜日(もくようび)　に　丸山(まるやま)さん　は　川田(かわだ)さん　の　代わり(かわり)　に　はたらいた。
　　Maruyama-san worked in place of Kawada-san on Thursday.

71-13. コンピュータはスライド・ルールに取って代わった。
　　　コンピュータ　は　スライド・ルール　に　取(と)って　代(か)わった。
　　The computer has supplanted the slide rule. (101)

71-14. 大正の代には、日本の人口はおよそ五千五百万人だった。
　　　大正(たいしょう)　の　代(よ)　に　は、　日本(にほん)　の　人口(じんこう)　は　およそ　五千(ごせん)　五百(ごひゃく)　万人(まんにん)　だった。
　　During the Taisho Period, the population of Japan was about fifty-five million.
　　「およそ～」 {凡そ～** 1629} ["generally __"; "roughly __"]: DJG v3 p526.

71-15. 土曜日にしゅっきんしてくれたので、その代わりに、月曜日か火曜日、一日休みを取って下さい。
　　　土曜日(どようび)　に　しゅっきん　して　くれた　ので、　その　代わり(かわり)　に、　月曜日(げつようび)　か　火曜日(かようび)、　一日(いちにち)　休み(やすみ)　を　取っ(とっ)て　下さい(ください)。
　　You did us the favor of coming to work on Saturday, so in return please take a day off on Monday or Tuesday.
　　「-てくれる」 {-て呉れる** 1478} ["do __ for (me)"]: DJG v1 p216; Genki ch16; Marx v2 day31; Tobira ch3 #12. 「～ので」 ["because __"]: DJG v1 p328; Genki ch12; Marx v1 day60. 「～(の)かわりに」 {～(の)代わりに 71} ["in place of __"; "in compensation for __"]: DJG v1 p184, v2 p116; Marx v2 day26; Tobira ch2 #5.

72：王

72-1. 大王イカ。
　　　大王(だいおう)イカ。

Giant squid. (100)

72-2. 王手をかける。

王手(おうて) を かける。

[Chess] Put the king in check.

「かける」 {掛ける*1117} ["hang"; "put", "put on"]: Marx v1 day52.

72-3. フランスの王。

フランス の 王(おう)。

The king of France. (100)

72-4. エドワード王の人生は無用だった。

エドワード王(おう) の 人生(じんせい) は 無用(むよう) だった。

King Edward's life was of no use.

73 : 玉

73-1. 火の玉。

火の玉(ひのたま)。

A ball of fire. (101)

73-2. レタス一玉を下さい。

レタス 一玉(ひとたま) を 下さい(ください)。

One head of lettuce please. (101)

73-3. 目玉をつき出してやる。

目玉(めだま) を つき出し(だし)て やる。

I will peck his eyes out. (99)

「-てやる」 ["do _ (for someone)"]: DJG v1 p67 (under あげる); Marx v2 day31.

73-4. 水玉のスカートがほしい。

水玉(みずたま) の スカート が ほしい。

I want a polka-dot skirt.

73-5. 小さな玉に丸めて下さい。

小(ちい)さな 玉(たま) に 丸め(まるめ)て 下さい(ください)。

Please roll it into small pellets.

73-6. ビリヤードの玉をラックに入れる。

ビリヤード の 玉(たま) を ラック に 入れる(いれる)。

Rack pool balls. (101)

73-7. 田代さんはポケットから百円玉を取り出した。

田代(たしろ)さん は ポケット から 百円玉(ひゃくえんだま) を 取り出し(とりだし)た。

Tashiro-san took a hundred-yen coin from his pocket.

73-8. この玉ねぎの中身がくさっています。代えてほしいのですが。

この 玉ねぎ(たまねぎ) の 中身(なかみ) が くさって います。 代え(かえ)て ほしい の です が。

The inside of this onion was rotten. I would like to exchange it.

「-てほしい」 {-て欲しい 1035} ["want(s) (someone) to __"]: DJG v1 p146; Genki ch21; Marx v1 day48.

74 : 宝

74-1. 明日宝さがしに行く。

明日(あした) 宝(たから)さがし に 行く(いく)。

Tomorrow I'm going treasure hunting.

「**Verb stem + に + verb of motion**」 ["(go) __ing"; "(go) to (do) __"]: DJG v1 p297; Genki ch7; Tobira ch3 #9.

74-2. 王さまの宝玉を手に入れたい。

王さま(おうさま) の 宝玉(ほうぎょく) を 手(て) に 入(い)れたい。

I would like to get my hands on [obtain] the king's jewels.

「-たい」 ["want to __"]: DJG v1 p441; Genki ch11; Marx v1 day48.

74-3. 一回宝くじにあたってみたいです。

一回(いっかい) 宝くじ(たからくじ) に あたって みたい です。

I'd like to win the lottery someday.

「-てみる」 ["try (out) __"; "check out __"]: DJG v1 p246; Genki ch13.

74-4. 千代さんは宝くじで三千万円も手に入れた。

千代(ちよ)さん は 宝くじ(たからくじ) で 三千万(さんぜんまん) 円(えん) も 手(て) に 入れ(いれ)た。

Chiyo won thirty million yen in the lottery.

75 : 国

75-1. アフリカの国々。

アフリカ の 国々(くにぐに)。

The countries of Africa.

75-2. インドは人口の大国だ。

インド は 人口(じんこう) の 大国(たいこく) だ。

India is a great power in terms of population.

75-3. スイスは中立国である。

スイス は 中立国(ちゅうりつこく) で ある。

Switzerland is a neutral country. (87)

75-4. 中国のケースを取り上げる。

中国(ちゅうごく) の ケース を 取り上げる(とりあげる)。

Take the case of China. (101)

75-5. この本は国宝のしていを受けた。

97

この 本(ほん) は 国宝(こくほう) の していを 受け(うけ)た。
This book was designated a national treasure.

75-6. その王国は小さく山がちであった。
その 王国(おうこく) は 小(ちい)さく 山(やま)がち で あった。
The kingdom was small and mountainous. (86)
「である vs. だ」: DJG v2 p30, v3 p35 of front matter; Tobira ch7 #5. 「-がち」 {-勝ち 460} ["tend to __"]: DJG v2 p47; Marx v2 day64.

75-7. この国の人口は三百万人ぐらいです。
この 国(くに) の 人口(じんこう) は 三百万人(さんびゃくまんにん) ぐらい です。
This country's population is about 3 million.

75-8. スロベニアはヨーロッパ中心部の小国だ。
スロベニア は ヨーロッパ 中心部(ちゅうしんぶ) の 小国(しょうこく) だ。
Slovenia is a small country in Central Europe.

75-9. そのあいだに中国の人口は五倍になった。
その あいだ に 中国(ちゅうごく) の 人口(じんこう) は 五倍(ごばい) に なった。
The population of China quintupled in that period. (101)
「～あいだに」 {～間に 448} ["while __"]: DJG v1 p67; Genki ch21; Marx v1 day88.

75-10. モルドヴァはヨーロッパ東部の小さな国です。
モルドヴァ は ヨーロッパ 東部(とうぶ) の 小(ちい)さな 国(くに) です。
Moldova is a small country in Eastern Europe.

75-11. あなたは中国人ですか、それとも日本人ですか。
あなた は 中国人(ちゅうごくじん) です か、それとも 日本人(にほんじん) です か。
Are you Chinese or Japanese? (87)
「それとも～」 {其れとも** 1757} ["or __"]: DJG v1 p421; Marx v2 day14.

76：白

76-1. 白ワイン用のブドウ。
白(しろ)ワイン用(よう) の ブドウ。
White wine grape. (100)

76-2. 東山には白人がたくさんいます。
東山(ひがしやま) に は 白人(はくじん) が たくさん います。
There are many white persons in Higashiyama.

76-3. この国には白人があまりいません。

この 国(くに) に は 白人(はくじん) が あまり いません。
There are few white persons in this country.
「あまり〜ない／あんまり〜ない」 {余り〜ない 995} ["not very (much) __"]: DJG v1 p72.

76-4. 東国さんが言ったことは明白なうそだ。
東国(ひがしくに)さん が 言っ(いっ)た こと は 明白(めいはく) な うそ だ。
What Higashikuni-san said is an overt lie. (101)

76-5. この金ぞくは白金とともに取り出される。
この 金(きん)ぞく は 白金(はっきん) とともに 取り出さ(とりださ)れる。
This metal is found together with platinum. (100)
「〜とともに」 {〜と共に 356} ["along with __"]: DJG v2 p532; Marx v2 day48; Tobira ch11 #8. 「-られる」 [passive]: DJG v1 p364; Genki ch21.

76-6. 白日の下では、ホールの上部はとても明るい。
白日(はくじつ) の 下(もと) で は、 ホール の 上部(じょうぶ) は とても 明るい(あかるい)。
The upper part of the hall is very bright under the midday sun.
「〜のもとで」 {〜の下で 40} ["under __"]: DJG v2 p310.

76-7. タイの国王の行いが白日の下にさらされました。
タイ の 国王(こくおう) の 行い(おこない) が 白日(はくじつ) の 下(もと) に さらされました。
The Thai king's conduct was brought to light.
「-られる」 [passive]: DJG v1 p364; Genki ch21. 「〜にさらされる」 [passive form of さらす ("expose"): "be exposed to __"].

76-8. そしてもう一つの足も、それから二本の白い足も目に付きました。
そして もう 一つ(ひとつ) の 足(あし) も、 それ から 二本(にほん) の 白い(しろい) 足(あし) も 目(め) に 付き(つき)ました。
And then a second foot, and then two little white legs came into view. (98)
「もう + (numeral) + (counter)」 ["__ more"]. 「そして」 ["and"]: DJG v1 p422. 「それから〜」 {其れから〜** 1757} ["and then __"]: DJG v1 p416.

77：皇

77-1. 日本は、むかし「皇国」とよばれたことがある。
日本(にほん) は、 むかし 「皇国(こうこく)」 と よばれた こと が ある。
Japan was once referred to as the "Imperial State".
「〜ことがある」 {〜事がある* 80} ["__ has occurred"]: DJG v1 p196; Genki ch11; Marx v1 day62; Tobira ch1 #6.

77-2. 上皇さまは成田で日本の国宝について話された。

上皇(じょうこう)さま は 成田(なりた) で 日本(にほん) の 国宝(こくほう) について 話され(はなされ)た。
The former Emperor spoke at Narita about Japan's National Treasures.
「～について」 {～に就いて** 1283} ["about __"]: DJG v2 p280; Marx v2 day42.
「**Honorific verbs**」: DJG v1 p36; Genki ch19; Marx v1 day89; Tobira ch2 (main body).

77-3. お正月には上皇さまご本人がお出ましになられたのです。
お正月(しょうがつ) には 上皇(じょうこう)さま ご本人(ほんにん) が お出まし(おでまし) に なられた の です。
At New Year's the former Emperor appeared personally.
「お-」 [prefix expressing politeness]: DJG v1 p343. 「**Honorific verbs**」: DJG v1 p36; Genki ch19; Marx v1 day89; Tobira ch2 (main body).

78：全

78-1. 全部上手く行くよ。
全部(ぜんぶ) 上手く(うまく) 行く(いく) よ。
Everything will be fine. (87)

78-2. 全ては明らかだった。
全て(すべて) は 明(あき)らか だった。
All was clear. (90)

78-3. パン全体をたべたい。
パン 全体(ぜんたい) を たべたい。
I want to eat a whole loaf of bread.
「-たい」 ["want to __"]: DJG v1 p441; Genki ch11; Marx v1 day48.

78-4. 全部話して上げよう。
全部(ぜんぶ) 話し(はなし)て 上げよ(あげよ)う。
I will tell you all about it. (99)
「**Volitional**」 ["let's __"; "I'll __"]: DJG v1 p576 & 578 second column from right; Genki ch15; Marx v1 day29.

78-5. お金が全ての人です。
お金(おかね) が 全て(すべて) の 人(ひと) です。
Money is everything to them.

78-6. 国のために万全のさくを取る。
国(くに) の ため に 万全(ばんぜん) の さく を 取る(とる)。
Take all possible measures for the sake of the country.
「～ため(に)」 {～為に* 1236} ["for (the sake of) __"]: DJG v1 p447; Tobira ch2 #6.

78-7. あの話が全国中でひろがった。
あの 話(はなし) が 全国中(ぜんこくじゅう) で ひろがった。
That story spread across the nation.

78-8. わたしの人生の全体のパターン。

わたし の 人生(じんせい) の 全体(ぜんたい) の パターン。
The overall pattern of my life. (101)

78-9. 全国ネットワークを活用します。
全国(ぜんこく) ネットワーク を 活用(かつよう) します。
We make use of our nationwide network. (10)

78-10. アジア中心部の国々全部へ行った。
アジア 中心部(ちゅうしんぶ) の 国々(くにぐに) 全部(ぜんぶ) へ 行っ(いっ)た。
I went to all the countries in Central Asia.

78-11. 白山さんの言うことは全く正しい。
白山(しらやま)さん の 言う(いう) こと は 全く(まったく) 正しい(ただしい)。
What Shirayama-san says is spot on.

78-12. ゆきはアイルランド全土にわたっていた。
ゆき は アイルランド 全土(ぜんど) に わたって いた。
Snow was general all over Ireland. (25)
「〜にわたって / 〜にわたる」 {〜に亘って* / 〜に亘る* 1395} ["spanning over __"]: DJG v3 p447.

78-13. 白田さんは全身白いペンキだらけになった。
白田(しらた)さん は 全身(ぜんしん) 白い(しろい) ペンキ だらけ に なった。
Shirata-san was covered all over with white paint.
「-だらけ」 ["covered all over with __"; "full of __"]: DJG v2 p25.

78-14. ヨーロッパ全体に一千百万人のユダヤ人がいた。
ヨーロッパ 全体(ぜんたい) に 一千(いっせん) 百万(ひゃくまん) 人(にん) の ユダヤ人(じん) が いた。
Eleven million Jews were spread throughout Europe. (101)
Note: 1,100 (一千百) * 10,000 (万) = 11,000,000 (一千百万).

78-15. 日本の全ての国宝がこの本でいちらんできます。
日本(にほん) の 全て(すべて) の 国宝(こくほう) が この 本(ほん) で いちらん できます。
You can look over all of Japan's national treasures in this one book.

78-16. 白川さんは不正な出金のことを全部人に話した。
白川(しらかわ)さん は 不正(ふせい) な 出金(しゅっきん) の こと を 全部(ぜんぶ) 人(ひと) に 話し(はなし)た。
Shirakawa-san told people about all the improper expenditures.
「〜のこと」 {〜の事* 80} ["about __"]: DJG v2 p304.

78-17. 水はその上、さらに十五キュービットみなぎって、山は全くおおわれた。

水(みず)は その 上(うえ)、さらに 十五(じゅうご) キュービット みなぎって、山(やま)は 全く(まったく) おおわれた。

Fifteen cubits upward did the waters prevail; and the mountain was covered. (33)

「さらに〜」{更に〜 889} ["still more __"]: DJG v3 p540.「おおわれる」{覆われる 1870} [passive form of おおう ("cover"): "be covered"].

79：書

79-1. イザヤ書。

イザヤ書(しょ)。

The book of Isaiah. (101)

79-2. 日本国宝全書。

日本(にほん) 国宝(こくほう) 全書(ぜんしょ)。

Encyclopedia of Japanese National Treasures.

79-3. ペンで書いて下さい。

ペン で 書い(かい)て 下さい(ください)。

Please write with a pen. (87)

「〜で」[instrument]: DJG v1 p106; Genki ch10.

79-4. スピーチを下書きする。

スピーチ を 下書き(したがき) する。

Draft a speech. (101)

79-5. 田代さんは上手に書く。

田代(たしろ)さん は 上手(じょうず) に 書く(かく)。

Tashiro-san writes well.

79-6. 千代さんは本を書くべきだ。

千代(ちよ)さん は 本(ほん) を 書く(かく) べき だ。

Chiyo ought to write a book.

「〜べきだ」["should __"; "must __"]: DJG v2 p11; Tobira ch11 #12.

79-7. スノーは中国について書いた。

スノー は 中国(ちゅうごく) について 書い(かい)た。

Snow wrote about China. (101)

「〜について」{〜に就いて** 1283} ["about __"]: DJG v2 p280; Marx v2 day42.

79-8. そのファイルを上書きして下さい。

その ファイル を 上書き(うわがき) して 下さい(ください)。

Please overwrite that file. (101)

79-9. 手で書かれたもの／手書きのもの。

手(て) で 書か(かか)れた もの ／ 手書き(てがき) の もの。

Something written by hand. (100)

79-10. あの白書に書いてあったことは全国で成立された。

あの 白書(はくしょ) に 書い(かい)て あった こと は 全国(ぜんこく) で 成立(せいりつ) された。
The things written in that white paper were established all across the country.
「-てある」 [indicates completed action and resulting condition]: DJG v1 p76 (under ある); Genki ch21; Marx v2 day7.

80：事

80-1. 小金を大事にする人。
小金(こがね) を 大事(だいじ) に する 人(ひと)。
A great nurser of pennies. (101)

80-2. 人の事に手を出すな。
人(ひと) の 事(こと) に 手(て) を 出す(だす) な。
Don't meddle in other people's affairs. (87)
「〜のこと」 {〜の事* 80} ["about __"]: DJG v2 p304. 「**infinitive + な**」 [prohibitive: "don't __"]: DJG v1 p266; Marx v1 day40.

80-3. 体を大事にしなさい。
体(からだ) を 大事(だいじ) に し なさい。
Take good care of yourself. (87)
「-なさい」 [imperative]: DJG v1 p284; Genki ch22; Marx v1 day40.

80-4. なにか大事な話がある？
なに か 大事(だいじ) な 話(はなし) が ある？
Do you have anything important to talk about?
「なにか」 {何か* 815} ["something"; "anything"]: Genki ch8; Marx v1 day18.

80-5. 明日は用事があります。
明日(あした) は 用事(ようじ) が あります。
I have things to do tomorrow. (87)

80-6. 万事上手く行っています。
万事(ばんじ) 上手く(うまく) 行っ(いっ)て います。
Everything is going well. (87)

80-7. お身体大事にして下さい。
お身体(からだ) 大事(だいじ) に して 下さい(ください)。
Please take care of your health.

80-8. 事の成り行きを受け入れる。
事(こと) の 成り行き(なりゆき) を 受け入れる(うけいれる)。
Accept things the way they go.
「こと」 {事 80} [intangible thing]: DJG v1 p191; Tobira ch7 (first page).

80-9. 明日はとくに用事はないです。
明日(あした) は とくに 用事(ようじ) は ない です。
Tomorrow I don't have anything in particular to do.

103

80-10. かれは無事だ、全く無事なんだ。
　　　かれ は 無事(ぶじ) だ、 全く(まったく) 無事(ぶじ) なん だ。
　　　He is safe, he is quite safe. (84)

80-11. どうぞご無事で行ってらっしゃい。
　　　どうぞ ご無事(ごぶじ) で 行っ(いっ)て らっしゃい。
　　　Do have a safe trip.
　　　「どうぞ」 ["please"]: DJG v3 p84 (under どうか〜).「-て/-で」 [connective form of adjectives]: DJG v1 p464; Marx v1 day66.

80-12. 人生にはもっと大事なことがある。
　　　人生(じんせい) に は もっと 大事(だいじ) な こと が ある。
　　　There are more important things in life. (87)

80-13. 国王は全国で大事を成したのです。
　　　国王(こくおう) は 全国(ぜんこく) で 大事(だいじ) を 成し(なし)た の です。
　　　The king did great things throughout the country.

80-14. 田代さんは三回中国に行った事がある。
　　　田代(たしろ)さん は 三回(さんかい) 中国(ちゅうごく) に 行っ(いっ)た 事(こと) が ある。
　　　Tashiro-san has been to China three times.
　　　「〜ことがある」{〜事がある* 80} ["__ has occurred"]: DJG v1 p196; Genki ch11; Marx v1 day62; Tobira ch1 #6.

80-15. 足立さんたちは全てを火事でなくした。
　　　足立(あだち)さんたち は 全て(すべて) を 火事(かじ) で なくした。
　　　The Adachis lost everything in the fire. (101)
　　　「-たち」{-達 1475} [plural personal pronoun suffix]: DJG v1 p28 bottom & 440, v3 p47 & 50-51 of front matter.

80-16. 言いたい事はなんでも言ってよろしい。
　　　言い(いい)たい 事(こと) は なん でも 言っ(いっ)て よろしい。
　　　You can say whatever you want to. (87)
　　　「こと」{事 80} [intangible thing]: DJG v1 p191; Tobira ch7 (first page).「〜でも」 ["even __"]: DJG v1 p111; Marx v1 day18.「なんでも」{何でも* 815} ["whatever"]: Marx v1 day18.

80-17. 白川さんはその事について、それ以上話さなかった。
　　　白川(しらかわ)さん は その 事(こと) について、 それ 以上(いじょう) 話さ(はなさ)なかった。
　　　Shirakawa-san didn't say anything more about that matter.
　　　「〜について」{〜に就いて** 1283} ["about __"]: DJG v2 p280; Marx v2 day42.

81：自

81-1. これは自明に正しい。
　　　これ　は　自明(じめい)　に　正しい(ただしい)。
　　　This is self-evidently true. (22)

81-2. 白川さんは全く自信が無い。
　　　白川(しらかわ)さん　は　全く(まったく)　自信(じしん)　が　無い(ない)。
　　　Shirakawa-san has absolutely no confidence in herself.

81-3. 丸でわたし自身が書いたように。
　　　丸(まる)　で　わたし　自身(じしん)　が　書(か)いた　よう　に。
　　　Just as if I had written it myself.
　　　「-じしん」{-自身 81; 60} ["__ oneself"]: DJG v3 p174 & 553 (under -じたい and そのもの). 「〜ように」["as __", "as if __"]: DJG v1 p554; Genki ch22; Tobira ch1 #3.

81-4. 自らはたらける人が人の上に立つ。
　　　自ら(みずから)　はたらける　人(ひと)　が　人(ひと)　の　上(うえ)　に　立つ(たつ)。
　　　Those who can work on their own initiative are leaders. (10)

81-5. 白書の成り立ち自体を大事にしたい。
　　　白書(はくしょ)　の　成り立ち(なりたち)　自体(じたい)　を　大事(だいじ)　に　したい。
　　　I want to take care with the white paper's structure itself.
　　　「-じたい」{-自体 81; 62} ["__ itself"]: DJG v3 p174.

81-6. 二人で一心に自活しようとしている。
　　　二人(ふたり)　で　一心に(いっしんに)　自活(じかつ)　しよう　と　している。
　　　The two of them are doing their best to support themselves.
　　　「-ようとする」["try to __"]: DJG v1 p246 (under みる).

81-7. 千代ちゃんはついに自らの行いを自白した。
　　　千代(ちよ)ちゃん　は　ついに　自ら(みずから)　の　行い(おこない)　を　白白(じはく)　した。
　　　Finally Chiyo-san confessed her conduct.
　　　「ついに〜」{遂に〜* 2210} ["at last __", "at length __"]: DJG v2 p531 (under とうとう〜); Tobira ch5 #7.

81-8. 王さんはこの上なく自信のある話し手だった。
　　　王(ワン)さん　は　この　上(うえ)　なく　自信(じしん)　の　ある　話し手(はなして)　だった。
　　　Wang-san was a supremely confident speaker.
　　　「このうえない」{この上ない / 此の上ない** 41; 1756} ["utterly __"; "supremely __"]: DJG v3 p226.

Note: This series displays Chinese and Korean names in kanji, with katakana phonetic guides to indicate the Japanese approximation of the <u>native</u> reading. Many persons in Japan of Chinese or Korean descent choose to use their Japanese name reading, which in this case would be「おう」*. Using the native reading*「ワン」*would be typical in international settings.*

105

81-9. 自信をもって正しい事をしなければいけない。
   自信(じしん) を もって 正しい(ただしい) 事(こと) を しなければいけない。
   We must confidently do what is right. (101)
   「-なければいけない」 [imperative]: DJG v1 p274; Genki ch12; Tobira ch2 #1.

81-10. 三川さん、そこにはご自身で行かれたのですか？
   三川(みかわ)さん、 そこ に は ご自身(ごじしん) で 行か(いか)れた の です か？
   Mikawa-san, have you been there yourself?

81-11. 田代さんは自らが行った事について自ら話さない。
   田代(たしろ)さん は 自ら(みずから) が 行っ(おこなっ)た 事(こと) について 自ら(みずから) 話さ(はなさ)ない。
   Tashiro-san does not speak of the things he has done himself.
   「〜について」 {〜に就いて** 1283} ["about __"]: DJG v2 p280; Marx v2 day42.

81-12. 自信はないけど、田代さんはこの白書を自らの手で書いていないとおもう。
   自信(じしん) は ない けど、 田代(たしろ)さん は この 白書(はくしょ) を 自(みずか)ら の 手(て) で 書(か)いて いない と おもう。
   I can't be certain, but I think Tashiro-san did not write this white paper himself.
   「〜とおもう」 {〜と思う 142} ["think(s) (that) __"]: Genki ch9&10.

82：貝

82-1. 貝の身を取り出す。
   貝(かい) の 身(み) を 取り出す(とりだす)。
   Remove the flesh from a shellfish.

82-2. ここの人はお金の代わりに宝貝をつかう。
   ここ の 人(ひと) は お金(おかね) の 代わり(かわり) に 宝貝(たからがい) を つかう。
   The people here use cowrie shells instead of money.
   「〜(の)かわりに」 {〜(の)代わりに 71} ["in place of __"; "in compensation for __"]: DJG v1 p184, v2 p116; Marx v2 day26; Tobira ch2 #5.

82-3. このあたりではカキの貝がらが取りやすい。
   この あたり で は カキ の 貝(かい)がら が 取り(とり)やすい。
   It's easy to find oyster shells around here.
   「-やすい」 {-易い* 443} ["easy to __"]: DJG v1 p541; Genki ch20; Marx v1 day61.

83：見

83-1. 一目見る。
   一目(ひとめ) 見る(みる)。

Shoot a glance. (101)

83-2. 見なかった？
見(み)なかった？
Didn't you see?

83-3. 心の中で見る。
心(こころ) の 中(なか) で 見る(みる)。
See in one's mind. (100)

83-4. 全く見えなかった。
全く(まったく) 見え(みえ)なかった。
I could see nothing. (4)
「～みえる」 {～見える 83} ["__ can be seen"; "looks __"]: DJG v1 p243.

83-5. 東日本で見つかる貝。
東日本(ひがしにほん) で 見つかる(みつかる) 貝(かい)。
A shellfish found in Eastern Japan.

83-6. なにも見えなかった。
なに も 見え(みえ)なかった。
I could see nothing.
「なにも」 {何も* 815} ["nothing"]: DJG v1 p250; Genki ch8; Marx v1 day18.

83-7. やっと火事を見付けた。
やっと 火事(かじ) を 見付け(みつけ)た。
We finally found the fire.

83-8. 80ページを見て下さい。
80ページ を 見(み)て 下さい(ください)。
Please see page 80.

83-9. 山の上から人を見下ろす。
山の上(やまのうえ) から 人(ひと) を 見下ろす(みおろす)。
Look down on people from atop a mountain.

83-10. 日本の本土と見なされる。
日本(にほん) の 本土(ほんど) と 見なさ(みなさ)れる。
Regarded as the Japanese mainland. (100)

83-11. 事の成り行きを見るしかない。
事(こと) の 成り行き(なりゆき) を 見る(みる) しか ない。
We just have to wait to see how things develop.
「こと」 {事 80} [intangible thing]: DJG v1 p191; Tobira ch7 (first page). 「しか～ない」 ["no more than __/no other than __"]: DJG v1 p398; Genki ch14.

83-12. それは一見では見えない事だ。
それ は 一見(いっけん) で は 見え(みえ)ない 事(こと) だ。
That's not something you can perceive at one glance.

「〜みえる」 {〜見える 83} ["__ can be seen"; "looks __"]: DJG v1 p243.

83-13. 無くした宝貝を見つけ出した。
無くし(なくし)た 宝貝(たからがい) を 見つけ出し(みつけだし)た。
I discovered the missing cowrie shells.
「-だす」 {-出す 38} ["__ out"; "start to __"]: DJG v1 p102; Tobira ch7 #6.

83-14. これから本日のビデオを見る。
これ から 本日(ほんじつ) の ビデオ を 見る(みる)。
Now we shall watch today's video. (10)

83-15. みんなレバーが回るのを見た。
みんな レバー が 回る(まわる) の を 見(み)た。
We all saw the lever turn. (89)
「の」 [nominalizer]: DJG v1 p318; Genki ch8.

83-16. アジア東部でよく見られる行い。
アジア 東部(とうぶ) で よく 見(み)られる 行い(おこない)。
An action that is common in eastern Asia. (100)

83-17. ひとみさんは人を見る目がある。
ひとみさん は 人(ひと) を 見る(みる) 目(め) が ある。
Hitomi is a good judge of character. (87)

83-18. 白川さんはよくテレビを見ます。
白川(しらかわ)さん は よく テレビ を 見(み)ます。
Shirakawa-san watches a lot of TV.

83-19. 目に見えるものは全部王国の中だ。
目(め) に 見える(みえる) もの は 全部(ぜんぶ) 王国(おうこく) の 中(なか) だ。
Everything you see before you is within the kingdom.
「〜みえる」 {〜見える 83} ["__ can be seen"; "looks __"]: DJG v1 p243.

83-20. 立ち上がってあたりを見回しました。
立ち上がっ(たちあがっ)て あたり を 見回し(みまわし)ました。
I stood up and looked round me. (89)

83-21. 火の明かりの中で、宝貝を見付けた。
火(ひ) の 明かり(あかり) の 中(なか) で、 宝貝(たからがい) を 見付け(みつけ)た。
In the light of the flame, I found the cowrie shells.

83-22. ここから火山が目にはっきりと見える。
ここ から 火山(かざん) が 目(め) に はっきり と 見(み)える。
From here the volcano is clearly visible.

83-23. 中身の一部をよく見ようと手に取った。

中身(なかみ) の 一部(いちぶ) を よく 見よ(みよ)う と 手(て) に 取っ(とっ)た。

I took up one part of the contents for a better look at it. (89)

83-24. 十九日目にはハドソン川が見えてきた。

十九日(じゅうくにち) 目(め) に は ハドソン川(がわ) が 見え(みえ)て きた。

On the 19th, the Hudson came into view. (7)

「-てくる」 {-て来る** 274} ["begin to __"; "come to __"; "up to now"]: DJG v1 p221.

83-25. 一行は中国東部ではなにも見なかった。

一行(いっこう) は 中国(ちゅうごく) 東部(とうぶ) で は なに も 見(み)なかった。

The party saw nothing of Eastern China.

「なにも」 {何も* 815} ["nothing"]: DJG v1 p250; Genki ch8; Marx v1 day18.

83-26. 34ページの下から7行目を見て下さい。

34 ページ の 下(した) から 7行(ぎょう) 目(め) を 見(み)て 下さい(ください)。

Please look at the seventh line from the bottom on page 34. (87)

83-27. 一見したところ、ただの本だなに見える。

一見(いっけん) した ところ、 ただ の 本(ほん)だな に 見える(みえる)。

At first glance it looks like a plain bookshelf.

「〜ところ」 ["when __"]: DJG v2 p500; Marx v2 day46. 「ただの〜」 {只の〜* 1194} ["ordinary __", "nothing but __"]: DJG v2 p449. 「〜みえる」 {〜見える 83} ["__ can be seen"; "looks __"]: DJG v1 p243; Marx v1 day50, v2 day69.

83-28. 小川さんのために、大目に見ておいてやる。

小川(おがわ)さん の ため に、 大目(おおめ) に 見(み)て おいて やる。

For Ogawa-san, I will look the other way.

「〜ため(に)」 {〜為に* 1236} ["for (the sake of) __"]: DJG v1 p447; Marx v2 day41; Tobira ch2 #6. 「-ておく」 {-て置く 843} [indicates act of prudence/getting something done]: DJG v1 p357; Genki ch15; Marx v2 day34. 「-てやる」 ["do __ (for someone)"]: DJG v1 p67 (under あげる); Marx v2 day31.

83-29. わたしはわたし自身の目でそれを見たのだ。

わたし は わたし 自身(じしん) の 目(め) で それ を 見(み)た の だ。

I saw it with my own eyes. (87)

「のである / のです / のだ / んだ」 [explanation or assertion]: DJG v1 p325; Genki ch12.

83-30. 十二月二十六日、山田さんは大事なことを見つけ出した。

十二月(じゅうにがつ) 二十六日(にじゅうろくにち)、 山田(やまだ)さん は 大事(だいじ) な こと を 見つけ出し(みつけだし)た。

109

On December the 26th, Yamada-san made an important discovery.

83-31. ドロシーにはなにも見えませんでしたが、トトには見えました。

ドロシー に は なに も 見え(みえ)ません でした が、 トト には 見え(みえ)ました。

Dorothy could not see at all, but Toto could. (99)

「なにも」 {何も* 815} ["nothing"]: DJG v1 p250; Genki ch8; Marx v1 day18. 「が」 ["but"]: DJG v1 p120, v2 p18; Marx v1 day59.

84：力

84-1. 体力の不足。

体力(たいりょく) の 不足(ふそく)。

Lack of physical strength. (100)

84-2. 全力で力む。

全力(ぜんりょく) で 力む(りきむ)。

Work with all one's strength.

84-3. 体力全部で力む。

体力(たいりょく) 全部(ぜんぶ) で 力む(りきむ)。

Try with all one's might.

84-4. 全国の力を活用する。

全国(ぜんこく) の 力(ちから) を 活用(かつよう) する。

Exploit the power of the whole country.

84-5. これから自力で生活したい。

これ から 自力(じりき) で 生活(せいかつ) したい。

I want to live independently from now on.

84-6. 田代さんには生活力があります。

田代(たしろ)さん に は 生活力(せいかつりょく) が あります。

Tashiro-san is a person of much vitality.

84-7. 成田さんはパスワードを入力した。

成田(なりた)さん は パスワード を 入力(にゅうりょく) した。

Narita-san entered his password.

84-8. 中国の人たちはとても活力がある。

中国(ちゅうごく) の 人(ひと)たち は とても 活力(かつりょく) が ある。

The people of China are full of energy.

84-9. 体力全部で力んだが、できなかった。

体力(たいりょく) 全部(ぜんぶ) で 力(りき)んだ が、 できなかった。

I tried with all my might, but I couldn't do it.

「が」 ["but"]: DJG v1 p120, v2 p18; Marx v1 day59.

84-10. 「人力」とは、人の力を用いる事を言う。
 「人力(じんりき)」 と は、 人(ひと) の 力(ちから) を 用いる(もちいる) 事(こと) を 言う(いう)。
  "Jinriki" means using the strength of a person.
  「こと」 {事 80} [nominalizer]: DJG v1 p193.

84-11. 東国さんはさらに力を入れることにした。
 東国(ひがしくに)さん は さらに 力(ちから) を 入れる(いれる) こと に した。
  Higashikuni-san redoubled his efforts.
  「さらに〜」 {更に〜 889} ["still more __"]: DJG v3 p540. 「〜ことにする」 {〜事にする* 80} ["decide to __"]: DJG v1 p204; Genki ch23; Marx v2 day80.

84-12. 部下にしては、白山さんは中々力があるな。
 部下(ぶか) に して は、 白山(しらやま)さん は 中々(なかなか) 力(ちから) が ある な。
  For an assistant, Shirayama-san sure has a lot of power.
  「〜にしては」 ["for (a) __"]: DJG v1 p309; Marx v2 day82. 「なかなか〜」 {中々〜* 35} ["quite __"; "not readily/quickly __"]: DJG v2 p206; Tobira ch6 #14. 「な」 [male alternative to ね]: DJG v1 p46 examples 9-11.

84-13. 「自力」とは、自らの力を用いる事を言う。
 「自力(じりき)」 と は、 自ら(みずから) の 力(ちから) を 用いる(もちいる) 事(こと) を 言う(いう)。
  "Jiriki" means using one's own strength.
  「こと」 {事 80} [nominalizer]: DJG v1 p193.

84-14. 一見白川さんは体力がないように見えるが、そうでもない。
 一見(いっけん) 白川(しらかわ)さん は 体力(たいりょく) が ない ように 見える(みえる) が、 そう でも ない。
  At first glance Shirakawa-san appears not to have strength, but that's not the case.
  「〜ように」 ["as __", "as if __"]: DJG v1 p554; Genki ch22; Tobira ch1 #3. 「〜みえる」 {〜見える 83} ["__ can be seen"; "looks __"]: DJG v1 p243; Marx v1 day50, v2 day69.

85 : 刀

85-1. 山刀を用いますか。
 山刀(やまがたな) を 用い(もちい)ます か。
  Do you use a hatchet?

85-2. 小刀一本で足りますか。
 小刀(こがたな) 一本(いっぽん) で 足り(たり)ます か。
  Will one knife be enough?

85-3. 日本刀を見た事がありますか。
 日本刀(にほんとう) を 見(み)た 事(こと) が あります か。

Have you ever seen a Japanese sword?

「〜ことがある」 {〜事がある* 80} ["__ has occurred"]: DJG v1 p196; Genki ch11; Marx v1 day62; Tobira ch1 #6.

85-4. 「大刀」とは、大きな刀の事を言う。

「大刀(だいとう)」 と は、 大(おお)きな 刀(かたな) の 事(こと) を 言う(いう)。

"Daito" means a long sword.

「〜のこと」 {〜の事* 80} ["about __"]: DJG v2 p304.

Note: 「大刀」 *can also be pronounced* 「たち」.

86 : 切

86-1. 一切れのパイ。

一切れ(ひときれ) の パイ。

A piece of pie. (101)

86-2. 切り口を付ける。

切り口(きりくち) を 付ける(つける)。

Cut a slit into. (100)

86-3. 下部を切り取る。

下部(かぶ) を 切り取る(きりとる)。

Cut away the underpart of. (100)

Note: This exercise is an example of the "Parallel definitions" described in the Introduction (in this case the word being defined is "undercut", as in "undercut a vein of ore"). Keep in mind that the English text is not a definition of the Japanese text, but its equivalent.

86-4. エンジンを切る。

エンジン を 切る(きる)。

Cut the engine. (101)

86-5. 千切りキャベツ。

千切り(せんぎり) キャベツ。

Shredded cabbage. (101)

86-6. メロンの一切れを切る。

メロン の 一切れ(ひときれ) を 切る(きる)。

Cut one segment of a melon.

86-7. 体をもっと大切にしたい。

体(からだ) を もっと 大切(たいせつ) に したい。

I'd like to take better care of my health.

86-8. ピザは一人二切れずつだ。

ピザ は 一人(ひとり) 二切れ(ふたきれ)ずつ だ。

There are two slices of pizza for each person. (87)

「-ずつ」 ["__ each"]: DJG v1 p572; Tobira ch11 #9.

86-9. ステレオを切って下さい。
　　　ステレオ　を　切っ(きっ)て　下さい(ください)。
　　　Turn off the stereo, please. (101)

86-10. ロースト用のラムの切り身。
　　　ロースト用(よう)　の　ラム　の　切り身(きりみ)。
　　　A cut of lamb suitable for roasting. (100)

86-11. 山田さんを信じ切っている。
　　　山田(やまだ)さん　を　信じ(しんじ)切っ(きっ)て　いる。
　　　I trust Yamada-san completely.

86-12. このはさみは、よく切れる。
　　　この　はさみ　は、　よく　切れる(きれる)。
　　　These scissors cut well. (87)

86-13. すると白川さんは口火を切った。
　　　すると　白川(しらかわ)さん　は　口火(くちび)　を　切っ(きっ)た。
　　　Then Shirakawa-san started in (on all that he had to say). (90)

86-14. 木の木目を切るための手のこぎり。
　　　木(き)　の　木目(もくめ)　を　切る(きる)　ため　の　手(て)のこぎり。
　　　A handsaw for cutting with the grain of the wood. (100)

86-15. 体の一部が自切を行うようにする。
　　　体(からだ)　の　一部(いちぶ)　が　自切(じせつ)　を　行う(おこなう)　ように　する。
　　　Cause a body part to undergo autotomy. (100)
　　　「～ようにする」 ["make sure (that) __"; "(act) so as to __"]: DJG v1 p562; Marx v2 day72; Tobira ch3 #13.

86-16. わたしはいつまでもそれを大切にする。
　　　わたし　は　いつ　まで　も　それ　を　大切(たいせつ)　に　する。
　　　I shall treasure it always. (101)

86-17. 木こりは手おのでレタスを千切りにした。
　　　木こり(きこり)　は　手(て)おの　で　レタス　を　千切り(せんぎり)　にした。
　　　The woodman shredded the lettuce with his hatchet.

86-18. 本人からの信書は一切受け取っていません。
　　　本人(ほんにん)　から　の　信書(しんしょ)　は　一切(いっさい)　受け取っ(うけとっ)て　いません。
　　　I never received any personal correspondence from this individual.
　　　「いっさい～ない」 {一切～ない 2; 86} ["no __ whatsoever"]: DJG v3 p159.

86-19. 田代さんは手を小刀で切ってしまいました。

113

田代(たしろ)さん は 手(て) を 小刀(こがたな) で 切っ(きっ)て しまいました。

Tashiro-san cut his hand with a pocketknife.

「-てしまう」 ["do (something regrettable)"; "finish __ing"]: DJG v1 p403; Genki ch18; Marx v2 day28.

86-20. これは大切なチャンスだから、みな力を入れよう。

これ は 大切(たいせつ) な チャンス だ から、 みな 力(ちから) を 入れよ(いれよ)う。

This is an important opportunity, so let's all give it our best effort.

「だから」 ["so", "that's why"; "since", "because"]: DJG v1 p413; Marx v2 day11.
「**Volitional**」 ["let's __"; "I'll __"]: DJG v1 p576 & 578 second column from right; Genki ch15; Marx v1 day29.

86-21. オズの国で、心のない木こりが手おのを用いて木を切った。

オズ の 国(くに) で、 心(こころ) の ない 木こり(きこり) が 手(て)おの を 用い(もちい)て 木(き) を 切っ(きっ)た。

In the Land of Oz, a woodman with no heart chopped wood with his hatchet.

86-22. もはや全国の人々は、トランプさんが言う事を一切信じない。

もはや 全国(ぜんこく) の 人々(ひとびと) は、 トランプさん が 言(い)う 事(こと) を 一切(いっさい) 信(しん)じない。

No longer will people across the country believe a word out of Trump's mouth.

「こと」 {事 80} [nominalizer]: DJG v1 p193. 「いっさい〜ない」 {一切〜ない 2; 86} ["no __ whatsoever"]: DJG v3 p159.

87：刃

87-1. この刀の刃はまだするどい。

この 刀(かたな) の 刃(は) は まだ するどい。

This knife's blade is still sharp.

87-2. この刀刃はとてもよく切れる。

この 刀刃(とうじん) は とても よく 切れる(きれる)。

This blade cuts very well.

87-3. 「白刃」とは、むき出しの刃の事を言う。

「白刃(はくじん)」 と は、 むき出し(むきだし) の 刃(は) の 事(こと) を 言(い)う。

"*Hakujin*" refers to a bare blade.

87-4. 中田さんが、自刃するため、刃をむき出した。

中田(なかた)さん が、 自刃(じじん) する ため、 刃(は) を むき出し(むきだし)た。

Nakata-san unsheathed the blade in order to take it to himself.

「-だす」 {-出す 38} ["__ out"; "start to __"]: DJG v1 p102; Tobira ch7 #6.

87-5. 千代さんは自らの足をするどい刃もので切った。

114

千代(ちよ)さん は 自ら(みずから) の 足(あし) を するどい 刃(は)もの で 切っ(きっ)た。
Chiyo cut her own feet with sharp knives.

87-6. するどい刃ものだから手を切らないようにしてね。
するどい 刃(は)もの だ から 手(て) を 切ら(きら)ない よう に して ね。
It's sharp cutlery so be careful not to cut your hands.

「だから」 ["so", "that's why"; "since", "because"]: DJG v1 p413; Marx v2 day11.
「〜ようにする」 ["make sure (that) __"; "(act) so as to __"]: DJG v1 p562; Tobira ch3 #13.
「ね」 [speaker seeks confirmation or agreement]: DJG v1 p45 & 286; Genki ch2.

88：分

88-1. 十二じ八分すぎ。
十二(じゅうに)じ 八分(はっぷん) すぎ。
Eight minutes past twelve.

88-2. 4分の1に分ける。
4分(ぶん) の 1 に 分ける(わける)。
Divide into quarters. (100)

88-3. ドリルの刃の部分。
ドリル の 刃(は) の 部分(ぶぶん)。
The cutting part of a drill. (100)

88-4. これで十分足りる。
これ で 十分(じゅうぶん) 足りる(たりる)。
This is plenty.

88-5. 十一じ十七分だった。
十一(じゅういち)じ 十七(じゅうなな)分(ふん) だった。
It was seventeen minutes past eleven.

88-6. もうすこしで三十分！
もう すこし で 三十分(さんじゅっぷん)！
Nearly the half-hour! (15)

88-7. それで十分以上ある。
それで 十分(じゅうぶん) 以上(いじょう) ある。
That's more than enough.

「〜で」 [instrument]: DJG v1 p106; Genki ch10.

88-8. 三ヶ月分の生ビール。
三ヶ月(さんかげつ) 分(ぶん) の 生(なま) ビール。
Three months' worth of draft beer. (58)

「-ぶん」 {-分 88} [portion]: DJG v2 p16.

88-9. 二、三分の話をした。
　　　二(に)、 三(さん) 分(ぷん) の 話(はなし) を した。
　　We had a brief chat.

88-10. 自分に全く自信が無い。
　　　自分(じぶん) に 全く(まったく) 自信(じしん) が 無い(ない)。
　　I have no confidence in myself. (10)

88-11. たっぷり二十分まった。
　　　たっぷり 二十分(にじゅっぷん) まった。
　　I waited a good twenty minutes.

88-12. 二万五千円で十分ですか。
　　　二万(にまん) 五千(ごせん) 円(えん) で 十分(じゅうぶん) です か。
　　Is twenty-five thousand yen enough?

88-13. 人口の大部分は白人です。
　　　人口(じんこう) の 大部分(だいぶぶん) は 白人(はくじん) です。
　　Most of the population is white. (101)

88-14. 自分のまわりをよく見回す。
　　　自分(じぶん) の まわり を よく 見回す(みまわす)。
　　Look about oneself. (100)

88-15. 大きな刀はお金が大分かかる。
　　　大(おお)きな 刀(かたな) は お金(おかね) が 大分(だいぶ) かかる。
　　A large knife is expensive.

88-16. それが一目ではっきり分かる。
　　　それ が 一目(ひとめ) で はっきり 分かる(わかる)。
　　That is clear at a glance. (10)

88-17. 目と耳は、体のよわい部分である。
　　　目(め) と 耳(みみ) は、 体(からだ) の よわい 部分(ぶぶん) である。
　　Eyes and ears are vulnerable parts of the body.

88-18. 川田さんは十分以上な水分を取る。
　　　川田(かわだ)さん は 十分(じゅうぶん) 以上(いじょう) な 水分(すいぶん) を 取る(とる)。
　　Kawada-san takes more than enough fluids.

88-19. この本はとても分かりやすいです。
　　　この 本(ほん) は とても 分かり(わかり)やすい です。
　　This book is very easy to follow.
　　「-やすい」 {-易い* 443} ["easy to __"]: DJG v1 p541; Genki ch20; Marx v1 day61.

88-20. お金が足りるかどうか分かりません。

116

お金(おかね) が 足りる(たりる) か どうか 分かり(わかり)ません。
I don't know whether I've enough money.
「～かどうか」 ["whether __ (or not)"]: DJG v1 p168; Marx v2 day26.

88-21. わたしは自分のチームを信じている。
わたし は 自分(じぶん) の チーム を 信じ(しんじ)て いる。
I have confidence in our team. (101)

88-22. 自分自身の事さえもかんがえなかった。
自分(じぶん) 自身(じしん) の 事(こと) さえ も かんがえなかった。
She thought not even of herself. (42)
「-じしん」 {-自身 81; 60} ["__ oneself"]: DJG v3 p174 & 553 (under -じたい and そのもの). 「～のこと」 {～の事* 80} ["about __"]: DJG v2 p304. 「～さえ」 ["even __"; "(if) just __"]: DJG v2 p363; Marx v2 day60-61; Tobira ch5 #6.

88-23. それは自分自身で見つけるしかないよ。
それ は 自分(じぶん) 自身(じしん) で 見つける(みつける) しか ない よ。
You must find that out for yourself. (99)
「しか～ない」 ["no more than __/no other than __"]: DJG v1 p398; Genki ch14.

88-24. 大部分の人はもうすでに行ったんです。
大部分(だいぶぶん) の 人(ひと) は もう すでに 行っ(いっ)た んです。
Almost everyone has already left. (87)

88-25. この話を信じるかどうか分かりません。
この 話(はなし) を 信じる(しんじる) か どうか 分かり(わかり)ません。
I can't tell whether to believe this story.

88-26. ここにいる大部分の人が日本ごを話せます。
ここ に いる 大部分(だいぶぶん) の 人(ひと) が 日本(にほん)ご を 話せ(はなせ)ます。
Almost everyone here can speak Japanese.

88-27. 自分が一体なにをしているか分かっているのか？
自分(じぶん) が 一体(いったい) なに を して いる か 分かっ(わかっ)て いる の か？
Have you any idea what you are doing? (87)

88-28. 下田さんの言った事はさっぱり分からなかった。
下田(しもだ)さん の 言っ(いっ)た 事(こと) は さっぱり 分から(わから)なかった。
I could make nothing of what Shimoda-san said. (87)

88-29. 中本さんは自分のいとこを用人の身分におとした。

117

中本(なかもと)さん は 自分(じぶん) の いとこ を 用人(ようにん) の 身分(みぶん) に おとした。
Nakamoto-san reduced her own cousin to the status of servant.

89：公

89-1. それは公にされた話だ。
それ は 公(おおやけ) に された 話(はなし) だ。
That story has been made public.

89-2. 公立に受かってよかったね。
公立(こうりつ) に 受かっ(うかっ)て よかった ね。
It's great that you passed the entrance exam for a public (school).
「-てよかった」 {-て良かった* 285} ["was good to have __ed"]: DJG v1 p89 (under -ばよかった; note typo: "yakatta" should be "yokatta"); Genki ch19. 「ね」 [speaker seeks confirmation or agreement]: DJG v1 p45 & 286; Genki ch2; Marx v2 day2.

89-3. 田代さんは公明正大な人だね。
田代(たしろ)さん は 公明正大(こうめいせいだい) な 人(ひと) だ ね。
Tashiro-san is a fair and upright person.

89-4. これは明白に不公正な行いだ。
これ は 明白(めいはく) に 不公正(ふこうせい) な 行い(おこない) だ。
This is a clearly unjust act.

89-5. このニュースはもう公になったの？
この ニュース は もう 公(おおやけ) に なった の？
Has this news become public?

89-6. 山口のチームは公正にプレーする。
山口(やまぐち) の チーム は 公正(こうせい) に プレー する。
The Yamaguchi team plays fairly.

89-7. 山下さんは正しいことを行って公正な人だ。
山下(やました)さん は 正しい(ただしい) こと を 行っ(おこなっ)て 公正(こうせい) な 人(ひと) だ。
Yamashita-san is a just person who does what is right.

89-8. 白川さんは、自分が信じている事をおもい切って公言した。
白川(しらかわ)さん は、 自分(じぶん) が 信じ(しんじ)て いる 事(こと) を おもい切っ(きっ)て 公言(こうげん) した。
Shirakawa-san boldly made a public declaration of her beliefs.

90：別

90-1. それは話が別です。

118

それ は 話(はなし) が 別(べつ) です。
That is another matter. (89)

90-2. 別人になったみたい。
別人(べつじん) に なった みたい。
I feel like another person. (87)
「〜みたい(だ)」 ["(is) like __"; "seems like __"]: DJG v3 p105 (under 〜ごとし); Genki ch17; Marx v2 day69.

90-3. 別のを見せて下さい。
別(べつ) の を 見せ(みせ)て 下さい(ください)。
Please show me another one. (87)

90-4. 別れの一言を言いたい。
別れ(わかれ) の 一言(ひとこと) を 言い(いい)たい。
I'd like to make a farewell remark.

90-5. わしには分別があるんだ。
わし に は 分別(ふんべつ) が ある ん だ。
I've a head on my shoulders, I have. (90)

90-6. その二人は土曜日に別れた。
その 二人(ふたり) は 土曜日(どようび) に 別れ(わかれ)た。
Those two broke up on Saturday.

90-7. あんな無分別なことをするな。
あんな 無分別(むふんべつ) な こと を する な。
Don't do such an injudicious thing.
「infinitive + な」 [prohibitive: "don't __"]: DJG v1 p266; Marx v1 day40.

90-8. ついに別れの日がやってきた。
ついに 別れ(わかれ) の 日(ひ) が やって きた。
The day to say good-bye finally came. (10)
「ついに〜」 {遂に〜* 2210} ["at last __", "at length __"]: DJG v2 p531 (under とうとう〜); Tobira ch5 #7. 「やってくる」 {やって来る 274} ["come (to)", "approach"; "come around"; "turn up"].

90-9. 別れ話はタイミングが大切だね。
別れ話(わかればなし) は タイミング が 大切(たいせつ) だ ね。
When it comes to discussing a breakup, timing is key.

90-10. 下川さんはとても分別のある人だ。
下川(しもかわ)さん は とても 分別(ふんべつ) の ある 人(ひと) だ。
Shimokawa-san is a very sensible person. (101)

90-11. 上田さんはかのじょに別れ話を切り出した。
上田(うえだ)さん は かのじょ に 別れ話(わかればなし) を 切り出し(きりだし)た。

119

Ueda-san started talking to his girlfriend about breaking up. (87)
「-だす」 {-出す 38} ["__ out"; "start to __"]: DJG v1 p102; Tobira ch7 #6.

90-12. 全国の分別のある人は、トランプさんが言う事を一切信じない。
全国(ぜんこく) の 分別(ふんべつ) の ある 人(ひと) は、 トランプさん が 言(い)う 事(こと) を 一切(いっさい) 信(しん)じない。
Wise folks across the country don't believe a word out of Trump's mouth.
「いっさい〜ない」 {一切〜ない 2; 86} ["no __ whatsoever"]: DJG v3 p159.

91：長

91-1. 四ミリ長いです。
四(よん)ミリ 長い(ながい) です。
It's four millimeters too long.

91-2. 人の体の長さだ。
人(ひと) の 体(からだ) の 長(なが)さ だ。
It's the length of a person's body. (100)
「-さ」 ["__ness"]: DJG v1 p381; Marx v1 day67; Tobira ch1 #2.

91-3. 長話はもう止めたら？
長話(ながばなし) は もう 止め(やめ)たら？
How about giving your tongue a rest?
「-たら(どうですか)」 ["why not __"]: DJG v1 p457; Genki ch14.

91-4. 長い目で見て下さい。
長い(ながい) 目(め) で 見(み)て 下さい(ください)。
I hope you won't expect results immediately. (87)

91-5. 話せば長くなります。
話せ(はなせ)ば 長く(ながく) なります。
It's a long story. (99)
「-ば」 ["if __"]: DJG v1 p81; Genki ch22.

91-6. 部長を長くじっと見た。
部長(ぶちょう) を 長く(ながく) じっと 見(み)た。
I gave the Division Chief a long, fixed look. (100)

91-7. 川上部長は身長190センチです。
川上(かわかみ) 部長(ぶちょう) は 身長(しんちょう) 190センチ です。
Division Chief Kawakami is 1.9 meters tall.

91-8. あんな生活で白田さんは長生きしないだろう。
あんな 生活(せいかつ) で 白田(しらた)さん は 長生き(ながいき) しない だろう。
With that lifestyle, I don't expect Shirata-san to make it to old age.
「〜だろう/〜でしょう」 ["probably __"]: DJG v1 p100; Genki ch12; Tobira ch2 #9.

120

91-9. 取り出されないならば、ポリープは成長できる。

　　取り出さ(とりださ)れない ならば、 ポリープ は 成長(せいちょう)できる。

　　Polyps can vegetate if not removed. (101)

　　「〜なら(ば)」 ["if __"]: DJG v1 p281; Genki ch13; Marx v2 day23; Tobira ch3 #5.

91-10. 長いハイキングで、下田さんの足は、水ぶくれになった。

　　長い(ながい) ハイキング で、 下田(しもだ)さん の 足(あし) は、水(みず)ぶくれ に なった。

　　Shimoda-san's feet blistered during the long hike. (101)

　　「〜で」 ["due to __"]: DJG v1 p107.

91-11. コドモはすぐに自分が成長するものだという事が分かるのです。

　　コドモ は すぐ に 自分(じぶん) が 成長(せいちょう) する もの だ という 事(こと) が 分かる(わかる) の です。

　　Children soon know that they will grow up. (64)

　　「すぐ」 ["immediately"; "directly"]: DJG v2 p439. 「〜という」 {〜と言う* 51} [links identifier with identified]: DJG v1 p486; Genki ch20; Tobira ch10 (first page).

91-12. 日本のいちばん長い川は三百六十七キロメートルの長さがあります。

　　日本(にほん) の いちばん 長(なが)い 川(かわ) は 三百(さんびゃく)六十(ろくじゅう) 七(なな) キロメートル の 長(なが)さ が あります。

　　Japan's longest river is three hundred sixty-seven kilometers long.

　　「いちばん」 {一番 2; 299} [superlative]: DJG v1 p148; Genki ch10; Marx v1 day70.

92：男

92-1. いまは白い男が見える。

　　いま は 白い(しろい) 男(おとこ) が 見える(みえる)。

　　I see a white man this time. (25)

92-2. 川上さんは男らしい人だ。

　　川上(かわかみ)さん は 男らしい(おとこらしい) 人(ひと) だ。

　　Kawakami-san is a masculine type.

　　「〜らしい」 ["(it) seems (that) __", "I heard (that) __"; "__-like"]: DJG v1 p373; Marx v2 day70; Tobira ch5 #13.

92-3. 二人は男に付いて行った。

　　二人(ふたり) は 男(おとこ) に 付い(つい)て 行っ(いっ)た。

　　Two followed the man. (9)

92-4. 大男はとても分別のある人だ。

　　大男(おおおとこ) は とても 分別(ふんべつ) の ある 人(ひと) だ。

　　The Giant is a sensible man.

92-5. 三人の男が手に手を取って行った。

121

三人(さんにん) の 男(おとこ) が 手(て) に 手(て) を 取っ(とっ)て 行っ(いっ)た。

Three men went together, hand in hand. (90)

92-6. その男はアンテナを取り付けようとした。

その 男(おとこ) は アンテナ を 取り付け(とりつけ)よう と した。

The man tried to install his own antenna. (87)

「-ようとする」 ["try to __"]: DJG v1 p246 (under みる).

92-7. 上田さんの長男は東大に受かったんだよ。

上田(うえだ)さん の 長男(ちょうなん) は 東大(とうだい) に 受かっ(うかっ)た ん だ よ。

Ueda-san's eldest son passed the Tokyo University entrance exam.

92-8. その男は明らかに目が見えないようだった。

その 男(おとこ) は 明(あき)らか に 目(め) が 見え(みえ)ない よう だった。

He was plainly blind. (90)

「〜ようだ」 ["looks like __"; "seems (that) __"]: DJG v1 p547; Marx v2 day66.

92-9. 長田さんは、ブラジル出身の男にひかれた。

長田(ながた)さん は、 ブラジル 出身(しゅっしん) の 男(おとこ) に ひかれた。

Nagata-san fell for a man from Brazil. (101)

「〜に」 [marks agent/source]: DJG v1 p292 & 303.

92-10. 大男は、ほかの男を足して二倍くらいすごかった。

大男(おおおとこ) は、 ほか の 男(おとこ) を 足し(たし)て 二倍(にばい) くらい すごかった。

The Giant was twice the man all the rest were. (75)

「〜くらい」 {〜位* 577} ["to __ extent"]: DJG v2 p151.

92-11. むかしは、「男なら男らしくしっかりしなさい」と言うことをよくきかされた。

むかし は、 「男(おとこ) なら 男らしく(おとこらしく) しっかり しなさい」 と 言う(いう) こと を よく きかされた。

In the past, one would often hear people say "Act like a man".

「〜なら(ば)」 ["if __"]: DJG v1 p281; Genki ch13; Marx v2 day23; Tobira ch3 #5.
「〜という」 {〜と言う* 51} [links identifier with identified]: DJG v1 p486; Genki ch20; Tobira ch10 (first page).

93 : 女

93-1. 女中の千代でした。

女中(じょちゅう) の 千代(ちよ) でした。

It was the housemaid, Chiyo. (1)

93-2. 正男さんは女を見る目がない。
　　　正男(まさお)さん は 女(おんな) を 見る(みる) 目(め) が ない。
　　　Masao has no eye for women. (87)

93-3. 長人さんがじっと女の人を見る。
　　　長人(ながと)さん が じっと 女(おんな) の 人(ひと) を 見(み)る。
　　　Nagato stares at women. (10)

93-4. 男女一人ずつ受付をすればどうですか？
　　　男女(だんじょ) 一人(ひとり)ずつ 受付(うけつけ) を すれば どう です か？
　　　How about we put one man and one woman at the reception?
　　　「-ずつ」 ["__ each"]: DJG v1 p572; Tobira ch11 #9. 「どう」 {如何** 2197; 815} ["how"]: DJG v1 p114.

93-5. 千代さんの長女は明日から休みを取るらしい。
　　　千代(ちよ)さん の 長女(ちょうじょ) は 明日(あした) から 休み(やすみ) を 取る(とる) らしい。
　　　It looks like Chiyo's eldest girl starts her vacation tomorrow.
　　　「～らしい」 ["(it) seems (that) __", "I heard (that) __"; "__-like"]: DJG v1 p373; Marx v2 day70; Tobira ch5 #13.

94 : 子

94-1. 男の子、女の子？
　　　男の子(おとこのこ)、 女の子(おんなのこ)？
　　　Boy or girl? (64)

94-2. DNAは分子の王である。
　　　DNA は 分子(ぶんし) の 王(おう) で ある。
　　　DNA is the king of molecules. (101)

94-3. 月子ちゃんは一人っ子だ。
　　　月子(つきこ)ちゃん は 一人っ子(ひとりっこ) だ。
　　　Tsukiko is an only child.
　　　Note: 「-ちゃん」 *is a diminutive and affectionate name suffix.*

94-4. 日本で子どもが生まれた。
　　　日本(にほん) で 子ども(こども) が 生まれ(うまれ)た。
　　　We had a baby in Japan. (10)

94-5. 王子の心はよく分かっていた。
　　　王子(おうじ) の 心(こころ) は よく 分かっ(わかっ)て いた。
　　　She knew the prince's feelings well. (55)

94-6. 別々のクラスの女の子と男の子。
　　　別々(べつべつ) の クラス の 女の子(おんなのこ) と 男の子(おとこのこ)。

Girls and boys in separate classes. (101)

94-7. 一つの玉子を二人で分けましょう。
一つ(ひとつ) の 玉子(たまご) を 二人(ふたり) で 分け(わけ)ましょう。
Let's split one egg between the two of us.

94-8. このクラスに男子はなん人いますか？
この クラス に 男子(だんし) は なん人(にん) います か？
How many boys are there in this class? (87)
「～いますか」 {～居ますか* 255} [inquire as to __'s existence/presence]: Genki ch4.

94-9. ぼくは男の子だし、きみは女の子だから。
ぼく は 男の子(おとこのこ) だ し、 きみ は 女の子(おんなのこ) だ から。
Because I am a boy and you are a girl. (64)
「し」 ["and", "besides"]: DJG v1 p395; Genki ch13. 「きみ」 {君 1407} [informal: "you"]: DJG v1 p28.

94-10. このクラスには女子は三人しかいません。
この クラス に は 女子(じょし) は 三人(さんにん) しか いません。
There are only three girls in the class. (87)
「しか～ない」 ["no more than __/no other than __"]: DJG v1 p398; Genki ch14.

94-11. きみのお子さんは男の子ですか、女の子ですか？
きみ の お子さん(おこさん) は 男の子(おとこのこ) です か、 女の子(おんなのこ) です か？
Is your child a boy or a girl? (87)

94-12. ドアのところに立っているあの男の子はだれですか。
ドア の ところ に 立っ(たっ)て いる あの 男の子(おとこのこ) は だれ です か。
Who's that boy standing at the door? (87)

94-13. ヨーロッパ人、中国人、日本人の男、女、子どもたち。
ヨーロッパ人(じん)、 中国人(ちゅうごくじん)、 日本人(にほんじん) の 男(おとこ)、 女(おんな)、 子ども(こども)たち。
Europeans and natives, Chinese and Japanese, men, women and children. (7)
「-ども」 {-共 356} [plural personal pronoun suffix]: DJG v1 p28 bottom & 440, v3 p47 & 50-51 of front matter (under -たち).

95 : 好

95-1. 長人さんは女好きだ。
長人(ながと)さん は 女好き(おんなずき) だ。
Nagato is a womanizer.

124

95-2. 月子さんの全部が好き。
　　　月子(つきこ)さん　の　全部(ぜんぶ)　が　好き(すき)。
　　　I like every part of Tsukiko. (87)

95-3. 人それぞれの好みがあります。
　　　人(ひと)　それぞれ　の　好み(このみ)　が　あります。
　　　Each person has his or her own preferences.
　　　「それぞれ」 {其々** 1757} ["each"; "respectively"]: DJG v2 p436; Tobira ch6 #6.

95-4. 明子さんのことが大好きです。
　　　明子(あきこ)さん　の　こと　が　大好き(だいすき)　です。
　　　I really like Akiko.
　　　「〜のこと」 {〜の事* 80} ["about __"]: DJG v2 p304.

95-5. 正男さんはコーヒーを好まない。
　　　正男(まさお)さん　は　コーヒー　を　好ま(このま)ない。
　　　Masao doesn't care for coffee.

95-6. 長田さんはコーヒーが大好きです。
　　　長田(ながた)さん　は　コーヒー　が　大好き(だいすき)　です。
　　　Nagata-san loves coffee.
　　　「すきだ」 {好きだ 95} ["be fond of"]: DJG v1 p426; Genki ch5; Marx v1 day41.

95-7. 成田さんはなっとうが大好きです。
　　　成田(なりた)さん　は　なっとう　が　大好き(だいすき)　です。
　　　Narita-san loves natto.

95-8. 日本人の大部分は生玉子を好みます。
　　　日本人(にほんじん)　の　大部分(だいぶぶん)　は　生玉子(なまたまご)を　好み(このみ)ます。
　　　Most Japanese like raw eggs.

95-9. 好きなだけテレビを見ていて下さい。
　　　好き(すき)　な　だけ　テレビ　を　見(み)て　いて　下さい(ください)。
　　　Please watch as much TV as you like.
　　　「〜だけ」 ["just __"]: DJG v1 p93; Marx v2 day39.
　　　Note: Here 「だけ」 does not mean "just"/"only", but "that much"/"as much as". See Makino & Tsutsui's Dictionary of Basic Japanese Grammar, page 96 note 4.

95-10. 人生または成長にとって好ましくない。
　　　人生(じんせい)　または　成長(せいちょう)　に　とって　好ましく(このましく)ない。
　　　Unfavorable to life or growth. (100)
　　　「〜にとって」 ["as far as __ is concerned", "for/to __"]: DJG v2 p278; Marx v2 day82; Tobira ch2 #4.

95-11. 大体で言うと、アメリカ人はコーヒーを好む。

大体(だいたい) で 言う(いう) と、 アメリカ人(じん) は コーヒー を 好む(このむ)。
Generally speaking, Americans like coffee. (87)

95-12. やっとボク好みの丸メガネを手に入れました。
やっと ボク 好み(ごのみ) の 丸(まる)メガネ を 手(て) に 入れ(いれ)ました。
I finally got the round glasses I love. (10)

95-13. わたしは女の子が一人で出かけるのを好まない。
わたし は 女の子(おんなのこ) が 一人(ひとり) で 出かける(でかける) の を 好ま(このま)ない。
I don't like girls going out alone. (87)
「の」 [nominalizer]: DJG v1 p318; Genki ch8.

95-14. 休日には好きなだけ月子さんと話すことができます。
休日(きゅうじつ) に は 好き(すき) な だけ 月子(つきこ)さん と 話す(はなす) こと が できます。
On my days off I get to talk with Tsukiko as much as I like. (87)
「〜ことができる」 {〜事ができる* 80} ["be able to __"]: DJG v1 p200.

95-15. 千代子さんはあの白いドレスが大好きだと言っている。
千代子(ちよこ)さん は あの 白い(しろい) ドレス が 大好き(だいすき) だ と 言っ(いっ)て いる。
Chiyoko says she loves that white dress. (87)

96：安

96-1. 不安定な生活。
不安定(ふあんてい) な 生活(せいかつ)。
An unsettled lifestyle. (101)

96-2. 安心して下さい。
安心(あんしん) して 下さい(ください)。
Please rest easy.

96-3. 円はドルより安い。
円(えん) は ドル より 安い(やすい)。
The yen is weaker than the dollar. (87)

96-4. 大体この国は安全だ。
大体(だいたい) この 国(くに) は 安全(あんぜん) だ。
In general this country is safe.

96-5. これから安らかな生活をしたい。
これ から 安らか(やすらか) な 生活(せいかつ) を したい。
I'd like to lead a peaceful lifestyle from now on.

96-6. そこで二人はやっと安心しました。
そこで 二人(ふたり) は やっと 安心(あんしん) しました。
And so with that, the two were quite relieved. (71)
「そこで〜」 {其処で〜** 1757; 553} ["(and) so __"]: DJG v2 p401/405; Tobira ch9 #8.

96-7. 安田さんはカラオケが大好きです。
安田(やすだ)さん は カラオケ が 大好き(だいすき) です。
Yasuda-san loves karaoke.

96-8. 安部さんの心は不安でいっぱいになった。
安部(あべ)さん の 心(こころ) は 不安(ふあん) で いっぱい に なった。
Abe-san's mind was filled with worry. (101)

96-9. 金子さんの手は白ワインをそそいだときに安定していなかった。
金子(かねこ)さん の 手(て) は 白(しろ) ワイン を そそいだ と き に 安定(あんてい) して いなかった。
Kaneko-san's hand was unsteady as she poured the wine. (101)
「〜とき」 {〜時* 383} ["when __"]: DJG v1 p490; Genki ch16.

96-10. このきれいな小さい人々には、なにか安心させるようなものがありました。
この きれい な 小(ちい)さい 人々(ひとびと) に は、 なにか 安心(あんしん) させる よう な もの が ありました。
There was something in these pretty little people that inspired confidence. (89)
「なにか」 {何か* 815} ["something"; "anything"]: Genki ch8; Marx v1 day18. 「〜ような」 ["like __"]: DJG v2 p340 bottom (under -っぽい); Genki ch22.

96-11. それから、見下ろして、自分がつかまっている不安定なフックを見なければなりませんでした。
それから、 見下ろ(みおろ)して、 自分(じぶん) が つかまって いる 不安定(ふあんてい) な フック を 見(み)なければ なりません でした。
Then I had to look down at the unstable hooks to which I clung. (89)
「それから〜」 {其れから〜** 1757} ["and then __"]: DJG v1 p416. 「-なければならない」 [imperative]: DJG v1 p274; Genki ch12; Marx v1 day54; Tobira ch2 #1.

97：案

97-1. 安田さんの案はよさそうだね。
安田(やすだ)さん の 案(あん) は よさそう だ ね。
Yasuda-san's idea sounds good.
「-そう(だ)」 ["look __"; "__-looking"]: DJG v1 p410; Genki ch13; Marx v2 day67.

97-2. これを立案した人はだれですか。
これ を 立案(りつあん) した 人(ひと) は だれ です か。
Who devised this plan?

127

97-3. 案の定、金子さんが部長になった。

案の定(あんのじょう)、 金子(かねこ)さん が 部長(ぶちょう) に なった。

As expected, Kaneko-san became the division chief.

97-4. 金曜日までにこの案を立てないといけない。

金曜日(きんようび) まで に この 案(あん) を 立て(たて)ない と いけない。

We have to draft this proposal by Friday.

「～までに」 {～迄に** 1806} ["by (a point in time)"]: DJG v1 p228. 「-ないといけない」 [imperative]: DJG v1 p274; Marx v1 day55.

97-5. ぼくはあたらしいアイデアを案出してみた。

ぼく は あたらしい アイデア を 案出(あんしゅつ) して みた。

I came up with a new idea.

「-てみる」 ["try (out) __"; "check out __"]: DJG v1 p246; Genki ch13.

97-6. そんな小さな事、案ずることはないですよ。

そんな 小(ちい)さな 事(こと)、 案ずる(あんずる) こと は ない です よ。

Such a trifle is not something to worry about.

「～ことはない」 {～事はない* 80} ["__ is not necessary"; "__ is not possible"]: DJG v2 p146; Tobira ch10 #15.

97-7. 安部さんはなにかを案出しているらしいんだ。

安部(あべ)さん は なに か を 案出(あんしゅつ) して いる らし いん だ。

Abe-san appears to be devising some plan.

「なにか」 {何か* 815} ["something"; "anything"]: Genki ch8; Marx v1 day18. 「～らしい」 ["(it) seems (that) __", "I heard (that) __"; "__-like"]: DJG v1 p373; Marx v2 day70; Tobira ch5 #13.

97-8. 部長がなにか不正な事を案出しているかと部下たちは案じている。

部長(ぶちょう) が なに か 不正(ふせい) な 事(こと) を 案出(あんしゅつ) して いる か と 部下(ぶか)たち は 案じ(あんじ)て いる。

The staff is concerned that the division chief is devising something unjust.

97-9. 月子さんが案じているのは、正男さんが別の女の人を好きかどうかと言うことです。

月子(つきこ)さん が 案じ(あんじ)て いる の は、 正男(まさお)さ ん が 別(べつ) の 女(おんな) の 人(ひと) を 好き(すき) か どうか と 言う(いう) こと です。

What Tsukiko is worried about is whether Masao favors another woman.

「～のは～だ」 [statement about a clause]: DJG v1 p337. 「～かどうか」 ["whether __ (or not)"]: DJG v1 p168; Marx v2 day26. 「～という」 {～と言う* 51} [links identifier with identified]: DJG v1 p486; Genki ch20; Tobira ch10 (first page).

98 : 字

98-1. これだれの字か分かる？
これ だれ の 字(じ) か 分かる(わかる)？
Do you know whose handwriting this is? (87)
「だれの」 {誰の 2155} ["whose"]: Genki ch2.

98-2. ちがう字体にしましょう。
ちがう 字体(じたい) に しましょう。
Let's use a different type [character form] (e.g., italics, bold, etc.).

98-3. 大きな字を用いて下さい。
大(おお)きな 字(じ) を 用い(もちい)て 下さい(ください)。
Please use large letters [characters].

98-4. 千代子ちゃんは字が上手だ。
千代子(ちよこ)ちゃん は 字(じ) が 上手(じょうず) だ。
Chiyoko has good handwriting. (87)

98-5. この部分はローマ字を入れて下さい。
この 部分(ぶぶん) は ローマ字(ろーまじ) を 入れ(いれ)て 下さい(ください)。
Please fill in Roman letters for this part.

98-6. この大きさの活字は見ることができますか。
この 大き(おおき)さ の 活字(かつじ) は 見る(みる) こと が できます か。
Are you able to read print of this size?
「〜ことができる」 {〜事ができる* 80} ["be able to __"]: DJG v1 p200.

98-7. 「宝」の正字は「寶」である。正字の一部としては「宝貝」の「貝」が入っている。
「宝(たから)」 の 正字(せいじ) は 「寶(たから)」 で ある。 正字(せいじ) の 一部(いちぶ) としては 「宝貝(たからがい)」 の 「貝(かい)」 が 入っ(はいっ)て いる。
The traditional form of 宝 is 寶. A portion of the traditional form is the 貝 (shell) of 宝貝 (cowrie shell).
「〜として」 ["in the capacity of __"]: DJG v1 p501; Tobira ch3 #6.

99 : 学

99-1. 学生の身分。
学生(がくせい) の 身分(みぶん)。
The position of student. (100)

99-2. 日本の学生さんですか？
日本(にほん) の 学生(がくせい)さん です か？

Are you a Japanese student? (87)

99-3. あの女の人は学生です。
あの 女(おんな) の 人(ひと) は 学生(がくせい) です。
That woman is a student.

99-4. 正男くんは中学生になった。
正男(まさお)くん は 中学生(ちゅうがくせい) に なった。
Masao entered junior high school.

99-5. 明日学力テストがあります。
明日(あした) 学力(がくりょく) テスト が あります。
Tomorrow is the scholastic aptitude test.

99-6. 学生は全部でなん人ですか？
学生(がくせい) は 全部(ぜんぶ) で なん人(にん) です か？
What is the total number of students? (87)

99-7. 日々学んで、成長したいです。
日々(ひび) 学ん(まなん)で、 成長(せいちょう) したい です。
I hope to study and learn each day.

99-8. かれらの大部分は大学生だった。
かれら の 大部分(だいぶぶん) は 大学生(だいがくせい) だった。
Most of them were university students. (87)

99-9. 入学生は、大学に入学した人だ。
入学生(にゅうがくせい) は、 大学(だいがく) に 入学(にゅうがく) した 人(ひと) だ。
"Matriculants" are persons who have been admitted to a college or university. (100)

99-10. 男子学生たちはイジメを止めることにした。
男子(だんし) 学生(がくせい)たち は イジメ を 止める(やめる) こと に した。
The schoolboys decided to give up bullying.
「～ことにする」 {～事にする* 80} ["decide to __"]: DJG v1 p204; Genki ch23.

99-11. あの男の学生はなにを学んでいるのですか。
あの 男(おとこ) の 学生(がくせい) は なに を 学ん(まなん)で いる の です か。
What is that male student studying?

99-12. 入学するために、全力で学ぶしかありません。
入学(にゅうがく) する ため に、 全力(ぜんりょく) で 学ぶ(まなぶ) しか ありません。
The only way to gain admission is to study as hard as you can.
「～で」 [instrument]: DJG v1 p106; Genki ch10.

99-13. 木の下で本をよんでいる学生は金子さんです。

木(き) の 下(した) で 本(ほん) を よんで いる 学生(がくせい) は 金子(かねこ)さん です。

The student reading a book under the tree is Kaneko-san.

99-14. 無学の人々は子どもが学ぶことを大切にする。

無学(むがく) の 人々(ひとびと) は 子ども(こども) が 学ぶ(まなぶ) こと を 大切(たいせつ) に する。

Unlearned persons place much importance on their children's studies.

99-15. このやりかたを、「学ぶ」より、身に付けるのだ。

この やりかた を、 「学ぶ(まなぶ)」 より、 身(み) に 付ける(つける) の だ。

Instead of "learning" this method, it's better to just practice until it's second nature.

「-かた」 {-方 173} ["way of __"; "how to __"]: DJG v1 p183; Genki ch23.

99-16. 大切なのはどの大学を出たかではなくて、大学でなにを学んだかだ。

大切(たいせつ) な の は どの 大学(だいがく) を 出(で)た か で は なくて、 大学(だいがく) で なに を 学ん(まなん)だ か だ。

What is important is not which university you've graduated from but what you've learned in the university. (87)

「〜のは〜だ」 [statement about a clause]: DJG v1 p337. 「〜を」 [indicates place from which one exits]: DJG v1 p351. 「-なくて」 ["not __, so __"]: DJG v1 p279; Marx v1 day39; Tobira ch2 #15.

100：父

100-1. 父は50代です。

父(ちち) は 50代(だい) です。

My father is in his fifties. (87)

100-2. 父はタバコを止めた。

父(ちち) は タバコ を 止め(やめ)た。

Father gave up cigarettes. (87)

100-3. お父さんがいますか。

お父さん(おとうさん) が います か。

Is your father in?

「〜いますか」 {〜居ますか* 255} [inquire as to __'s existence/presence]: Genki ch4.

100-4. 父はハムを切り分けた。

父(ちち) は ハム を 切り分け(きりわけ)た。

Father carved the ham. (101)

100-5. 父は中国に行きました。

父(ちち) は 中国(ちゅうごく) に 行き(いき)ました。

My father went to China. (87)

100-6. 父が大金を出してくれた。

131

父(ちち) が 大金(たいきん) を 出し(だし)て くれた。
My father gave me a lot of money.

「-てくれる」 {-て呉れる** 1478} ["do __ for (me)"]: DJG v1 p216; Genki ch16; Marx v2 day31; Tobira ch3 #12.

100-7. お父さんにそっくりだね。
お父さん(おとうさん) に そっくり だ ね。
You're just like your father. (87)

100-8. お父さんには話しましたか？
お父さん(おとうさん) に は 話し(はなし)ました か？
Did you tell your father? (4)

100-9. お父さんはオーストラリア人です。
お父さん(おとうさん) は オーストラリア人(じん) です。
Father is Australian.

100-10. 長田さんは父子二人で生活しています。
長田(ながた)さん は 父子(ふし) 二人(ふたり) で 生活(せいかつ) して います。
The Nagatas live together as father and child.

100-11. このあいだ父が書いた本を見つけ出した。
この あいだ 父(ちち) が 書い(かい)た 本(ほん) を 見つけ出し(みつけだし)た。
The other day I discovered a book written by my father. (87)

「この〜」 {此の〜** 1756} ["this (past) __"; "this (coming) __"]: DJG v2 p127.

100-12. 父の代わりに代父が受付してもいいですか？
父(ちち) の 代わり(かわり) に 代父(だいふ) が 受付(うけつけ) して も いい です か？
May my godfather receive it in my father's place?

「〜(の)かわりに」 {〜(の)代わりに 71} ["in place of __"; "in compensation for __"]: DJG v1 p184, v2 p116; Tobira ch2 #5. 「-てもいい」 ["all right if __"]: DJG v1 p471.

100-13. 子どものとき、父から自分自身の行いを正すことを学んだ。
子(こ)ども の とき、 父(ちち) から 自分(じぶん) 自身(じしん) の 行(おこな)い を 正(ただ)す こと を 学(まな)んだ。
When I was a child, I learned from my father to correct my own behavior.

「〜とき」 {〜時* 383} ["when __"]: DJG v1 p490; Genki ch16. 「-じしん」 {-自身 81; 60} ["__ oneself"]: DJG v3 p174 & 553 (under -じたい and そのもの).

祝 Congratulations! 祝

You have now attained the second *dan*:

子

こ

LITTLE ONE

See the full list of KLC kanji ranks at
keystojapanese.com/kanji-ranks

Color badges & custom mounting sheet available at
keystojapanese.com/stickers

Volume 2

Volume 2 takes you to kanji 200 and the third *dan*:

素

ソ
NATURAL

For printed versions of this series, visit keystojapanese.com/klcgrs-printed.
For ebook versions, visit keystojapanese.com/klcgrs-volumes.

Companion Resources

Kanji Dan Badges

**24 stickers cover all KLC kanji *dan* (stages)
from 50 "Newborn" to 2300 "Spectrum"**

Each badge's kanji is associated with a stage of learning; for example, the badge for Stage 1 (ichi-dan) stands for "Newborn", while the badges for advanced stages stand for "Kanjinaut", "Kanjisseur", "Kanjedi", etc. Badge colors progress in gradients through the full spectrum of colors, culminating in a rainbow badge for completing the last kanji in the course, #2300 虹 (RAINBOW). The custom tabloid-size mounting sheet shows the KLC stage progression, Japanese pronunciation, and English title for each stage.

Learn more at keystojapanese.com/stickers.

The KLC Green Book
Writing Practice Workbook
漢字書き方練習帳

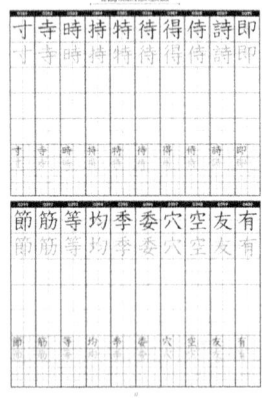

Even today when most learners are focused on learning to read kanji rather than to write them, handwriting practice remains essential. Integrating hand-eye coordination with the kinesthetic experience of each kanji's stroke sequence, handwriting improves your ability to recognize each kanji, grasp intuitively how it is put together, and distinguish it from lookalikes. Designed to help you use your study time most efficiently, this simple little workbook contains just the right quantity of writing spaces -- four large spaces followed by seven small spaces -- to give you enough practice for each character.

Learn more at keystojapanese.com/klc-green-book.

The KLC Wall Chart
漢字学習図表

A sequential mosaic of 2300 characters
and 4400 illustrative example words
(91×61cm / 36×24in)

Learn more at keystojapanese.com/klc-wall-chart

The Ultimate Kana Wall Chart
A visual guide to Japanese phonetic writing
(31×44cm / 12.25×17.25in)

There are many hidden nuances involved with mastering kana spelling and keyboard input, as well as managing the full range of roughly 250 kana combinations and variations. This chart organizes all this information into an illuminating visual framework that allows you to readily perceive the underlying phonological structure of the Japanese language. Far more than a simple "50 sounds table", it systematizes the kana in all their complexity, reinforcing your grasp of kana order and clarifying the principles behind how kana are written, pronounced and romanized. Post it beside your desk for easy reference as you learn to read, write and type in Japanese.

Learn more at keystojapanese.com/kana-wall-chart.

Index of Grammar Glosses

This index, which lists every gloss in this series, is long and may be cumbersome to navigate in book format. To download this index in spreadsheet form, visit keystojapanese.com/klcgrs-ggindex.

Expressions are listed with romanized headings to simplify searching, followed by a kana version in Japanese quotation brackets 「」, followed in curved brackets {} by a kanji version, if one exists. Asterisks in the kanji version indicate that it is used less frequently (single asterisk) or much less frequently (double asterisk) than the kana-only version. Numerals inside the curved brackets indicate the kanji's KLC entry number(s).

The English glosses have been prepared as concise keywords intended to encapsulate the basic meaning of the expression. However these are no substitute for reading a full explanation in a specialized grammar resource (the Makino & Tsutsui series being by far the most comprehensive and detailed).

The end of each gloss contains references to other resources for more information on how the pattern is used:

DJG1, DJG2, DJG3: *A Dictionary of Basic Japanese Grammar* (DJG1), *A Dictionary of Intermediate Japanese Grammar* (DJG2), and *A Dictionary of Advanced Japanese Grammar* (DJG3), all by Seiichi Makino & Michio Tsutsui.

Genki: *Genki: An Integrated Course in Elementary Japanese, 2nd Edition*, by Eri Banno et al. References to chapters 1-2 refer to Volume 1, while those to chapters 13-23 refer to Volume 2.

Marx: *Speak Japanese in 90 Days*, by Kevin Marx. "Marx v1" refers to the first volume, and "v2" to the second volume.

Tobira: *Tobira: Gateway to Advanced Japanese*, by Mayumi Oka, et al. Tobira references point to numbered items in the 「文法ノート」 sections at the end of each chapter.

Examples of each expression can be found at the numbered exercises appearing below its gloss.

To avoid technical issues with displaying macrons in the ebook format, the alphabetical headings diverge from Hepburn romanization by rendering long vowels as follows: おお = oo; おう = ou; うう = uu.

Expressions are listed in alphabetical order, ignoring spaces (e.g., "aa…" precedes "A ba…").

139

aa iu ~ 「ああいう〜」 {ああ言う〜 51} ["such __"]: Tobira ch4 #10.
  Examples: 1593-45.

A ba B hodo 「**A**ば**B**ほど」 {AばB程* 588} ["the more A, the more B"]: DJG v2 p6; Marx v2 day58; Tobira ch8 #5.
  Examples: 143-3; 588-8; 934-17.

aete ~ 「あえて〜」 {敢えて〜* 809} ["dare to __", "venture to __"]: DJG v3 p3; Tobira ch2 #3.
  Examples: 809-2; 809-9; 1017-16; 1191-26.

~ ageku (ni) 「〜あげく(に)」 {〜挙げ句に* / 〜揚げ句に* 1247; 166} ["after much __ing"]: DJG v3 p7.
  Examples: 1144-31; 1589-10.

ageru 「あげる」 {上げる* 41} ["give (to someone)"]: DJG v1 p63; Genki ch14; Marx v2 day30.
  Examples: 3-2; 29-7; 104-10.

~ aida ni 「〜あいだに」 {〜間に 448} ["while __"]: DJG v1 p67; Genki ch21; Marx v1 day88.
  Examples: 4-3; 10-2; 75-9.

akumade (mo) 「あくまで(も)」 {飽くまで(も)* / 飽く迄(も)** 1964; 1806} ["to the last"]: DJG v3 p11.
  Examples: 1971-20.

~ amari 「〜あまり」 {〜余り 995} ["on account of too much __"]: DJG v2 p3.
  Examples: 941-12; 1237-9; 1597-8; 1990-7.

amari ~ nai/anmari ~ nai 「あまり〜ない / あんまり〜ない」 {余り〜ない 995} ["not very (much) __"]: DJG v1 p72.
  Examples: 76-3; 114-8; 226-3; 274-17; 383-31.

amari ni (mo) ~/anmari ni (mo) ~ 「あまりに(も)〜 / あんまりに(も)〜」 {余りに(も)〜 995} ["too __"]: Tobira ch13 #10.
  Examples: 217-3; 302-6; 315-12; 453-23; 611-7; 621-5.

anata 「あなた」 {貴方 1177; 173} [formal: "you"]: DJG v1 p28.
  Examples: 21-3; 46-8; 232-6.

A no wa B no koto da 「**A**のは**B**のことだ」 {AのはBの事だ* 80} [time of occurrence: "It was/will be B when A"]: DJG v2 p313; Tobira ch1 #13.
  Examples: 1737-5.

~ arimasu ka 「〜ありますか」 {〜有りますか* 400} ["is/are there any __?"; "do you have any __?"]: Genki ch4; Marx v1 day15.
  Examples: 1-5.

aru 「ある」 {有る 400} ["exist"; "have"]: DJG v1 p73.
  Examples: 1-5; 2-3; 3-4; 3-7.

aruiwa 「あるいは」 {或は* 1152} ["or"]: DJG v3 p16; Tobira ch9 #5.
  Examples: 454-6; 976-26; 1152-2.

ataka mo ~ 「あたかも〜」 ["as if __"]: DJG v3 p21.
  Examples: 1525-44; 1803-8; 1877-13.

~ ato 「〜あと」 {〜後 114} ["after __"].
  Examples: 114-11; 138-2.

140

ato ~ 「あと〜」 {後〜 114} ["__ left", "__ longer", "__ until"].
    Examples: 1-4; 1-7.

A to iu no wa B (to iu) koto da 「AというのはB(という)ことだ」
{Aと言うのはB(と言う)ことだ* / Aと言うのはB(と言う)事だ** 51; 80} ["A means B"]: DJG v2 p487.
    Examples: 1207-7.

A wa B da 「AはBだ」 ["A is B"]: DJG v1 p521; Genki ch1; Marx v1 day8.
    Examples: 3-5; 4-5; 5-4; 7-5; 8-3; 8-7; 9-3; 9-8.

A wa B ga C 「AはBがC」 [C describes something about B, as an attribute of subject A]: DJG v1 p525.
    Examples: 10-6; 29-4; 29-5; 29-8; 30-5; 173-18.

-ba 「-ば」 ["if __"]: DJG v1 p81; Genki ch22.
    Examples: 58-4; 64-14; 91-5; 91-9.

~ bakari 「〜ばかり」 ["just __"]: DJG v1 p84 & 402; Marx v2 day39; Tobira ch4 #18.
    Examples: 134-2; 179-14; 269-10; 553-9.

~ bakari ka 「〜ばかりか」 ["not just __"].
    Examples: 1062-21; 1497-4.

-ba yokatta 「-ばよかった」 {-ば良かった* 285} ["should have __ed"; "wish had __ed"]: DJG v1 p87; Genki ch18.
    Examples: 143-8; 148-7; 274-8.

~ bekarazu/~ bekarazaru 「〜べからず/〜べからざる」 ["do not __"]: DJG v3 p29.
    Examples: 1153-13; 1273-5.

~ beki da 「〜べきだ」 ["should __"; "must __"]: DJG v2 p11; Marx v1 day53; Tobira ch11 #12.
    Examples: 79-6; 159-10; 189-4.

~ beku 「〜べく」 ["in order to __"; "so that __"]: DJG v3 p32.
    Examples: 1223-17; 1481-21; 1605-17.

~ beku mo nai 「〜べくもない」 ["there is no way to __"]: DJG v3 p34.
    Examples: 2222-9.

boku 「ぼく」 {僕 1358} [informal: "I"]: DJG v1 p28.
    Examples: 15-17; 17-4; 40-2; 1358-1.

-bun 「-ぶん」 {-分 88} [portion]: DJG v2 p16.
    Examples: 88-8.

-buri 「-ぶり」 {-振り* 903} ["for the first time in __"]: DJG v2 p343 (under -らい).
    Examples: 6-2; 904-3.

-cha 「-ちゃ」 [colloquial contraction of -ては: links a verb with a negative statement]: DJG v2 p461 (under -ては).
    Examples: 1160-10.

-chau 「-ちゃう」 [colloquial contraction of -てしまう: "do (something regrettable)"; "finish __ing"]: DJG v1 p384 (under -てしまう); Marx v2 day28.
    Examples: 529-18; 1941-6.

chinami ni ~ 「ちなみに〜」 {因みに〜** 1725} ["incidentally __"]: DJG v3 p40.
    Examples: 632-24.

141

chittomo ~ nai　「ちっとも〜ない」　{些とも〜ない* 1789}　["no __ whatsoever"]: DJG v3 p334 (under なんら〜ない).
　　　　Examples: 942-28; 2050-13.
Compound verbs: DJG v1 p610, v2 p626; Marx v1 day33.
　　　　Examples: 59-2; 64-7; 67-6.
Counters: DJG v1 p604; Genki ch9; Marx v1 day81.
　　　　Examples: 2-1; 3-2.
da ga　「だが」　["but"]: DJG v2 p18; Tobira ch10 #13.
　　　　Examples: 106-7; 791-9.
dai　「だい」　[male alternative to か]: DJG v1 p48 middle & 90.
　　　　Examples: 1332-4.
da kara　「だから」　["so", "that's why"; "since", "because"]: DJG v1 p413; Marx v2 day11.
　　　　Examples: 43-4; 86-20; 63-10; 87-6.
da kara to itte　「だからといって〜」　{だからと言って〜 51}　["but it doesn't follow that __"]: DJG v2 p21.
　　　　Examples: 2225-11.
~ dake　「〜だけ」　["just __"]: DJG v1 p93; Marx v2 day39.
　　　　Examples: 15-7; 19-4; 51-6; 65-11; 95-9.
~ dake de　「〜だけで」　["just by __ing"]: DJG v2 p23; Tobira ch13 #9.
　　　　Examples: 850-21; 981-24; 1260-32.
~ dake de (wa) naku/~ dake ja nakute　「〜だけで(は)なく / 〜だけじゃなくて」　["not just __"]: Tobira ch1 #14.
　　　　Examples: 418-4; 983-14; 1101-21.
da kedo　「だけど」　["but"]: DJG v1 p120, v2 p18; Marx v1 day59.
　　　　Examples: 231-3; 258-5; 280-17.
~ dake no koto wa aru　「〜だけのことはある」　{〜だけの事はある* 80}　["not __ for nothing"]: DJG v3 p51.
　　　　Examples: 1462-14.
~ dano　「〜だの」　["__ and __ and the like"]: DJG v3 p57.
　　　　Examples: 1475-58.
-darake　「-だらけ」　["covered all over with __"; "full of __"]: DJG v2 p25.
　　　　Examples: 78-13; 198-5; 878-15; 882-20.
dare ka　「だれか」　{誰か 2155}　["someone"]: Marx v1 day18.
　　　　Examples: 159-19; 266-22; 400-14; 412-4.
dare mo　「だれも」　{誰も 2155}　["no one"; "anyone"]: DJG v1 p250; Marx v1 day18.
　　　　Examples: 47-10; 51-3; 66-9; 194-6; 269-15; 281-8; 393-14.
dare no　「だれの」　{誰の 2155}　["whose"]: Genki ch2.
　　　　Examples: 98-1.
darou/deshou　「〜だろう / 〜でしょう」　["probably __"]: DJG v1 p100; Genki ch12; Tobira ch2 #9.
　　　　Examples: 36-5; 62-2; 91-8; 265-3; 280-11.
~ darou ga/to ~ darou ga/to　「〜だろうが〜だろうが / 〜だろうと〜だろうと」　["be it __ or __"]: DJG v3 p644 (under 〜といわず).
　　　　Examples: 815-17; 923-18; 2179-19.

darou ka/deshou ka　「〜だろうか/〜でしょうか」　["I wonder __"]: DJG v3 p715; Tobira ch6 #4.
    Examples: 55-4; 67-10; 115-7; 118-4.

-dasu　「-だす」　{-出す 38}　["__ out"; "start to __"]: DJG v1 p102; Tobira ch7 #6.
    Examples: 59-2; 83-13; 87-4; 90-11; 166-5.

datta　「だった」　[past tense of copula だ]: DJG v1 p580 bottom; Genki ch9; Marx v1 day37.
    Examples: 2-4; 33-11; 48-3.

datte　「だって〜」　["because __"]: DJG v3 p60.
    Examples: 613-12.

~ datte　「〜だって」　["__ too"; "even __"]: DJG v3 p63.
    Examples: 189-12; 1247-12; 1350-30.

~ de　「〜で」　["due to __"]: DJG v1 p107.
    Examples: 91-10; 108-7.

~ de　「〜で」　[instrument]: DJG v1 p106; Genki ch10.
    Examples: 8-5; 17-3; 21-10; 22-4; 35-12; 40-10; 44-8; 54-6; 55-17; 79-3; 88-7; 99-12.

~ de　「〜で」　[location]: DJG v1 p105.
    Examples: 2-7; 33-8; 36-2; 37-4; 80-13; .

~ de　「〜で」　[time]: DJG v1 p109.
    Examples: 10-1; 35-13; 50-6.

~ de are　「〜であれ」　["though it may be __"]: DJG v3 p67.
    Examples: 953-11; 1863-10; 2052-8.

~ de are ~ de are　「〜であれ〜であれ」　["be it __ or __"]: DJG v3 p70.
    Examples: 1596-21; 1761-20; 1984-22; 2037-12.

~ de arou　「〜であろう」　[expression of conjecture or resoluteness]: DJG v2 p29.
    Examples: 455-16; 1046-12.

de aru vs. da　「である vs. だ」: DJG v2 p30, v3 p35 of front matter; Tobira ch7 #5.
    Examples: 15-10; 75-6.

~ de atte mo　「〜であっても」　["though it may be __"]: DJG v3 p70 (under であれ).
    Examples: 1121-32; 1198-12; 1223-23.

~ de dekiru　「〜でできる」　{〜で出来る 38; 274}　["be made of __"]: Tobira ch1 #1.
    Examples: 28-6; 211-2; 212-2.

~ de gozaimasu　「〜でございます」　{〜で御座います** 862; 749}　["be __"]: DJG v1 p41.
    Examples: 1595-37.

dekiru dake ~　「できるだけ〜」　["as __ as possible", "as much as possible __"]: Marx v2 day4.
    Examples: 407-10; 651-14; 669-14; 922-27.

~ demo　「〜でも」　["even __"]: DJG v1 p111; Marx v1 day18.
    Examples: 80-16; 142-23; 232-8; 832-24.

de wa nai vs. ja nai　「ではない vs. じゃない」: DJG v3 p35 of front matter.
    Examples: 15-20; 126-25.

doko ka　「どこか」　{何処か** 815; 553}　["somewhere"]: Genki ch10; Marx v1 day18.
    Examples: 339-9; 992-14.

doko mo 「どこも」 {何処も** 815; 553} ["everywhere"; "anywhere"]: DJG v1 p250; Genki ch10; Marx v1 day18.
    Examples: 899-15.

~ dokoro ka 「～どころか」 ["far from __"]: DJG v2 p34.
    Examples: 1748-8; 2092-9.

-domo 「-ども」 {-共 356} [plural personal pronoun suffix]: DJG v1 p28 bottom & 440, v3 p47 & 50-51 of front matter (under -たち).
    Examples: 94-13; 486-26; 546-40; 1510-19; 1510-22.

donna ni ~ 「どんなに～」 ["no matter how __"]: DJG v3 p135 & 138.
    Examples: 232-8; 423-17; 832-24; 1236-34.

donna ni ~ ka 「どんなに～か」 ["how __(!)"]: DJG v2 p39.
    Examples: 703-5; 1380-12; 1470-22.

dore hodo ~ ka 「どれほど～か」 {どれ程～か* 588} ["how __(!)"]: DJG v2 p39.
    Examples: 1878-12; 2145-15.

dou 「どう」 {如何** 2197; 815} ["how"]: DJG v1 p114.
    Examples: 93-4; 104-6; 222-12.

dou ka ~ 「どうか～」 {如何か～** 2197; 815} ["please by all means __"; "pray __"]: DJG v3 p82.
    Examples: 402-10; 794-14; 1160-11; 1402-3; 1427-13; 1562-5.

doumo 「どうも」 ["somehow"; "no matter how"]: DJG v2 p36.
    Examples: 15-21; 276-19; 385-9; 546-31.

dou ni ka ~ 「どうにか～」 {如何にか～** 2197; 815} ["somehow"]: DJG v3 p341 (under なんとか～).
    Examples: 1448-19.

-doushi 「-どうし」 {-同士 182; 350} ["fellow __"; "between/among __"]: DJG v3 p94; Tobira ch11 #11.
    Examples: 350-8; 498-12; 758-39; 777-6; 963-10.

douzo 「どうぞ」 ["please"]: DJG v3 p84 (under どうか～).
    Examples: 35-7; 41-1; 80-11.

e 「へ」 [indicates direction]: DJG v1 p116.
    Examples: 41-1; 55-2.

Ellipsis: DJG v1 p23.
    Examples: 1-5; 2-6; 2-9.

~ fuu ni 「～ふうに」 {～風に 425} ["in (such a) way"]: DJG v2 p44.
    Examples: 425-16; 1026-18; 1472-22.

ga 「が」 ["but"]: DJG v1 p120, v2 p18; Marx v1 day59.
    Examples: 63-11; 83-31; 84-9.

ga 「が」 [subject marker]: DJG v1 p118; Genki ch8; Marx v1 day8.
    Examples: 1-2; 1-5; 1-8.

-gachi 「-がち」 {-勝ち 460} ["tend to __"]: DJG v2 p47; Marx v2 day64.
    Examples: 75-6; 422-25; 1524-39; 1662-14.

~ ga hoshii 「～がほしい」 {～が欲しい 1035} ["want __"]: DJG v1 p144; Genki ch14; Marx v1 day48.

Examples: 6-6; 10-6; 12-5.

-garu　「-がる」　[have or express a feeling; pretend]: DJG v1 p123; Marx v2 day63.
Examples: 252-3; 309-15; 432-11; 659-1.

-gata　「-がた」　{-方 173} [plural personal pronoun suffix]: DJG v1 p28 bottom & 440, v3 p47 of front matter.
Examples: 232-6; 869-43; 873-12; 988-11.

-gatai　「-がたい」　{-難い* 712} ["un__able"]: DJG v2 p50.
Examples: 151-8; 548-10; 683-24; 843-31; 1013-8.

-ge　「-げ」　["__-looking", "__-like"]: Marx v2 day68.
Examples: 336-6; 452-5; 460-4; 506-3; 597-25; 779-6; 934-15; 1152-6; 1218-5.

~ goro　「～ごろ」　{～頃* 1916} ["around __"]: DJG v1 p126.
Examples: 35-2; 115-4; 265-2.

-goto ni　「-ごとに」　{-毎に* 105} ["every __"]: DJG v1 p128.
Examples: 1-1; 55-15; 105-1.

~ gotoshi　「～ごとし」　{～如し* 2197} ["as if __"]: DJG v3 p103.
Examples: 2197-6.

gyaku ni　「ぎゃくに」　{逆に 1775} ["on the contrary"]: DJG v2 p53; Tobira ch8 #8.
Examples: 1775-21.

-hajimeru　「-はじめる」　{-始める 956} ["begin to __"]: DJG v1 p131; Tobira ch1 #8.
Examples: 498-8; 889-20; 1225-13.

hatashite　「はたして～」　{果たして～* 599} ["indeed __"]: DJG v3 p111.
Examples: 1231-4; 1248-8.

hazu　「はず」　{筈* 1442} [expectation]: DJG v1 p133; Genki ch19; Marx v1 day53; Tobira ch8 #9.
Examples: 106-7; 237-26; 284-9.

~ hazu ga nai　「～はずがない」　{～筈がない 1442} ["__ is impossible"]: DJG v2 p580.
Examples: 864-17.

~ hodo　「～ほど」　{～程* 588} ["to __ extent"]: DJG v1 p135, v2 p57; Marx v2 day57; Tobira ch10 #1.
Examples: 61-7; 136-19; 208-6; 239-14; 313-3.

Honorific verbs: DJG v1 p36; Genki ch19; Marx v1 day89; Tobira ch2 (main body of chapter).
Examples: 77-2; 77-3; 302-3; 371-17; 407-5; 787-17; 1103-6; 1170-20; 2195-3.

hotondo ~ nai　「ほとんど～ない」　{殆ど～ない* 2192} ["almost no(t) __"; "almost never __"]: DJG v3 p252; Tobira ch5 #16.
Examples: 53-15; 63-7; 67-3; 237-25.

~ hou ga ii　「～ほうがいい」　{～方がいい / ～方が良い* 173} ["had better __"]: DJG v1 p138; Genki ch12; Marx v1 day53.
Examples: 42-5; 173-21; 184-3.

~ hou ga ~yori　「～ほうが～より」　{～方が～より 173} [comparison]: DJG v1 p140; Genki ch10; Marx v1 day69.
Examples: 314-12; 1695-2.

Humble expressions: DJG v1 p36; Genki ch20; Marx v1 day89.
Examples: 53-4; 251-1; 280-16; 1238-9.

hyotto shitara ~/hyotto shite ~/hyotto suru to ~　「ひょっとしたら〜／ひょっとして〜／ひょっとすると〜」 ["possibly __"].
    Examples: 2173-9.

ichi/hito + counter + toshite ~ nai　「一 + counter + として〜ない」 ["not a single __"]: DJG v3 p117.
    Examples: 276-20; 1502-29; 1885-7.

ichiban　「いちばん」 {一番 2; 299} [superlative]: DJG v1 p148; Genki ch10; Marx v1 day70.
    Examples: 54-9; 71-7; 91-12; 130-8; 299-1.

~ igai　「〜いがい」 {〜以外 66; 266} ["besides __"]: DJG v2 p60; Marx v2 day39; Tobira ch9 #9.
    Examples: 266-17; 291-2.

~ijou (wa)　「〜いじょう(は)」 {〜以上は 66; 41} ["given that __"]: DJG v2 p64.
    Examples: 2037-8.

ikaga　「いかが」 {如何** 2197; 815} ["how"; "would you like __"]: DJG v1 p114.
    Examples: 2-9; 787-14; 2197-31.

ikanaru ~　「いかなる〜」 {如何なる〜** 2197; 815} ["any __"]: DJG v3 p132.
    Examples: 552-9; 636-7; 684-14.

ika ni ~　「いかに〜」 {如何に〜** 2197; 815} ["how __"]: DJG v3 p135; Tobira ch14 #9.
    Examples: 946-3; 1117-11; 1806-2; 2197-26; 2197-30.

ika nimo ~　「いかにも〜」 {如何にも〜** 2197; 815} ["truly __"]: DJG v2 p66.
    Examples: 1656-15; 2197-13.

iku　「いく」 {行く 55} ["go"]: DJG v1 p149.
    Examples: 30-7; 55-1.

~ imasu ka　「〜いますか」 {〜居ますか* 255} [inquire as to __'s existence or presence]: Genki ch4; Marx v1 day15.
    Examples: 94-8; 100-3.

Imperative verb ending: DJG v1 p577 & 579 right column, v2 p70; Marx v1 day28 ("-E form verbs").
    Examples: 138-7; 274-12; 497-6; 581-4; 639-1; 642-10; 653-4; 1356-8.

infinitive + na　「infinitive + な」 [prohibitive: "don't __"]: DJG v1 p266; Marx v1 day40.
    Examples: 19-6; 51-3; 80-2; 90-7; 125-8.

~ ippou (da)　「〜いっぽう(だ)」 {〜一方(だ) 2; 173} ["only __"; "keep on __ing"]: DJG v3 p146.
    Examples: 173-17; 173-18; 185-12; 239-4; 239-13; 277-2; 353-9; 555-17.

ippou (de)　「いっぽう(で)」 {一方(で) 2; 173} ["while"]: DJG v3 p149; Tobira ch9 #4.
    Examples: 173-23; 669-22; 815-28; 1166-13; 1551-9.

ippou de ~ tahou de　「いっぽうで〜たほうで」 {一方で〜他方で 2; 173; 189; 173} ["on one hand, __; on the other hand, __"]: DJG v2 p73; Marx v2 day4.
    Examples: 1912-46; 2024-7.

Irregular humble polite forms: DJG v1 p40; Genki ch20.
    Examples: 21-7; 226-8; 251-1; 276-10; 313-5; 315-1; 407-7; 1238-9; 1642-2.

Irregular verb: kuru　「くる」: DJG v1 p578-79.
    Examples: 21-9; 210-7; 274-12; 274-20; 369-6; 699-27; 1419-20.

Irregular verb: suru　「する」: DJG v1 p578-79.
　　　　Examples: 1-8; 4-6; 6-4; 15-24; 16-6; 53-16; 54-3; 274-20.
iru　「いる」　{居る* 255} ["exist"; "be present"]: DJG v1 p153.
　　　　Examples: 1-6; 34-2; 35-8; 36-10; 40-8; 51-20.
iru　「いる」　{要る* 547} ["need"]: DJG v1 p157.
　　　　Examples: 143-11; 547-3.
issai ~ nai　「いっさい〜ない」　{一切〜ない 2; 86} ["no __ whatsoever"]: DJG v3 p159.
　　　　Examples: 86-18; 86-22; 90-12; 1771-20; 2213-29.
issho ni　「いっしょに」　{一緒に 2; 1450} ["together"]: DJG v3 p97 (under どうし).
　　　　Examples: 377-7; 379-14; 649-9; 763-8; 1450-5.
issou　「いっそう〜」　{一層〜 2; 1224} ["still more __"]: DJG v3 p344 (under なお).
　　　　Examples: 528-19; 1224-5; 1435-39; 1468-5.
itsu ka　「いつか」　{何時か** 815; 383} ["sometime"]: Marx v1 day18.
　　　　Examples: 21-7; 326-3.
itsu mo　「いつも」　{何時も** 815; 383} ["always"]: DJG v1 p253.
　　　　Examples: 2-5; 50-9; 55-12; 67-7.
ittan ~　「いったん〜」　{一旦〜 2; 1392} ["once __"; "__ for a time"]: DJG v3 p161.
　　　　Examples: 1392-1; 1392-3; 1468-7; 1517-12; 1662-14; 1689-23.
iwaba ~　「いわば〜」　{言わば〜 51} ["__, so to speak"]: DJG v3 p170.
　　　　Examples: 1761-21.
iwayuru ~　「いわゆる〜」　["so-called __"]: DJG v3 p172.
　　　　Examples: 592-11; 642-14; 780-18; 852-8; 1715-36.
izen (to shite)　「いぜん(として)」　{依然(として) 701; 760} ["as ever"]: DJG v3 p347 (under なお).
　　　　Examples: 760-23; 1257-52.
-jishin　「-じしん」　{-自身 81; 60} ["__ oneself"]: DJG v3 p174 & 553 (under -じたい and そのもの).
　　　　Examples: 81-3; 88-22; 100-13; 252-5; 420-14.
-jitai　「-じたい」　{-自体 81; 62} ["__ itself"]: DJG v3 p174.
　　　　Examples: 81-5; 569-20; 987-4.
-jou　「-じょう」　{-上 41} ["for __"]: DJG v2 p76.
　　　　Examples: 246-5; 454-6; 501-12.
ka　「か」　["or"]: DJG v1 p164.
　　　　Examples: 3-7; 39-13; 173-16.
ka　「か」　[question marker]: DJG v1 p166; Marx v1 day11.
　　　　Examples: 1-5; 2-10.
~ ka dou ka　「〜かどうか」　["whether __ (or not)"]: DJG v1 p168; Marx v2 day26.
　　　　Examples: 88-20; 88-25; 97-9; 134-14; 160-4; 452-7.
kaette ~　「かえって〜」　{却って〜* / 反って〜* 733; 374} ["on the contrary __"]: DJG v2 p80; Marx v2 day38; Tobira ch15 #11.
　　　　Examples: 1570-18.
~ kagiri　「〜かぎり」　["as long as __"; "unless __"]: Tobira ch9 #14.
　　　　Examples: 282-12; 650-26; 892-28; 1323-2; 1407-22.

147

~ kagiri da 「〜かぎりだ」 {〜限りだ 282} ["extremely __"]: DJG v3 p177.
    Examples: 1524-36; 2040-1.

kai 「かい」 [male alternative to か]: DJG v1 p48 middle & 170.
    Examples: 26-4; 1269-17.

~ ka ina ka 「〜かいなか」 {〜か否か 552} ["whether __ (or not)"]: DJG v3 p182; Genki ch20.
    Examples: 552-2; 1097-21; 1503-18.

~ ka ~ ka 「〜か〜か」 ["whether __ or __"]: DJG v2 p87; Tobira ch2 #8.
    Examples: 36-12; 829-16; 1073-12.

~ ka ~ ka 「〜か〜か」 ["either __ or __"]: DJG v1 p164; Marx v2 day14.
    Examples: 478-10; 969-2; 984-13; 1503-7.

kakaru 「かかる」 {掛かる* 1117} ["hang"; "be caught"]: Marx v1 day52.
    Examples: 18-7; 21-7; 180-15.

kakeru 「かける」 {掛ける* 1117} ["hang"; "put", "put on"]: Marx v1 day52.
    Examples: 27-3; 53-11; 72-2.

~ ka mo shirenai 「〜かもしれない」 {〜かも知れない* 560} ["might __"]: DJG v1 p173, v3 p513; Genki ch14.
    Examples: 142-23; 315-9; 431-6; 502-9.

~ ka na/~ ka naa 「〜かな/〜かなあ」 [male: "I wonder __"]: DJG v1 p48 bottom, v2 p90, v3 p185; Tobira ch3 #14.
    Examples: 1028-13; 1269-22.

kanarazu shimo ~ nai 「かならずしも〜ない」 {必ずしも〜ない 549} ["not necessarily __"]: DJG v2 p92.
    Examples: 574-22; 721-20; 936-13; 950-31; 1087-30; 1269-25.

-kaneru 「-かねる」 {-兼ねる 1006} ["cannot __"]: DJG v2 p96.
    Examples: 534-13; 1006-2; 1006-6; 1717-2.

~ ka no you ni 「〜かのように」 ["as though __"]: DJG v3 p187.
    Examples: 580-15; 802-13; 815-16; 1075-21; 1305-8; 1342-24; 1469-14; 1525-44.

~ kara 「〜から」 ["because __"]: DJG v1 p179; Genki ch6&9; Marx v1 day60.
    Examples: 43-4; 62-9.

~ kara 「〜から」 ["from __"]: DJG v1 p176.
    Examples: 17-5; 24-7; 32-3; 34-4; 36-5.

~ kara dekiru 「〜からできる」 {〜から出来る 38; 274} ["be made from __"]: Tobira ch1 #1.
    Examples: 34-4; 654-6.

~ kara ~ made 「〜から〜まで」 ["from __ to __"]: DJG v2 p99.
    Examples: 5-5; 28-5; 37-2; 185-13.

~ kara ~ ni itaru made 「〜から〜にいたるまで」 {〜から〜に至るまで 250} ["from A to Z"]: DJG v2 p100; Tobira ch11 #10.
    Examples: 1264-6; 1656-14.

~ kara ~ ni kakete 「〜から〜にかけて」 ["from __ through __"]: DJG v2 p101; Tobira ch11 #3.
    Examples: 114-14; 117-15; 402-5.

~ kara to itte 「〜からといって」 {〜からと言って 51} ["just because __"]: DJG v2 p103.

Examples: 760-47; 1505-22; 1505-25.

kari ni ~ 「かりに〜」 {仮に〜 921} ["assuming __"]: DJG v3 p201.
Examples: 921-9; 921-13; 921-17; 1405-14.

-karou 「-かろう」 ["probably __"]: DJG v2 p106.
Examples: 679-33; 1757-2; 1798-5; 2165-24; 2227-21.

kashira 「かしら」 [female: "I wonder"]: DJG v1 p48 bottom & 181.
Examples: 971-35.

-kata 「-かた」 {-方 173} ["way of __"; "how to __"]: DJG v1 p183; Genki ch23.
Examples: 99-15; 173-11; 236-9.

-kata wo suru 「-かたをする」 {-方をする 173} ["in (such a) way"]: DJG v2 p109.
Examples: 169-14; 245-7.

katsu 「かつ」 {且つ* 263} ["and"]: DJG v3 p209.
Examples: 263-1; 633-21; 926-35; 1092-5.

~ kekka 「〜けっか」 {〜結果 516; 599} ["after __"; "as a result of __"]: DJG v2 p121.
Examples: 839-43; 949-21; 1087-32; 1128-24; 1339-14; 1696-26.

kekkou ~ 「けっこう〜」 {結構〜 516; 917} ["rather __"]: DJG v2 p123; Tobira ch6 #13.
Examples: 917-17; 917-28; 917-37.

~ keredomo 「〜けれども」 ["although __"]: DJG v1 p187.
Examples: 279-12; 1135-6; 1156-14.

kesshite ~ nai 「-けっして〜ない」 ["never __", "by no means __"]: Tobira ch9 #10.
Examples: 330-6; 330-12; 330-15.

~ ki ga suru 「〜きがする」 ["I get the impression that __", "I think __"]: Marx v2 day74; Tobira ch5 #17.
Examples: 126-4; 126-17; 136-16; 169-16.

kikoeru 「〜きこえる」 {〜聞こえる 453} ["__ can be heard"; "sounds __"]: DJG v1 p188; Marx v1 day50.
Examples: 453-8; 453-18; 579-16; 1089-24; 1518-5.

kimi 「きみ」 {君 1407} [informal: "you"]: DJG v1 p28.
Examples: 2-10; 43-2; 94-9; 94-11; 126-29.

~ kirai da 「〜がきらいだ」 {〜が嫌いだ* 2058} ["dislike __"]: DJG v1 p190; Genki ch5; Marx v1 day41.
Examples: 15-5; 161-2; 578-5.

~ kirai ga aru 「〜きらいがある」 ["have a propensity to __"]: DJG v3 p214.
Examples: 2035-9.

-kke 「-っけ」 [informal question marker]: DJG v3 p223; Marx v2 day3; Tobira ch15 #14.
Examples: 597-17.

(k)kiri 「〜(っ)きり」 ["since __"; "only __"]: DJG v3 p219.
Examples: 15-17; 1015-12; 1035-21; 1142-7; 2162-8.

ko/so/a/do 「こ / そ / あ / ど」 : DJG v1 p600; Genki ch2; Marx v1 day16-17.
Examples: 2-8; 8-7; 9-8; 15-5; 15-12; 15-18; 19-6; 36-5; 50-5; 53-7.

kono ~ 「この〜」 {此の〜** 1756} ["this (past) __"; "this (coming) __"]: DJG v2 p127.
Examples: 100-11.

kono ue nai　「このうえない」 {この上ない / 此の上ない** 41; 1756} ["utterly __"; "supremely __"]: DJG v3 p226.
　　　　Examples: 81-8; 2058-38; 2062-26.

~ **koso**　「～こそ」 [places focus on the particular person, object, place, time, etc. that was just mentioned]: DJG v2 p132; Tobira ch12 #9.
　　　　Examples: 296-2; 465-9; 1133-33; 1197-31; 1232-18.

~ **koto**　「～こと」 [imperative]: DJG v2 p135.
　　　　Examples: 880-17.

koto　「こと」 {事 80} [intangible thing]: DJG v1 p191; Marx v1 day34; Tobira ch7 (first page).
　　　　Examples: 19-6; 23-5; 33-1; 43-4; 50-9; 51-17; 51-23; 55-12; 58-4; 80-2; 80-8; 80-16; 83-11.

koto　「こと」 {事 80} [nominalizer]: DJG v1 p193.
　　　　Examples: 84-10; 84-13; 86-22; 109-8; 112-3; 152-15; 159-19; 280-11; 312-5; 668-6; 1062-4.

~ **koto de**　「～ことで」 {～事で* 80} ["by virtue of __"]: DJG v2 p137.
　　　　Examples: 350-6; 682-25; 704-32; 793-29; 948-6; 1026-17.

~ **koto ga aru**　「～ことがある」 {～事がある* 80} ["__ has occurred"]: DJG v1 p196; Genki ch11; Marx v1 day62; Tobira ch1 #6.
　　　　Examples: 51-22; 55-11; 57-2; 77-1; 80-14; 85-3; 122-3; 129-4; 180-16.

~ **koto ga aru**　「～ことがある」 {～事がある* 80} ["__ does occur"]: DJG v1 p198.
　　　　Examples: 412-13; 619-22; 701-6; 748-20.

~ **koto ga dekiru**　「～ことができる」 {～事ができる* 80} ["be able to __"]: DJG v1 p200; Marx v1 day50.
　　　　Examples: 95-14; 98-6; 147-17; 165-5; 172-18; 323-2.

~ **koto ni naru**　「～ことになる」 {～事になる* 80} ["be decided that __"]: DJG v1 p202; Marx v2 day80; Tobira ch3 #7&10.
　　　　Examples: 55-21; 648-17; 780-39.

~ **koto ni naru**　「～ことになる」 {～事になる* 80} ["end up that __"]: DJG v2 p140; Marx v2 day73.
　　　　Examples: 454-14; 650-33; 944-15; 1127-13; 1147-25.

~ **koto ni suru**　「～ことにする」 {～事にする* 80} ["decide to __"]: DJG v1 p204; Genki ch23; Marx v2 day80.
　　　　Examples: 84-11; 99-10; 226-15; 272-4.

~ **koto ni yoru**　「～ことによる」 {～事による* 80} ["result from __"]: DJG v2 p143.
　　　　Examples: 2024-6.

~ **koto wa**　「～ことは」 {～事は* 80} ["indeed __ (but)"]: DJG v1 p206.
　　　　Examples: 950-34.

~ **koto wa nai**　「～ことはない」 {～事はない* 80} ["__ is not necessary"; "__ is not possible"]: DJG v2 p146; Tobira ch10 #15.
　　　　Examples: 97-6; 169-11; 232-8; 443-10; 563-14; 760-32; 953-11.

kou iu ~/kou itta ~　「こういう～/ こういった～」 {こう言う～ / こう言った～ 51} ["such __"]: DJG v2 p131; Tobira ch4 #10.
　　　　Examples: 478-15; 618-9; 839-43; 1474-3; 1503-6.

kou shita ~ 「こうした~」 ["such __"]: DJG v2 p130.
    Examples: 697-11; 710-34; 804-13; 884-5.
kou shite 「こうして」 ["like this"]: DJG v2 p131.
    Examples: 467-11; 470-3; 1045-19.
-ku 「-く」 ["and"; "so"]: DJG v2 p148.
    Examples: 185-8; 199-7.
kudasaru 「くださる」 {下さる 40} ["give"].
    Examples: 867-9; 973-35; 1224-13; 2037-2.
~ kurai 「~くらい」 {~位* 577} ["about __"]: DJG v1 p212; Marx v2 day78.
    Examples: 33-11; 35-6; 62-4; 107-10; 182-12.
~ kurai 「~くらい」 {~位* 577} ["to __ extent"]: DJG v2 p151.
    Examples: 92-10; 183-19; 355-13; 403-7; 805-19; 830-22; 864-17; 878-24.
~ kure 「~くれ」 {~呉れ** 1478} [impolite request]: DJG v1 p210.
    Examples: 51-6; 51-13; 427-9; 605-24; 659-1.
~ kureru 「~くれる」 {~呉れる** 1478} ["give"]: DJG v1 p213; Genki ch14; Marx v2 day30.
    Examples: 237-33; 307-4; 478-16.
kuru 「くる」 {来る 274} ["come"]: DJG v1 p219.
    Examples: 21-9; 31-6; 135-5; 219-15.
~ kuse ni 「~くせに」 {~癖に 1468} ["__ and yet"]: DJG v2 p155; Marx v2 day12; Tobira ch7 #13.
    Examples: 643-15.
kuwaete ~ 「くわえて~」 {加えて~ 1147} ["in addition, __"]: DJG v3 p240.
    Examples: 1147-17; 1162-17; 1195-21.
machigai naku 「まちがいなく」 {間違いなく 448; 663} ["unmistakably"]: DJG v3 p750 (under ずにはおかない); Marx v2 day3.
    Examples: 294-5; 663-18; 663-24.
mada ~ 「まだ~」 ["still __"; "not yet __"]: DJG v1 p224; Genki ch9; Marx v1 day87.
    Examples: 4-1; 4-4; 36-6; 109-10; 136-19; 154-4.
~ made 「~まで」 {~迄** 1806} ["until __"]: DJG v1 p225; Genki ch23.
    Examples: 1-7; 5-5; 7-6; 36-13.
~ made mo nai 「~までもない」 {~迄もない** 1806} ["no need to __"]: DJG v2 p159; Tobira ch10 #5.
    Examples: 1624-7; 1811-14.
~ made ni 「~までに」 {~迄に** 1806} ["by (a point in time)"]: DJG v1 p228.
    Examples: 97-4; 103-10; 152-19; 167-2.
~ mai 「~まい」 ["isn't/aren't/won't __"]: DJG v2 p161.
    Examples: 478-15; 1907-16; 2027-20; 2037-12.
mai ~ no you ni 「まい~のように」 ["almost every __"]: Tobira ch4 #1.
    Examples: 2141-11.
~ mama 「~まま」 ["as is/was"]: DJG v1 p236; Marx v2 day49; Tobira ch12 #15.
    Examples: 220-4; 236-8; 253-6; 300-14; 308-7; 329-11.
masaka ~ 「まさか~」 ["surely not __"]: DJG v2 p165; Marx v2 day3.

Examples: 1407-26.

-masen ka 「-ませんか」 ["won't you __"]: Genki ch3; Marx v1 day49.
Examples: 61-3; 179-19; 221-6; 258-3; 280-8.

mashi (da) 「まし(だ)」 ["(is) less undesirable"]: DJG v2 p169.
Examples: 1965-6.

mashite (ya) ~ 「まして(や)~」 ["to say nothing of __"]: DJG v3 p245.
Examples: 2198-4.

-mashou 「-ましょう」 ["I/we shall __"; "let's __"]: DJG v1 p240; Genki ch5; Marx v1 day29.
Examples: 9-4; 14-4; 21-7.

-mashou ka 「-ましょうか」 ["shall I/we __"]: Genki ch6; Marx v1 day49.
Examples: 223-5; 467-30; 959-9; 1765-5.

mata wa 「または」 {又は* 58} ["or"]: DJG v2 p171.
Examples: 58-1; 60-10.

matomeru 「まとめる」 ["gather", "put together", "unify"; "arrange", "summarize"].
Examples: 102-9; 183-18; 478-14; 989-12; 1587-20.

-me 「-め」 {-目 21} ["__th"]: DJG v2 p174.
Examples: 11-3.

meimei 「めいめい」 {銘々 1546} ["each (person)"]: DJG v2 p439 (under それぞれ).
Examples: 1546-4; 1546-7; 2233-6.

-men 「-めん」 {-面 175} ["aspect of __"]: DJG v2 p176.
Examples: 175-5; 189-10; 305-9.

metta ni ~ nai 「めったに~ない」 {滅多に~ない 1149; 267} ["seldom __"]: DJG v3 p252.
Examples: 611-3; 1149-7; 1149-14; 1575-7; 1605-20.

mieru 「~みえる」 {~見える 83} ["__ can be seen"; "looks __"]: DJG v1 p243; Marx v1 day50, v2 day69.
Examples: 21-10; 22-4; 83-4; 83-12; 83-19; 83-27; 84-14; 117-6.

miru kara ni ~ 「みるからに~」 {見るからに~ 83} ["visibly __"]: DJG v3 p254.
Examples: 1804-12.

~ mitai (da) 「~みたい(だ)」 ["(is) like __"; "seems like __"]: DJG v3 p105 (under ~ごとし); Genki ch17; Marx v2 day69.
Examples: 90-2; 231-5; 341-6; 560-28; 564-4; 677-19.

~ mo 「~も」 ["also __"]: DJG v1 p247; Genki ch2&4.
Examples: 27-11; 113-6; 103-12; 151-5; 161-6; 182-3; 222-10.

~ mo 「~も」 ["even __"]: DJG v1 p250; Genki ch14.
Examples: 2-3; 2-6; 15-18; 50-6; 51-24; 64-14.

~ mo ~ mo 「~も~も」 ["both __ and __"; "neither __ nor __"]: DJG v1 p255, v2 p185; Marx v2 day14; Tobira ch6 #3.
Examples: 3-6; 15-16; 23-4.

mon 「もん」 [colloquial contraction of もの].
Examples: 341-6; 676-2; 1317-25; 1427-16; 2275-24.

mono 「もの」 {物 172} [tangible thing]: DJG v1 p193 (under こと); Marx v1 day34; Tobira ch7 (first page).

Examples: 47-12; 59-7; 59-13; 172-9.
~ **mono (da)**　「〜もの(だ)」　[emphasis on a particular situation]: DJG v1 p257.
Examples: 404-11; 475-24; 476-13; 575-5; 676-2.
~ **mono (da)**　「〜もの(だ)」　["(is) something that __"]: DJG v2 p189.
Examples: 60-7; 130-9; 257-4; 266-20; 341-6.
~ **mono ka**　「〜ものか」　["no way __"]: DJG v3 p266.
Examples: 2275-24.
~ **mono (darou) ka**　「〜もの(だろう)か」　[expression of uncertainty or wish]: DJG v3 p268.
Examples: 425-16; 1589-9.
~ **mono nara(ba)**　「〜ものなら(ば)」　["were it the case that __"]: DJG v3 p272.
Examples: 2032-23.
~ **mono no**　「〜ものの」　["although __"]: DJG v3 p274.
Examples: 973-33; 1153-13; 1852-10; 1893-10.
mono wo　「ものを」　["but (alas)"]: DJG v3 p279.
Examples: 2014-27.
morau　「もらう」　{貰う* 1160} ["receive"]: DJG v1 p261; Genki ch14; Marx v2 day30.
Examples: 30-6; 105-8; 1160-1.
moshika shitara ~/moshika shite ~/moshika suru to　「もしかしたら〜/もしかして〜/もしかすると〜」　{若しかしたら* / 若しかして* / 若しかすると* 404} ["perhaps __"].
Examples: 2062-38.
moshi (mo) ~　「もし(も)〜」　["if __"]: DJG v3 p205 bottom (under かりに〜); Marx v2 day21.
Examples: 55-3; 143-11; 226-7; 954-13; 995-16.
motarasu　「もたらす」　["bring"; "bring about"; "introduce"].
Examples: 849-52; 884-5; 1021-22; 1257-55; 1260-36; 1466-28.
mou ~　「もう〜」　[changed state]: DJG v1 p254; Marx v1 day87.
Examples: 4-6; 10-7; 15-22; 38-3; 48-6; 63-1.
mou + (numeral) + (counter)　「もう + (numeral) + (counter)」　["__ more"].
Examples: 2-9; 2-10; 51-6; 67-14; 76-8; 113-24.
mushiro　「むしろ」　["rather"]: DJG v3 p295; Marx v2 day56.
Examples: 632-22; 1234-8; 1237-11; 1526-8; 1617-4.
-n　「-ん」　[colloquial contraction of -ない: "not __"].
Examples: 478-20; 1133-33.
na　「な」　[male alternative to ね]: DJG v1 p46 examples 9-11.
Examples: 62-5; 84-12; 126-8; 150-8; 206-1; 218-5; 336-14; 492-14; 1317-25.
naa　「なあ」　[exclamation]: DJG v1 p47 bottom, v2 p193.
Examples: 143-5; 143-8; 274-8; 1149-4.
~ **nado**　「〜など」　{〜等* 393} ["such as __"]: DJG v1 p267; Tobira ch2 #2.
Examples: 172-6; 179-18; 245-7; 393-8; 409-1; 506-3; 1130-46.
~ **nado to**　「〜などと」　{〜等と* 393} [paraphrase]: DJG v2 p197.
Examples: 644-14; 741-27; 1269-24; 1668-18; 1748-7.
~ **nagara**　「〜ながら」　["while __"]: DJG v1 p269; Genki ch18; Marx v1 day88.

153

Examples: 339-11; 355-16; 439-9; 476-10; 565-10; 578-7.

~ **nagara(mo)** 「〜ながら(も)」 ["though __"]: DJG v2 p199.
Examples: 760-36; 1327-13; 1407-20; 1634-25; 1988-8.

nai 「ない」 [informal negative of ある]: DJG v1 p576.
Examples: 1-4; 2-3.

-nai de 「-ないで」 ["do not __"; "without __ing"]: DJG v1 p271; Genki ch8&20; Marx v1 day39.
Examples: 51-9; 51-24; 57-5; 114-5; 255-4.

naishi (wa) 「ないし(は)」 {乃至は* 1754; 250} ["from __ to__"; "between __ and __"; "__ or __"]: DJG v3 p307.
Examples: 1048-6; 1761-21; 2037-9; 1754-1.

-nai to ikenai 「-ないといけない」 [imperative]: DJG v1 p274; Marx v1 day55.
Examples: 97-4; 143-12; 267-20; 304-5.

nakanaka ~ 「なかなか〜」 {中々〜* 35} ["quite __"; "not readily/quickly __"]: DJG v2 p206; Marx v2 day47; Tobira ch6 #14.
Examples: 46-16; 84-12; 231-3; 378-6; 239-15.

nakatta 「なかった」 [negative past tense of ある]: DJG v1 p577; Genki ch9; Marx v1 day37.
Examples: 2-6.

-nakereba ikenai 「-なければいけない」 [imperative]: DJG v1 p274; Genki ch12; Marx v1 day54; Tobira ch2 #1.
Examples: 81-9; 306-13.

-nakereba naranai 「-なければならない」 [imperative]: DJG v1 p274; Genki ch12; Marx v1 day54; Tobira ch2 #1.
Examples: 96-11; 145-5.

-naku 「-なく」 ["not __, so __"; "not __, but __"]: DJG v2 p211; Tobira ch2 #15.
Examples: 61-12; 294-5; 623-24.

-naku naru 「-なくなる」 ["no longer __"]: DJG v1 p277.
Examples: 183-20; 301-11; 313-5; 448-26.

-nakute 「-なくて」 ["not __, so __"]: DJG v1 p279; Marx v1 day39; Tobira ch2 #15.
Examples: 99-16; 411-3.

-nakute mo 「-なくても」 ["even without __"]: DJG v1 p280; Genki ch17; Marx v1 day39.
Examples: 55-8; 305-11.

-nakute wa naranai/ikenai/dame 「-なくてはならない/-なくてはいけない/-なくてはだめ」 [imperative]: DJG v1 p274; Genki ch12; Marx v1 day54; Tobira ch2 #1.
Examples: 272-3; 442-8; 526-17.

-nakya (ikenai/naranai) 「-なきゃ(いけない/ならない)」 [colloquial contraction of -なければ(いけない/ならない): "must __"].
Examples: 582-14; 1133-33; 1167-2.

nan demo 「なんでも」 {何でも* 815} ["whatever"]: Marx v1 day18.
Examples: 80-16; 293-4; 837-22.

nani ka 「なにか」 {何か* 815} ["something"; "anything"]: Genki ch8; Marx v1 day18.
Examples: 39-2; 80-4; 96-10; 97-7; 126-17.

nani mo 「なにも」 {何も* 815} ["nothing"]: DJG v1 p250; Genki ch8; Marx v1 day18.

Examples: 51-16; 83-6; 83-25; 83-31; 143-9.

nanishiro 「なにしろ」 {何しろ* 815} ["indeed" - used to emphasize a description]: DJG v2 p216.
   Examples: 1514-19.

~ **nanka** 「〜なんか」 ["such (things)/such (a thing)"]: DJG v3 p341 (under 〜なんて).
   Examples: 337-3; 443-10; 573-7; 698-15; 1027-6; 1063-12; 1260-29; 1622-8.

~ **na no de** 「〜なので」 ["since __"]: DJG v1 p322; Marx v1 day60.
   Examples: 144-7; 390-4; 409-3.

nanraka no ~ 「なんらかの〜」 {何らかの〜* 815} ["some (kind of) __"]: DJG v3 p333.
   Examples: 488-5; 555-37; 1872-29.

nanra ~ nai 「なんら〜ない」 {何ら〜ない* 815} ["no __ whatsoever"]: DJG v3 p334.
   Examples: 1639-27; 1849-25; 2056-6.

nante 「なんて」 {何て〜* 815} ["what __"]: DJG v3 p337.
   Examples: 878-17; 1356-1; 1681-33.

~ **nante** 「〜なんて」 ["such (things)/such (a thing)"]: DJG v3 p339; Tobira ch4 #3.
   Examples: 51-23; 126-29; 171-3; 274-18; 617-21; 584-26.

nanto ~ 「なんと〜」 {何と〜* 815} ["how __"]: DJG v3 p138 (under いかに〜).
   Examples: 1079-7; 1648-23; 1662-10.

nan to ka 「なんとか」 {何とか* 815} ["somehow"]: DJG v3 p341.
   Examples: 526-23; 1214-2; 1317-13.

nao ~ 「なお〜」 {尚〜* 184} ["still (more) __"]: DJG v3 p344.
   Examples: 358-3; 373-10; 1343-8; 1453-27.

naosara 「なおさら」 {尚更* 184; 889} ["still (more) __"]: DJG v3 p348.
   Examples: 889-19; 1143-18; 1553-25.

~ **nara(ba)** 「〜なら(ば)」 ["if __"]: DJG v1 p281; Genki ch13; Marx v2 day23; Tobira ch3 #5.
   Examples: 55-13; 91-9; 92-11; 143-11.

~ **nari** 「〜なり」 ["the moment __"]: DJG v3 p355.
   Examples: 1017-22.

~ **nari ~ nari** 「〜なり〜なり」 [listing of two examples/possibilities]: DJG v2 p223; Marx v2 day14.
   Examples: 2095-34.

nari no ~ 「なりの〜」 ["(one's) own particular __"]: DJG v2 p227.
   Examples: 173-24; 1149-14; 2156-18.

narubeku 「なるべく」 ["as __ as possible", "as much as possible __"]: Marx v2 day4; Tobira ch3 #15.
   Examples: 214-6; 1518-10; 2048-21.

naruhodo 「なるほど」 ["indeed"; "Ah, that makes sense."]: DJG v3 p359.
   Examples: 595-13; 1931-12.

-nasai 「-なさい」 [imperative]: DJG v1 p284; Genki ch22; Marx v1 day40.
   Examples: 55-7; 80-3; 180-10.

~ **nashi de wa** 「〜なしでは」 ["without __"]: DJG v2 p230.
   Examples: 36-9.

~ **nashi ni** 「〜なしに」 ["without __ing"]: DJG v3 p362.

155

Examples: 159-9; 1233-3.

~ nashi ni wa　「〜なしには」　["without __"]: DJG v2 p231.
Examples: 38-8.

nasu　「なす」　{為す* 1236}　["(to) effect" (i.e., bring about, realize, perform, etc.)]: DJG v3 p365.
Examples: 518-15; 954-14; 1743-20; 1748-1; 2048-29; 2056-5; 2075-27; 2103-14.

naze ka ~　「なぜか〜」　{何故か** 815; 257}　["for some reason __"]: DJG v3 p370.
Examples: 530-5; 2014-15.

naze nara(ba) ~ kara da　「なぜなら(ば)〜からだ」　{何故なら(ば)〜からだ** 815; 257}　["because __"]: DJG v3 p371; Marx v2 day11.
Examples: 180-16.

-n bakari (ni)　「-んばかり(に)」　["practically __"]: DJG v3 p374.
Examples: 1764-18; 2043-8; 2136-11.

ne　「ね」　[speaker seeks confirmation/agreement]: DJG v1 p45 & 286; Genki ch2; Marx v2 day2.
Examples: 15-8; 15-14; 24-9; 87-6; 89-2.

ne/nee　「ねえ / ねぇ」　[exclamation]: DJG v1 p47 bottom.
Examples: 39-10; 1607-25; 1712-17; 2213-28.

ne/nee　「ねえ / ねぇ」　[vulgar pronunciation of ない].
Examples: 643-20; 2267-10.

-neba naranai　「-ねばならない」　[imperative]: DJG v2 p232.
Examples: 500-5.

negau/negaimasu　「ねがう / ねがいます」　{願う / 願います 214} [request]: DJG v3 p377.
Examples: 17-3; 190-5; 214-1.

~ ni　「〜に」　[time of occurrence]: DJG v1 p289 & 303.
Examples: 1-6; 1-8; 3-1; 4-3; 9-4; 25-3; 30-4; 30-6; 30-7; 55-14.

~ ni　「〜に」　[marks indirect object]: DJG v1 p291 & 303.
Examples: 2-10; 28-3; 29-7; 51-3; 51-9; 51-13; 51-19; 53-11.

~ ni　「〜に」　[marks agent/source]: DJG v1 p292 & 303.
Examples: 21-7; 21-8; 47-10; 56-5; 92-9; 135-8; 137-4; 330-4.

~ ni　「〜に」　["on __"]: DJG v1 p295 & 303.
Examples: 14-1; 27-3; 60-2; 62-8; 64-4; 64-7; 64-9; 124-8; 125-9.

~ ni　「〜に」　[location of existence]: DJG v1 p299 & 303.
Examples: 3-7; 15-18; 22-2; 27-5; 31-8; 33-5; 34-2; 35-8.

~ ni　「〜に」　["to __", "toward __"]: DJG v1 p302 & 303.
Examples: 10-8; 21-4; 21-5; 24-3; 26-3; 28-1; 29-6; 30-7; 38-1; 38-12.

~ ni atari/~ ni atatte　「〜にあたり / 〜にあたって」　{〜に当たり / 〜に当たって 141}　["on the occasion of __", "when __"; "for __"]: DJG v2 p237.
Examples: 1510-25; 1668-22; 1953-9; 2164-6.

~ ni chigainai　「〜にちがいない」　{〜に違いない 663}　["no doubt __"]: DJG v1 p304; Tobira ch5 #10.
Examples: 663-35; 741-10; 893-26; 903-19; 1211-3.

~ ni hanshite/~ ni hansuru　「〜にはんして / 〜にはんする」　{〜に反して / 〜に反する 374}　["contrary to __"]: DJG v2 p241.

Examples: 374-1; 374-6; 532-28; 543-3.

~ **ni hoka naranai** 「〜にほかならない」 {〜に他ならない 189} ["be nothing but __"]: DJG v2 p245.
    Examples: 815-39.

~ **ni kagirazu** 「〜にかぎらず」 {〜に限らず 282} ["not limited to __"]: DJG v2 p249.
    Examples: 795-15; 869-44.

~ **ni kagitte** 「〜にかぎって」 {〜に限って 282} ["only (this one) of all (its group)"]: DJG v2 p250.
    Examples: 637-7; 1927-8.

~ **ni kakawarazu** 「〜にかかわらず」 {〜に関わらず 451} ["regardless of __"]: DJG v3 p386.
    Examples: 975-16; 1052-10.

~ **ni kakete wa** 「〜にかけては」 ["when it comes to __"]: DJG v3 p391.
    Examples: 298-20.

~ **ni kanshite/~ ni kansuru** 「〜にかんして / 〜にかんする」 {〜に関して / 〜に関する 451} ["with regard to __", "about __"]: DJG v2 p252; Marx v2 day42; Tobira ch12 #4.
    Examples: 451-9; 451-11; 495-4; 540-21; 582-29.

~ **ni kawatte** 「〜にかわって」 {〜に代わって 71} ["in place of __"]: DJG v2 p254.
    Examples: 1661-26; 1922-35.

~ **ni ki ga tsuku** 「〜にきがつく」 ["notice __"]: Tobira ch6 #1.
    Examples: 126-6; 238-15; 327-14; 382-4.

~ **ni kimatte iru** 「〜にきまっている」 {〜に決まっている 330} ["be bound to __"]: DJG v3 p395.
    Examples: 653-24.

-nikui 「-にくい」 {-難い* 712} ["hard to __"]: DJG v1 p307, v2 p52 & 96; Genki ch20; Marx v1 day61.
    Examples: 46-12; 135-4; 235-4.

~ **ni kuraberu to/~ ni kurabete** 「〜にくらべると / 〜にくらべて」 {〜に比べると / 〜に比べて 123} ["compared to __"]: DJG v2 p256.
    Examples: 123-5; 1118-10; 1227-14.

~ **ni mo kakawarazu** 「〜にもかかわらず」 {〜にも関わらず 451} ["although __"]: DJG v2 p257; Tobira ch9 #15.
    Examples: 650-29; 1238-25; 1430-26; 1760-32.

~ **ni motozuite/~ ni motozuku** 「〜にもとづいて / 〜にもとづく」 {〜に基づいて / 〜に基づく 485} ["based on __"]: DJG v2 p261.
    Examples: 485-4; 499-7; 499-23; 532-32; 1165-24.

~ **ni naru to** 「〜になると」 ["when __ comes"]: DJG v2 p262; Genki ch18.
    Examples: 238-11; 239-15; 243-3; 454-13; 467-33.

~ **ni oite/~ ni okeru** 「〜において / 〜における」 {〜に於いて* / 〜に於ける* 1885} ["in/on/at/to __"]: DJG v2 p265; Tobira ch13 #13.
    Examples: 194-10; 282-11; 371-10; 379-14; 427-5; 539-24; 1885-1; 1885-2.

~ **ni oujite/~ ni oujita** 「〜におうじて / 〜におうじた」 {〜に応じて / 〜に応じた 850} ["in response to __"; "corresponding to __"]: DJG v3 p412.
    Examples: 860-12; 1036-13; 1039-13; 1099-13; 1147-11; 1224-10.

~ ni sarasareru　「～にさらされる」 [passive form of さらす ("expose"): "be exposed to __"].
　　　Examples: 76-7; 425-6; 799-40; 888-11.
~ ni shiro/~ ni seyo　「～にしろ／～にせよ」 [imperative]: DJG v2 p70.
　　　Examples: 1377-21.
~ ni shiro/~ ni seyo　「～にしろ／～にせよ」 ["regardless of (whether) __"]: DJG v3 p418.
　　　Examples: 923-18; 1276-17; 1874-18; 2179-19; 2189-43.
~ ni shitagatte/~ ni shitagai　「～にしたがって／～にしたがい」 {～に従って／～に従い 869} ["in accordance with __"; "as __"]: DJG v2 p268; Tobira ch10 #8.
　　　Examples: 544-21; 869-17; 869-36; 892-19; 1712-37.
~ ni shite　「～にして～」 ["both __ and __"]: DJG v3 p429.
　　　Examples: 1304-18.
~ ni shite　「～にして」 ["at/in (such a) time"]: DJG v3 p426.
　　　Examples: 167-5; 1432-28; 1484-31.
~ ni shite mo　「～にしても」 ["regardless of (whether) __"]: DJG v3 p435; Marx v2 day25.
　　　Examples: 1260-28; 1466-27; 2150-33.
~ ni shite wa　「～にしては」 ["for (a) __"]: DJG v1 p309; Marx v2 day82.
　　　Examples: 84-12; 676-5; 1022-17; 1498-9.
~ ni suginai　「～にすぎない」 {～に過ぎない 464} ["be merely __"]: DJG v2 p245 & 271; Marx v2 day36.
　　　Examples: 674-13; 799-30; 838-24; 1454-4.
~ ni sumu　「～にすむ」 {～に住む 366} ["live in (a particular place)" - generally conjugated in -ている form].
　　　Examples: 22-2; 254-11; 366-2.
~ ni suru　「～にする」 ["opt for __"]: DJG v1 p310; Marx v2 day80.
　　　Examples: 6-4; 16-6; 42-5; 53-10.
~ ni taishite/~ ni taishi　「～にたいして／～にたいし」 {～に対して／～に対し 650} ["toward __"; "(as) against __"]: DJG v2 p275; Tobira ch9 #13.
　　　Examples: 185-12; 502-10; 551-7; 611-7; 650-30; 738-42; 744-12; 760-43.
~ ni todomarazu　「～にとどまらず」 {～に止まらず 42} ["go beyond __"]: DJG v3 p440.
　　　Examples: 2222-11.
~ ni totte　「～にとって」 ["as far as __ is concerned", "for/to __"]: DJG v2 p278; Marx v2 day82; Tobira ch2 #4.
　　　Examples: 33-7; 95-10; 201-6; 244-8; 245-6; 277-10.
~ ni tsuite　「～について」 {～に就いて** 1283} ["about __"]: DJG v2 p280; Marx v2 day42.
　　　Examples: 51-21; 77-2; 79-7; 80-17; 81-11; 106-4; 118-6.
~ ni tsuke　「～につけ」 {～に付け* 64} ["whenever __"]: DJG v3 p444.
　　　Examples: 2032-18.
~ ni tsuki　「～につき」 {～に付き* 64} ["per __"]: DJG v2 p283.
　　　Examples: 15-1; 38-6; 394-8; 1743-13.
~ ni tsurete/~ ni tsure　「～につれて／～につれ」 {～に連れて*／～に連れ* 582} ["as __"; "in proportion to __"]: DJG v2 p285; Tobira ch13 #6.
　　　Examples: 375-4; 424-6; 553-12; 1388-17; 1483-20; 1512-16; 1686-7.
~ ni wa　「～には」 ["for the purpose of __"]: DJG v2 p289; Tobira ch13 #11.

Examples: 125-10; 204-7; 303-11; 315-12.

~ ni watatte/~ ni wataru 「〜にわたって / 〜にわたる」 {〜に亘って* / 〜に亘る* 1395} ["spanning over __"]: DJG v3 p447.
Examples: 78-12; 778-14; 968-3; 1118-8; 1155-21; 1395-1.

~ ni yoranai 「〜によらない」 {〜に依らない* 701} ["without (being based on) __"].
Examples: 1473-18; 1608-17; 1657-32; 2190-37; 2191-15.

~ ni yorazu 「〜によらず」 {〜に依らず* 701} ["independent of (whether) __"]: DJG v3 p452.
Examples: 1197-33.

~ ni yoreba 「〜によれば」 {〜に依れば* 701} ["according to __"]: DJG v3 p459 (under 〜によると).
Examples: 1260-31; 1472-43; 1576-17; 1761-19.

~ ni yoru 「〜による」 {〜に依る* 701} ["based on __"; "by __"].
Examples: 182-2; 227-19; 348-2; 368-12; 387-9; 389-3.

~ ni yoru to 「〜によると」 {〜に依ると* 701} ["according to __"]: DJG v3 p459; Marx v2 day43.
Examples: 51-20; 256-5; 546-41.

~ ni yotte/~ ni yori 「〜によって / 〜により」 {〜に依って* / 〜に依り* 701} ["based on/depending on __"; "due to __"]: DJG v2 p292; Marx v2 day43; Tobira ch8 #2.
Examples: 45-6; 129-5; 135-7; 420-7; 1005-39; 1078-30; 1266-7; 1399-9.

~ ni yotte + passive 「〜によって + passive」 {〜に依って* 701} ["(done) by __"]: DJG v1 p366.
Examples: 45-6; 154-10; 155-7; 235-3; 302-7; 341-4.

no 「の」 [nominalizer]: DJG v1 p318; Genki ch8.
Examples: 43-6; 47-8; 51-10; 70-11; 83-15; 95-13; 97-9; 112-4; 180-3; 185-9.

no 「の」 [marks end of modifying phrase]: DJG v1 p312; Genki ch10.
Examples: 2-5; 2-7; 2-10; 3-7; 4-3; 6-7; 9-6; 10-2.

no 「の」 [female: explanation or assertion]: DJG v1 p322; Genki ch1.
Examples: 384-21; 802-8; 1111-11.

no(?) 「の(?)」 [female: question marker]: DJG v1 p48; Marx v1 day11.
Examples: 5-8; 37-4; 55-2; 152-10; 847-26; 1987-11.

~ no de 「〜ので」 ["because __"]: DJG v1 p328; Genki ch12; Marx v1 day60.
Examples: 44-12; 67-11; 71-15; 103-12; 142-25.

(no) de areba 「(の)であれば」 ["if it's the case that __"]: DJG v3 p617 (under とあっては).
Examples: 815-39.

no de aru/no desu/no da/n da 「のである / のです / のだ / んだ」 [explanation or assertion]: DJG v1 p325; Genki ch12.
Examples: 21-10; 22-4; 33-9; 35-13; 36-5; 38-9; 46-8; 71-6; 83-29; 113-20; 294-6; 423-18.

~ (no) kawari ni 「〜(の)かわりに」 {〜(の)代わりに 71} ["in place of __"; "in compensation for __"]: DJG v1 p184, v2 p116; Marx v2 day26; Tobira ch2 #5.
Examples: 71-5; 71-9; 71-15; 82-2; 100-12; 315-10.

~ no koto 「〜のこと」 {〜の事* 80} ["about __"]: DJG v2 p304.
Examples: 29-2; 53-15; 63-10; 78-16; 80-2; 85-4; 88-22; 95-4; 134-17; 142-24; 321-5.

159

~ nomi 「〜のみ」 ["only __"]: DJG v2 p307.
> Examples: 282-4; 412-7; 549-21; 760-34.

~ nomi narazu 「〜のみならず」 ["not only __"]: DJG v3 p461.
> Examples: 1260-36; 2083-12.

~ no moto de 「〜のもとで」 {〜の下で 40} ["under __"]: DJG v2 p310.
> Examples: 76-6; 393-14; 398-11; 542-18; 753-6; 923-12; 932-37; 1213-9.

~ no nasa 「〜のなさ」 {〜の無さ* 48} ["lack of __"]: DJG v3 p468.
> Examples: 1818-4; 2217-11.

~ no ni 「〜のに」 ["even though __"]: DJG v1 p331; Genki ch22; Marx v2 day12.
> Examples: 148-7; 148-14; 221-10; 266-15; 286-2.

~ no ni 「〜のに」 ["in order to __"]: DJG v1 p335.
> Examples: 190-7; 272-2; 294-2; 302-21; 368-16; 368-19.

~ (no) ue de 「〜(の)うえで」 {〜(の)上で 41} ["upon __"]: DJG v2 p547; Tobira ch11 #15.
> Examples: 2278-13.

~ no ue de wa 「〜のうえでは」 {〜の上では 41} ["as far as __ is concerned"]: DJG v2 p312.
> Examples: 1113-12.

~ no wa ~ da 「〜のは〜だ」 [statement about a clause]: DJG v1 p337.
> Examples: 97-9; 99-16; 111-5; 117-11; 1466-23.

-n to suru 「-んとする」 ["try to __"; "be about to __"]: DJG v3 p474.
> Examples: 1999-33; 2197-32.

-nu 「-ぬ」 ["not __"]: DJG v2 p315; Tobira ch11 #14.
> Examples: 560-13; 642-17; 658-1; 956-38.

Numerals: DJG v1 p602; Genki ch1-2; Marx v1 day78-80.
> Examples: 5-2.

o- 「お-」 [prefix expressing politeness]: DJG v1 p343.
> Examples: 10-6; 23-4; 27-2; 29-1; 35-10; 53-8; 77-3.

~ okage 「〜おかげ」 {〜お陰* 1311} ["thanks to __"]: DJG v2 p382 (under せい); Marx v2 day44; Tobira ch8 #14.
> Examples: 438-4; 564-8; 607-12; 615-2; 1640-25; 1982-9.

o- ~ kudasai/go- ~ kudasai 「お-〜ください/ご-〜ください」 {お-〜下さい/ご-〜下さい 40} ["please __"]: DJG v2 p322; Genki ch19.
> Examples: 126-22; 162-4; 338-4; 366-4; 1133-24; 1256-33.

o-mae 「おまえ」 {お前 113} [very informal: "you"]: DJG v1 p28.
> Examples: 113-9; 113-20.

omake ni ~ 「おまけに〜」 {お負けに〜* / 御負けに〜** 829; 862} ["what's more, __"]: DJG v2 p390 & 413 & 427.
> Examples: 521-12.

omoikitte ~ 「おもいきって〜」 {思い切って〜 142} ["boldly/resolutely __"]: DJG v3 p3 (under あえて〜).
> Examples: 142-22; 249-9; 1558-17; 1913-19; 2020-46.

omou ni ~ 「おもうに〜」 {思うに〜 142} ["in my view __", "I think __"]: DJG v3 p496.
> Examples: 588-19; 1374-7; 1621-7; 1829-38; 2289-13.

160

o- ~ ni naru 「お-〜になる」 [polite description of outgroup person's action]: DJG v1 p358.
>Examples: 299-13; 560-30; 1112-13.

ono'ono 「おのおの」 {各々 786} ["each"]: DJG v2 p439 (under それぞれ).
>Examples: 786-5; 1186-2.

oomune 「おおむね」 {概ね 1821} ["on the whole"; "roughly"]: DJG v3 p530 bottom (under およそ).
>Examples: 1885-6.

oowareru 「おおわれる」 {覆われる 1870} [passive form of おおう ("cover"): "be covered"].
>Examples: 78-17; 607-13; 899-7; 912-4; 1652-11; 1870-6.

ore 「おれ」 {俺 1356} [very informal: "I"]: DJG v1 p28.
>Examples: 113-23; 124-8; 182-10; 1356-1.

~ ori (ni) 「〜おり(に)」 {〜折りに* 1698} [at a particular time/opportunity/occasion]: DJG v3 p502.
>Examples: 1698-23.

o- ~ suru 「お-〜する」 [polite description of action by oneself or another ingroup person]: DJG v1 p39 bottom; Genki ch20.
>Examples: 17-3; 18-6; 53-4.

oyobi 「および」 {及び* 1760} ["and"]: DJG v3 p521.
>Examples: 356-11; 393-20; 581-10; 636-7; 696-4; 1760-25.

oyoso ~ 「およそ〜」 {凡そ〜** 1629} ["generally __"; "roughly __"]: DJG v3 p526.
>Examples: 71-14; 129-5; 554-16; 596-9; 652-4; 2062-32.

Past tense adjectives: DJG v1 p580; Genki ch5&9; Marx v1 day65.
>Examples: 2-6; 36-13.

Past tense verbs: DJG v1 p576; Genki ch4&9; Marx v1 day31.
>Examples: 1-2; 1-6; 2-4; 3-6; 5-2; 5-3; 7-3.

-ppanashi 「-っぱなし」 {-放し* 574} [leave in an improper state]: DJG v2 p333; Marx v2 day49; Tobira ch15 #15.
>Examples: 67-11; 574-13; 1881-6.

-ppoi 「-っぽい」 [" __like"]: DJG v2 p337; Marx v2 day68.
>Examples: 27-6; 240-4; 128-10; 160-1; 180-13; 631-17.

-ra 「-ら」 {-等* 393} [plural personal pronoun suffix]: DJG v1 p28 bottom & 440, v3 p47 & 50-51 of front matter (under -たち); Tobira ch9 #12.
>Examples: 15-16; 223-7; 264-11.

-rareru 「-られる」 [passive]: DJG v1 p364; Genki ch21.
>Examples: 40-13; 42-4; 45-7; 47-11; 47-12; 51-23; 53-16; 55-21; 76-5; 76-7.

~ rashii 「〜らしい」 ["(it) seems (that) __", "I heard (that) __"; "__-like"]: DJG v1 p373; Marx v2 day70; Tobira ch5 #13.
>Examples: 15-20; 92-2; 93-5; 97-7; 152-2; 171-1.

rei no ~ 「れいの〜」 {例の〜 721} [reference to an understood object: "the aforementioned __", "that __", "the customary __"]: DJG v2 p346.
>Examples: 743-7; 1078-27; 1080-6; 1472-12; 1636-12; 1774-5.

roku ni ~ nai 「ろくに〜ない」 ["not properly __"]: DJG v2 p355.

161

Examples: 1009-26.

-sa 「-さ」 ["__ness"]: DJG v1 p381; Marx v1 day67; Tobira ch1 #2.
Examples: 33-11; 62-4; 91-2; 120-6; 186-6; 260-6.

~ sa 「〜さ」 ["__, I tell you."]: DJG v2 p358; Marx v2 day1; Tobira ch12 #11.
Examples: 910-17; 1167-10; 1731-15; 1916-28; 1925-17.

~ sae 「〜さえ」 ["even __"; "(if) just __"]: DJG v2 p363; Marx v2 day60-61; Tobira ch5 #6.
Examples: 35-13; 88-22; 142-15; 403-8; 422-32; 461-15; 503-24; 1204-19.

~ sai (ni) 「〜さい(に)」 {〜際に 638} ["on the occasion of __", "when __"]: DJG v2 p369.
Examples: 638-6; 638-15; 642-6; 669-31.

sara ni ~ 「さらに〜」 {更に〜 889} ["still more __"]: DJG v3 p540.
Examples: 78-17; 84-11; 237-33; 708-22; 774-14; 889-7.

sarasu 「さらす」 ["expose"].
Examples: 398-19; 1031-25.

-saserareru 「-させられる」 [causative-passive verbs]: DJG v1 p392; Genki ch23; Marx v2 day9.
Examples: 383-17; 823-15; 859-25; 947-8; 1142-6; 1182-10; 1419-18; 1564-28; 1949-12.

-saserareru 「-させられる」 [causative {-させる} + potential {-られる}; cf. causative-passive {-させられる, DJG 1 p 392}].
Examples: 706-37.

-saseru/-aseru 「-させる」 [causing/permitting]: DJG v1 p387; Genki ch22; Marx v2 day8.
Examples: 135-8; 145-4; 289-8; 303-6; 303-10; 357-5; 677-28; 826-5; 827-23.

-sasu 「-さす」 [causing/permitting]: DJG v1 p391 number 6.
Examples: 2154-8.

sasuga 「さすが」 ["as one might expect"]: DJG v2 p374.
Examples: 560-29.

sate 「さて」 [initiates a new matter]: DJG v3 p543; Tobira ch8 #6.
Examples: 467-30; 483-4; 568-18; 664-13; 732-19; 1017-22; 1418-13.

sazo(kashi) ~ 「さぞ(かし)〜」 ["must be __"]: DJG v3 p547.
Examples: 775-42.

sei 「せい」 ["because of __"]: DJG v2 p378; Marx v2 day44; Tobira ch8 #14.
Examples: 321-8; 452-10; 927-36; 1018-28; 1105-2; 1466-23; 1580-9; 1593-43.

sekkaku ~ 「せっかく〜」 {折角〜** 1698; 342} [indicates a situation that should be taken advantage of]: DJG v1 p392; Marx v2 day76; Tobira ch9 #16.
Examples: 253-8; 1252-1; 1683-17.

semete ~ 「せめて〜」 ["at least __"]: DJG v2 p383; Marx v2 day62.
Examples: 1876-12.

shi 「し」 ["and", "besides"]: DJG v1 p395; Genki ch13.
Examples: 94-9; 218-9; 263-2; 1317-25.

~ shidai 「〜しだい」 {〜次第 1191} ["as soon as __"; "depends on __"]: DJG v2 p385; Tobira ch14 #13.
Examples: 1191-2; 1191-3; 1434-1; 1505-13; 1675-4.

shika mo ~ 「しかも〜」 ["and __"; "and yet __"]: DJG v2 p390.

Examples: 1494-2; 1924-4; 1596-21; 1620-16; 1638-3; 1659-14; 1912-46.

shika ~ nai　「しか〜ない」　["no more than __/no other than __"]: DJG v1 p398; Genki ch14; Marx v2 day40.
Examples: 1-4; 10-7; 51-12; 83-11; 88-23; 94-10.

shikashi　「しかし」　["but"]: DJG v1 p120, v2 p18; Marx v1 day59.
Examples: 464-21; 478-16.

shiru　「しる」　{知る 560}　["know"]: DJG v1 p406.
Examples: 560-15.

shitagatte ~　「したがって〜」　{従って〜 869}　["accordingly, __"]: DJG v2 p395.
Examples: 869-39; 926-36; 1040-5; 1113-11; 1302-5.

soko de ~　「そこで〜」　{其処で〜** 1757; 553}　["(and) so __"]: DJG v2 p401 & 405; Tobira ch9 #8.
Examples: 96-6; 142-21; 194-12; 569-21; 582-31; 679-33.

somosomo (no)　「そもそも(の)」　{抑** / 抑抑** 1137}　["to begin with", "originally"]: DJG v3 p550.
Examples: 1613-8; 1821-10; 2206-4.

~ sono mono　「〜そのもの」　["__ itself"]: DJG v3 p553.
Examples: 831-31; 1062-21; 1130-41; 1756-9.

sono ue ~　「そのうえ〜」　{その上〜 41}　["furthermore, __"]: DJG v2 p413; Tobira ch7 #2.
Examples: 1191-24; 2179-19.

sore dake　「それだけ」　{其れだけ** 1757}　["that much"]: DJG v3 p557.
Examples: 942-30.

sore de ~　「それで〜」　{其れで〜** 1757}　["that's why __"]: DJG v1 p413; Marx v2 day13; Tobira ch4 #14.
Examples: 1064-18; 1260-30.

sore demo ~　「それでも〜」　{其れでも〜** 1757}　["yet __"]: DJG v2 p418; Marx v2 day13.
Examples: 179-13.

sore de wa ~　「それでは〜」　{其れでは〜** 1757}　["then __"]: DJG v1 p414.
Examples: 237-23.

sore dokoroka　「それどころか」　{其れどころか** 1757}　["far from it"]: DJG v2 p420.
Examples: 1033-18.

sore kara ~　「それから〜」　{其れから〜** 1757}　["and then __"]: DJG v1 p416.
Examples: 61-10; 76-8; 96-11; 170-9; 183-19.

sore mo ~　「それも〜」　{其れも〜** 1757}　["what's more, __"]: DJG v2 p425.
Examples: 1323-5; 1530-10.

sore nara ~　「それなら〜」　{其れなら〜** 1757}　["in that case, __"]: DJG v1 p419; Tobira ch10 #17.
Examples: 184-3; 1735-19.

sore nari ni/no　「それなりの」　{其れなりの** 1757}　["(one's) own particular __"]: DJG v3 p559.
Examples: 1149-14; 1585-15.

sore ni ~　「それに〜」　{其れに〜** 1757}　["in addition, __"]: DJG v2 p427; Tobira ch3 #4.
Examples: 298-23; 310-9; 344-12; 631-22.

sore to ~　「それと〜」　{其れと〜** 1757}　["in addition, __"]: DJG v2 p431.

Examples: 1356-12.

sore tomo ~ 「それとも〜」 {其れとも** 1757} ["or __"]: DJG v1 p421; Marx v2 day14.
Examples: 36-12; 75-11; 1296-3; 1672-18; 1917-36; 2062-36.

sorezore 「それぞれ」 {其々** 1757} ["each"; "respectively"]: DJG v2 p436; Tobira ch6 #6.
Examples: 65-12; 95-3; 113-14; 298-23; 384-11; 437-3.

soshite 「そして」 ["and"]: DJG v1 p422.
Examples: 76-8; 141-20; 157-10; 183-14; 278-10.

-sou (da) 「-そう(だ)」 ["look __"; "__-looking"]: DJG v1 p410; Genki ch13; Marx v2 day67.
Examples: 97-1; 180-12; 230-1; 563-13; 726-7; 780-30.

~ sou da 「〜そうだ」 ["I heard that __"]: DJG v1 p407; Genki ch17; Marx v2 day70.
Examples: 600-10; 617-16; 775-37; 845-12.

sou iu ~/sou itta ~ 「そういう〜/そういった〜」 {そう言う〜/そう言った〜 51} ["such __"]: DJG v2 p131; Tobira ch4 #10.
Examples: 310-10; 577-25; 628-28; 633-21; 683-19.

-sou ni naru 「-そうになる」 ["on the verge of __"]: DJG v2 p409.
Examples: 941-10; 1373-11.

sou shita ~ 「そうした〜」 ["such __"]: DJG v2 p131.
Examples: 691-11; 838-29; 981-23.

sou shite 「そうして」 ["like this"]: DJG v2 p131.
Examples: 669-29; 927-36.

~ sue (ni) 「〜すえ(に)」 {〜末(に) 272} ["at the end of __"]: DJG v3 p562.
Examples: 233-6; 272-3; 272-4; 2109-27.

-sugiru 「-すぎる」 {-過ぎる 464} ["__ too much", "over-__"]: DJG v1 p423; Genki ch12; Marx v1 day61.
Examples: 113-9; 143-10; 171-3; 185-5; 202-2; 464-3.

sugu 「すぐ」 ["immediately"; "directly"]: DJG v2 p439.
Examples: 21-5; 39-3; 55-5; 64-11; 91-11; 114-10.

suki da 「すきだ」 {好きだ 95} ["be fond of"]: DJG v1 p426; Genki ch5; Marx v1 day41.
Examples: 95-6.

sukunai 「すくない」 {少ない 677} ["few"; "little"]: DJG v1 p427.
Examples: 30-5; 37-5; 107-4; 677-3.

sukunaku to mo ~ 「すくなくとも〜」 {少なくとも〜 677} ["at least __"]: DJG v2 p383 (under せめて〜); Tobira ch15 #1.
Examples: 677-32; 842-31.

sunawachi ~ 「すなわち〜」 {即ち〜* 390} ["namely, __", "that is, __"]: DJG v2 p538 (under つまり); Tobira ch14 #2.
Examples: 471-1; 557-9; 1197-25; 1459-17.

~ sura 「〜すら」 ["even __"]: DJG v2 p368 (under さえ).
Examples: 549-27; 795-15; 1083-10; 1607-33.

suru to ~ 「すると〜」 ["then __"]: DJG v1 p437; Tobira ch8 #3.
Examples: 316-13; 450-23; 579-15.

-ta ato de 「-たあとで」 {-た後で 114} ["after __ing"]: DJG v1 p78.
Examples: 793-28; 1024-5.

~ tabi ni 「～たびに」 {～度に* 280} ["every time __"]: DJG v2 p442; Marx v2 day84; Tobira ch8 #16.
    Examples: 280-13; 355-20; 1028-24.

-tachi 「-たち」 {-達 1475} [plural personal pronoun suffix]: DJG v1 p28 bottom & 440, v3 p47 & 50-51 of front matter.
    Examples: 15-17; 71-8; 80-15.

tada ~ 「ただ～」 {只～* 1194} ["just __", "only __"]: DJG v2 p445.
    Examples: 303-14; 349-4; 431-4; 597-24; 648-14; 1194-5.

tada no ~ 「ただの～」 {只の～* 1194} ["ordinary __", "nothing but __"]: DJG v2 p449.
    Examples: 83-27; 515-21; 706-30; 1454-4.

tadashi ~ 「ただし～」 {但し～ 1393} [proviso: "however, __"]: DJG v3 p573.
    Examples: 1393-3.

-tai 「-たい」 ["want to __"]: DJG v1 p441; Genki ch11; Marx v1 day48.
    Examples: 15-11; 51-21; 53-14; 61-11; 67-11; 68-12; 74-2; 78-3.

taihen ~ 「たいへん～」 {大変～ 33; 775} ["terribly __"]: DJG v2 p210 (under なかなか～).
    Examples: 775-25.

~ tai to omotte iru 「～たいとおもっている」 {～たいと思っている 142} ["would like to __"].
    Examples: 142-18; 237-21.

takaga ~ 「たかが～」 {高が～** 185} ["mere __"]: DJG v3 p576.
    Examples: 392-2.

-taku nai 「-たくない」 [negative form of -たい ("want to __"): "do not want to __"]: DJG v1 p441; Genki ch11; Marx v1 day48.
    Examples: 33-6; 51-15; 58-3.

takusan 「たくさん」 {沢山* 1504; 37} ["a lot of"]: DJG v1 p356 (under おおい); Genki ch4.
    Examples: 29-7; 30-8; 68-12.

-tamae 「-たまえ」 {-給え* 526} [male, familiar: imperative]: Marx v1 day40.
    Examples: 1448-9; 1561-9; 1652-10.

tama ni wa ~ 「たまには～」 ["occasionally __"]: DJG v3 p252 (under めったに～ない).
    Examples: 873-9; 2125-9.

~ tame (ni) 「～ため(に)」 {～為に* 1236} ["for (the sake of) __"]: DJG v1 p447; Marx v2 day41; Tobira ch2 #6.
    Examples: 15-9; 38-13; 45-7; 46-9; 78-6; 83-28.

~ tame (ni) 「～ため(に)」 {～為に* 1236} ["because of __"]: DJG v1 p447; Tobira ch2 #7.
    Examples: 154-8; 266-18; 361-7; 368-17; 415-8.

-tara 「-たら」 ["if __"; "when __"]: DJG v1 p452; Genki ch17; Marx v2 day21.
    Examples: 18-8; 55-3; 130-6; 136-15; 142-23; 148-10.

-tara (dou desu ka) 「-たら(どうですか)」 ["why not __"]: DJG v1 p457; Genki ch14.
    Examples: 91-3; 1505-10.

~ -tari ~ -tari suru 「～-たり～-たりする」 [partial enumeration of actions/states]: DJG v1 p458; Genki ch11.
    Examples: 201-8; 505-14; 605-25.

tari to mo ~ nai 「たりとも～ない」 ["not a single __"]: DJG v3 p117 (under 一 + counter + としては～ない).

Examples: 386-10; 1464-11; 1802-3.

~ **taruya** 「～たるや」 ["when it comes to __"]: DJG v3 p591.
Examples: 2166-16.

tashika ni ~ ga 「たしかに～が」 {確かに～が 1133} ["indeed __, but __"]: DJG v2 p450.
Examples: 1743-18.

tatoe ~ 「たとえ～」 ["even if __", "no matter __"]: Marx v2 day25.
Examples: 1681-50; 1988-6; 2014-23.

-ta tokoro de 「-たところで」 ["even if __"]: DJG v2 p452.
Examples: 811-5.

tatta ~ 「たった～」 ["just __", "only __"]: DJG v2 p448 (under ただ～); Tobira ch15 #7.
Examples: 13-6; 63-9; 1057-16; 1330-25; 1801-1.

-tatte 「-たって」 ["even if __", "no matter __"]: DJG v1 p461 bottom, v2 p105 & 510, v3 p594.
Examples: 761-13; 2014-23.

-te ageru 「-てあげる」 {-て上げる* 41} ["do __ (for someone)"]: DJG v1 p65; Genki ch16; Marx v2 day31.
Examples: 60-6; 78-4; 276-23; 788-20.

-te aru 「-てある」 [indicates completed action and resulting condition]: DJG v1 p76 (under ある); Genki ch21; Marx v2 day7.
Examples: 79-10; 340-11; 343-6.

-te/-de 「-て / -で」 [connective form of verbs]: DJG v1 p464, v2 p64 of front matter; Genki ch6; Marx v1 day30.
Examples: 5-7; 7-5; 12-8; 28-1; 28-6; 38-5; 46-14; 47-3; 51-24; 55-5; 56-2.

-te/-de 「-て / -で」 [connective form of adjectives]: DJG v1 p464; Marx v1 day66.
Examples: 33-11; 48-7; 80-11; 176-4; 185-8; 215-6; 262-11.

-te hajimete 「-てはじめて」 {-て初めて 710} ["not until __", "for the first time in __"]: DJG v2 p456.
Examples: 710-27; 752-12; 1971-27; 2299-17.

-te hoshii 「-てほしい」 {-て欲しい 1035} ["want(s) (someone) to __"]: DJG v1 p146; Genki ch21; Marx v1 day48.
Examples: 71-6; 73-8; 103-10; 1035-26; 1373-9.

-te iku 「-ていく」 {-て行く 55} ["go on __ing"]: DJG v1 p151.
Examples: 239-14; 336-9; 521-9; 817-21.

-te iru 「-ている」 ["be __ing"; "have (done) __"]: DJG v1 p155; Genki ch7; Marx v1 day36.
Examples: 4-6; 12-7; 15-21; 21-6; 22-2; 29-8; 33-8; 34-3; 67-13.

-te iru hito 「-ているひと」 {-ている人 15} ["person (who is) __ing"]: Genki ch9.
Examples: 35-9; 67-13.

-te itadaku 「-ていただく」 {-て頂く / -て戴く* 1913; 1914} ["do __ for (me)"]: DJG v1 p265 (under -てもらう); Genki ch16.
Examples: 280-16; 282-7; 309-17; 1913-5.

-te kara 「-てから」 ["after __ing"; "since __"]: DJG v1 p177.
Examples: 117-23; 226-11; 233-1; 253-7; 423-18.

-te kudasai 「-てください」 {-て下さい 40} ["please __"]: DJG v1 p209; Genki ch6.

Examples: 6-4; 8-6.

-te kudasaru　「-てくださる」　{-て下さる 40} ["do __ for (me)"]: DJG v1 p210 & 215 & 218.
Examples: 225-5; 231-6; 348-7.

-te kureru　「-てくれる」　{-て呉れる** 1478} ["do __ for (me)"]: DJG v1 p216; Genki ch16; Marx v2 day31; Tobira ch3 #12.
Examples: 71-3; 71-15; 100-6; 160-2; 165-3; 179-19.

-te kuru　「-てくる」　{-て来る** 274} ["begin to __"; "come to __"; "up to now"]: DJG v1 p221.
Examples: 83-24; 246-3; 294-6; 336-15; 735-11.

-te miru　「-てみる」　["try (out) __"; "check out __"]: DJG v1 p246; Genki ch13; Marx v2 day35.
Examples: 74-3; 97-5; 104-3; 106-1; 298-11.

-te miseru　「-てみせる」　{-て見せる* 83} ["am determined to __"]: DJG v2 p177.
Examples: 461-11; 809-9.

-te mo　「-ても」　["even if __"]: DJG v1 p468; Genki ch23; Marx v2 day25.
Examples: 191-21; 239-13; 282-11.

-te mo ii　「-てもいい」　["all right if __"]: DJG v1 p471; Marx v1 day56.
Examples: 55-8; 100-12; 125-5; 132-6; 249-11.

-te morau　「-てもらう」　{-て貰う** 1160} ["do __ for (me)"]: DJG v1 p263; Genki ch16; Marx v2 day31; Tobira ch3 #12.
Examples: 135-9; 223-3; 279-10; 302-17; 311-4; 1160-3.

-te naranai　「-てならない」　["cannot help/bear __"]: DJG v2 p219.
Examples: 1184-6; 2034-14.

~ ten (de)　「〜てん(で)」　{〜点(で) 349} ["in terms of __"]: DJG v2 p458; Tobira ch8 #10.
Examples: 349-3; 349-4; 349-10; 349-12; 767-3.

-te oku　「-ておく」　{-て置く 843} [indicates act of prudence/getting something done]: DJG v1 p357; Genki ch15; Marx v2 day34.
Examples: 52-3; 83-28; 109-7; 174-6; 240-3; 274-21.

-te ori　「-ており」　[written equivalent of verbal connective -ていて]: DJG v2 p329 & 64 of front matter if unclear about -ていて.
Examples: 669-30; 797-17; 812-19; 889-13; 932-56; 1102-13.

-teru　「-てる」　[colloquial contraction of -ている: "be __ing"; "have (done) __"]: DJG v1 p155; Genki ch7; Marx v1 day36.
Examples: 113-23; 303-4; 398-5; 551-4; 565-13; 578-9; 597-12.

-te shikata ga nai/-te shiyou ga nai/-te shou ga nai　「-てしかたがない / -てしようがない / -てしょうがない」　{-て仕方がない / -て仕様がない 371; 173; 501} ["cannot help/bear __"]: DJG v3 p605; Tobira ch15 #8.
Examples: 371-25; 1084-2.

-te shimau　「-てしまう」　["do (something regrettable)"; "finish __ing"]: DJG v1 p403; Genki ch18; Marx v2 day28.
Examples: 86-19; 102-8; 134-16; 152-19; 288-20; 334-21; 371-30.

-te sumasu/-te sumaseru　「-てすます / -てすませる」　{-て済ます / -て済ませる 1260} ["make do (with __)"]: DJG v3 p569 (under -てすむ).
Examples: 1616-14.

-te sumu　「-てすむ」　{-て済む 1260} ["be enough"]: DJG v3 p565.
　　　Examples: 1260-32; 1811-19.

-teta　「-てた」　[colloquial contraction of -ていた: "was ＿ing"; "had (done) ＿"]: DJG v1 p155; Genki ch7; Marx v1 day36.
　　　Examples: 113-20; 703-2; 1478-7.

-te tamaranai　「-てたまらない」　["cannot help/bear ＿"]: DJG v1 p445, v2 p222 (under -てならない).
　　　Examples: 597-22; 619-23.

-te wa　「-ては」　[links a verb with a negative statement]: DJG v2 p461.
　　　Examples: 1078-30; 1220-13; 1549-24.

-te wa dame (da)　「-てはだめ(だ)」　{-ては駄目(だ)* 2275} ["must not ＿"]: DJG v1 p274.
　　　Examples: 1160-10.

-te wa ikenai　「-てはいけない」　["must not ＿"]: DJG v1 p528, v2 p70; Genki ch6.
　　　Examples: 191-19; 486-27; 525-3; 540-35; 849-43; 1042-14.

-te yaru　「-てやる」　["do ＿ (for someone)"]: DJG v1 p67 (under あげる); Marx v2 day31.
　　　Examples: 73-3; 83-28; 555-37; 1061-4.

-te yokatta　「-てよかった」　{-て良かった* 285} ["was good to have ＿ed"]: DJG v1 p89 (under -ばよかった; note typo: "yakatta" should be "yokatta"); Genki ch19.
　　　Examples: 89-2.

to　「と」　["and" within an exhaustive list; cf. や]: DJG v1 p473; Genki ch4; Marx v1 day57.
　　　Examples: 2-8; 3-5; 55-19; 57-4; 70-14; 70-15.

~ to　「〜と」　["with ＿"]: DJG v1 p476; Genki ch4.
　　　Examples: 33-12; 36-13; 38-14; 55-18.

to　「と」　[marks sound/manner or quoted speech]: DJG v1 p478.
　　　Examples: 14-4; 15-26; 27-11; 39-13; 51-15; 51-22; 53-9; 53-14; 59-9; 61-11; 161-6; 222-10.

~ to　「〜と」　["if ＿"; "when ＿"]: DJG v1 p480; Genki ch18; Marx v2 day24.
　　　Examples: 5-8; 44-5; 59-13.

~ to atte　「〜とあって」　["because ＿"]: DJG v3 p612.
　　　Examples: 2258-14.

~ to atte wa　「〜とあっては」　["if it's the case that ＿"]: DJG v3 p615.
　　　Examples: 829-17.

~ to ieba　「〜といえば」　{〜と言えば* 51} ["speaking of ＿"]: DJG v1 p484; Tobira ch1 #11.
　　　Examples: 792-5.

~ to ie domo　「〜といえども」　{〜と言えども** 51} ["even though ＿"; "any ＿"]: DJG v3 p624.
　　　Examples: 1130-53; 2160-8.

~ to ii　「〜といい」　{〜と言い 51} ["it would be good if ＿", "I hope ＿"]: Genki ch16.
　　　Examples: 253-7; 2095-35.

~ to issho ni　「〜といっしょに」　{〜と一緒に 2; 1450} ["along with ＿"]: DJG v2 p535 (under 〜とともに).
　　　Examples: 1257-44; 1450-10.

-toita　「-といた」 [colloquial contraction of -ておいた, past tense of -ておく: indicates act of prudence/getting something done].
　　　　Examples: 173-21.
~ to itta　「〜といった」 {〜と言った* 51} ["such as __"]: DJG v3 p629; Tobira ch9 #3.
　　　　Examples: 1223-24; 1266-8; 1484-29.
~ to itte mo　「〜といっても」 {〜と言っても* 51} [introduces qualification of preceding statement]: DJG v2 p474; Tobira ch9 #17.
　　　　Examples: 1762-15.
~ to iu　「〜という」 {〜と言う* 51} [links identifier with identified]: DJG v1 p486; Genki ch20; Tobira ch10 (first page).
　　　　Examples: 58-4; 91-11; 92-11; 97-9; 121-7; 169-16; 245-7.
~ to iu fuu ni　「〜というふうに」 {〜と言う風に* 51; 425} ["in (such a) way"]: DJG v2 p478.
　　　　Examples: 315-7; 436-4.
~ to iu koto wa　「〜ということは」 {〜と言うことは* / 〜と言う事は** 51; 80} [presents preceding clause as the subject of the sentence: "that __"]: DJG v2 p480; Marx v2 day18.
　　　　Examples: 649-19; 653-27; 1518-12; 1554-11.
~ to iu to　「〜というと」 {〜と言うと* 51} ["at the mention of __", "when (one) says __"]: DJG v2 p492.
　　　　Examples: 134-17.
~ to iwazu　「〜といわず」 {〜と言わず 51} ["be it __ (or any other)"]: DJG v3 p643.
　　　　Examples: 1971-31.
~ toka　「〜とか」 [non-exhaustive examples]: DJG v1 p488, v2 p227; Marx v1 day57; Tobira ch1 #12.
　　　　Examples: 791-9; 1430-24; 1595-33; 1631-20.
tokaku ~　「とかく〜」 ["apt to __", "liable to __"].
　　　　Examples: 760-46.
~ toki　「〜とき」 {〜時* 383} ["when __"]: DJG v1 p490; Genki ch16.
　　　　Examples: 56-9; 96-9; 100-13; 124-7; 137-14; 157-8; 215-11.
~ tokoro　「〜ところ」 ["when __"]: DJG v2 p500; Marx v2 day46.
　　　　Examples: 83-27; 127-2; 460-14; 607-13; 934-20.
~ tokoro da　「〜ところだ」 ["be just about to __", "be just now __ing", "have just now __ed"]: DJG v1 p496; Tobira ch5 #18.
　　　　Examples: 43-5; 148-9; 249-4; 371-20; 716-23; 726-13; 804-11; 941-17; 1650-12.
tokoro ga　「ところが〜」 ["however, __"]: DJG v2 p503; Tobira ch5 #9.
　　　　Examples: 147-19; 380-8.
-toku　「-とく」 [colloquial contraction of -ておく: indicates act of prudence/getting something done].
　　　　Examples: 113-23.
~ tomo　「〜とも」 ["both/all __"; "(n)either (of) __"].
　　　　Examples: 15-14; 63-3; 104-5; 142-8; 237-23; 262-11.
tomokaku　「ともかく」 ["anyway"].
　　　　Examples: 1798-10.
~ to naru　「〜となる」 ["become __"]: DJG v2 p511.

Examples: 12-8; 15-25; 30-1; 186-9; 209-6; 210-3.

~ **to naru to**　「〜となると」　["when it comes to ___"; "if it is the case that ___"]: DJG v2 p512.
Examples: 2275-31.

tonikaku　「とにかく」　["anyway"]: DJG v2 p216 (under なにしろ); Marx v2 day4.
Examples: 196-9; 273-18; 712-7.

~ **to omou**　「〜とおもう」　{〜と思う 142}　["think(s) (that) ___"]: Genki ch9&10.
Examples: 81-12; 114-6; 142-3.

~ **to onajiku**　「〜とおなじく」　{〜と同じく 182}　["as well as ___"; "in the same way as ___"]: DJG v2 p535 (under 〜とともに).
Examples: 1143-22; 1527-14; 1598-34; 1668-14; 1672-17; 2190-32.

~ **toori (ni)/~ doori (ni)**　「〜とおり(に)/〜どおり(に)」　{〜通りに 159}　["just as ___"]: DJG v2 p514; Marx v2 day3; Tobira ch8 #4.
Examples: 51-14; 136-15; 159-1; 159-11.

toriaezu ~　「とりあえず〜」　{取り敢えず〜* 59; 809}　["___ at once"; "___ for now"].
Examples: 14-4; 144-6; 809-1.

~ **to shite**　「〜として」　["in the capacity of ___"]: DJG v1 p501; Tobira ch3 #6.
Examples: 47-11; 98-7; 148-12; 313-5; 325-15; 333-15; 420-13; 480-5; 484-1.

~ **to shite wa**　「〜としては」　["for (a) ___"]: DJG v1 p502.
Examples: 1310-19.

~ **to suru**　「〜とする」　[follows description of an impression or sensation]: DJG v2 p523; Marx v2 day35.
Examples: 36-4; 176-1; 220-4; 238-3; 320-2; 456-2.

~ **to suru**　「〜とする」　["assume ___"]: DJG v2 p518.
Examples: 533-10; 921-9; 1405-14; 2008-9.

~ **totan (ni)**　「〜とたん(に)」　{〜途端に* 1000; 2114}　["the moment ___"]: DJG v2 p525.
Examples: 494-7; 965-9; 1800-9; 2114-19; 2300-2.

totemo ~　「とても〜」　["quite ___"]: DJG v2 p210 (under なかなか〜); Marx v2 day47.
Examples: 24-10; 27-8; 29-6; 68-7.

~ **to tomo ni**　「〜とともに」　{〜と共に 356}　["along with ___"]: DJG v2 p532; Marx v2 day48; Tobira ch11 #8.
Examples: 76-5; 142-21; 179-12; 423-18.

toutou ~　「とうとう〜」　["finally ___"]: DJG v2 p528; Tobira ch8 #17.
Examples: 7-3; 312-7; 387-21; 454-10; 578-14.

~ **to wa ie**　「〜とはいえ」　{〜とは言え* 51}　["even if ___"]: DJG v3 p664.
Examples: 1748-4; 2133-11; 2231-8.

~ **to wa kagiranai**　「〜とはかぎらない」　{〜とは限らない 282}　["not necessarily ___"]: DJG v2 p536; Tobira ch14 #14.
Examples: 936-13; 1087-30; 1269-25; 1505-25; 1586-6; 2032-7.

Transitive and intransitive verbs: DJG v1 p585; Genki ch18; Marx v1 day51.
Examples: 12-2; 12-7; 36-2; 36-7; 44-4; 44-5.

tsuide ni　「ついでに」　{序でに** 1209}　["while you're at it, ___"]: DJG v3 p671.
Examples: 179-19.

tsui ni ~　「ついに〜」　{遂に〜* 2210}　["at last ___", "at length ___"]: DJG v2 p531 (under とうとう〜); Tobira ch5 #7.

Examples: 62-5; 81-7; 90-8; 137-8; 173-22; 235-4; 2210-1.

tsumari ~　「つまり〜」 {詰まり〜* 515} ["that is, __", "in sum, __"]: DJG v2 p538; Marx v2 day4; Tobira ch9 #7.
Examples: 723-18; 887-44; 903-30; 984-13; 1138-12; 1158-10; 1191-25; 1236-35.

~ tsumori　「〜つもり」 {〜積もり* 832} [intention/conviction]: DJG v1 p503; Genki ch10; Marx v1 day63.
Examples: 43-7; 55-18; 59-14; 136-20; 137-15; 287-3; 352-5; 371-31; 448-29.

~ tsutsu　「〜つつ」 ["while __"]: DJG v2 p542.
Examples: 1191-26; 1661-59; 1775-23; 1849-19; 1912-40; 1915-20.

-tsutsu aru　「-つつある」 ["__ing"]: DJG v2 p542.
Examples: 251-6; 445-38; 812-19; 938-29; 1089-27; 1245-14; 1593-35; 2020-57.

~ (t)tatte/~ datte　「〜(っ)たって/〜だって」 ["even if __"]: DJG v3 p594.
Examples: 445-40.

-tte　「-って」 [colloquial topic marker]: DJG v1 p507; Tobira ch1 #15.
Examples: 120-2; 122-6; 1468-4.

-tte　「-って」 [colloquial quote marker]: DJG v1 p510; Genki ch17; Tobira ch1 #16.
Examples: 117-1; 117-22; 460-13.

-tte　「-って」 [colloquial contraction of という].
Examples: 526-23; 1317-25.

~ uchi ni　「〜うちに」 {〜内に* 215} ["while __", "before __ ends"]: DJG v1 p512; Tobira ch4 #16.
Examples: 138-5; 145-4; 194-11; 226-5; 390-5; 639-5; 675-8.

ue (ni)　「うえ(に)」 {上に 41} ["(and) moreover"]: DJG v2 p551; Tobira ch10 #11.
Examples: 1839-46.

-uru/-eru　「-うる/-える」 {-得る* 387} ["can/could __"]: DJG v2 p553.
Examples: 387-19; 893-19; 995-20; 1236-30; 1257-58.

Verbal connectives akin to -te　「-て」: DJG v1 p464, v2 p64 of front matter; Tobira ch1 #5.
Examples: 67-12; 142-20; 183-19; 187-9; 199-7; 219-14; 224-11; 357-18; 450-24.

Verbs of potential ["can __"]: DJG v1 p370; Genki ch13; Marx v1 day50.
Examples: 10-1; 15-8; 18-8; 33-12; 36-9; 37-4; 55-4; 63-2; 67-8; 135-9; 280-16.

Verb stem + ni　「に」 **+ verb of motion** ["(go) __ing"; "(go) to (do) __"]: DJG v1 p297; Genki ch7; Tobira ch3 #9.
Examples: 21-9; 38-14; 74-1; 252-19.

Volitional ["let's __"; "I'll __"]: DJG v1 p576 & 578 second column from right; Genki ch15; Marx v1 day29.
Examples: 2-10; 12-6; 16-6; 32-2; 60-6; 78-4; 86-20.

Volitional + to omou　「とおもう」 {Volitional + と思う 142} ["think about __ing"]: Genki ch15.
Examples: 142-21; 274-13; 352-14.

wa　「わ」 [female speech marker]: DJG v1 p47 & 520; Marx v2 day1.
Examples: 38-14; 141-20; 173-27; 218-9; 219-2; 377-9; 385-8.

~ wa iu made mo naku/~ wa noberu made mo naku 「〜はいうまでもなく / 〜はのべるまでもなく」 {〜は言うまでもなく / 〜は述べるまでもなく 51; 994} ["__ is needless to mention"]: DJG v2 p568.
    Examples: 1624-7; 2197-34.

waa 「わあ」 [female: exclamation]: DJG v1 p47 bottom.
    Examples: 2015-4.

wakaru 「わかる」 {分かる 88} ["understand"]: DJG v1 p529.
    Examples: 5-8; 47-9.

~ wake da 「〜わけだ」 {〜訳だ* 1505} ["the fact is/was that __"]: DJG v1 p531, v2 p570; Marx v2 day77; Tobira ch6 #11.
    Examples: 153-7; 273-18; 301-9; 518-13; 726-9; 793-37; 839-43.

~ wake de wa nai 「〜わけではない」 {〜訳ではない* 1505} ["it is/was not the case that __"]: DJG v2 p574; Tobira ch7 #15.
    Examples: 153-7; 269-15; 618-10; 683-31; 800-12; 870-14.

~ wake ga nai 「〜わけがない」 {〜訳がない* 1505} ["__ is impossible"]: DJG v2 p578.
    Examples: 1958-20.

~ wake ni wa ikanai 「〜わけにはいかない」 {〜訳にはいかない* 1505} ["cannot __"]: DJG v2 p581.
    Examples: 1037-24.

~ wa oroka 「〜はおろか」 {〜は疎か* 1142} ["let alone __"]: DJG v3 p694.
    Examples: 1970-51.

~ wari ni (wa) 「〜わりに(は)」 {〜割に(は) / 〜割りに(は) 416} ["considering __", "for (a) __"]: DJG v3 p697.
    Examples: 416-10; 629-11; 676-9.

wazawaza ~ 「わざわざ〜」 {態態〜** 893} ["take the trouble to __"]: DJG v1 p394 (under せっかく〜); Marx v2 day76.
    Examples: 1481-20; 1637-3.

~ wo 「〜を」 [indicates direct object]: DJG v1 p347; Genki ch3; Marx v1 day9.
    Examples: 2-8; 2-9; 2-10; 3-2; 5-7.

~ wo 「〜を」 [indicates space of motion]: DJG v1 p349.
    Examples: 215-10; 228-4; 255-5; 475-6; 475-14; 679-18; 704-30.

~ wo 「〜を」 [indicates place from which one exits]: DJG v1 p351.
    Examples: 38-4; 51-24; 99-16; 104-5; 272-3; 1377-7; 1521-23; 1970-40.

~ wo 「〜を」 [indicates source of emotion]: DJG v1 p352.
    Examples: 1212-3; 1245-8; 1633-4.

~ wo hajime (to shite) 「〜をはじめ(として)」 {〜を始めとして 956} ["starting with __"]: DJG v2 p320; Tobira ch5 #4.
    Examples: 1238-26.

~ wo meguru/~ wo megutte 「〜をめぐる/〜をめぐって」 {〜を巡る* / 〜を巡って* 1553} ["over __"]: DJG v3 p486.
    Examples: 1447-13; 1553-17; 1620-18; 1694-8.

~ wo mono to mo sezu 「〜をものともせず」 ["undaunted by __"]: DJG v3 p493.
    Examples: 1946-12.

~ wo towazu 「〜をとわず」 {〜を問わず 452} ["irrespective of __"]: DJG v3 p514.

Examples: 1661-50; 1712-44; 1872-29.

~ wo tsuujite/~ wo tooshite 「〜をつうじて / 〜をとおして」 {〜を通じて / 〜を通して 159} [instrument/means: "through __"]: DJG v2 p330; Tobira ch11 #2.
    Examples: 327-14; 953-11; 1066-36; 1257-60; 1264-5.

~ wo tsuujite/~ wo tooshite 「〜をつうじて / 〜をとおして」 {〜を通じて / 〜を通して 159} [duration: "throughout __"]: DJG v2 p330.
    Examples: 426-6; 954-14; 2189-44.

ya 「や」 ["and" within a non-exhaustive list; cf. と]: DJG v1 p536; Genki ch11; Marx v1 day57.
    Examples: 27-11; 131-6; 420-14; 435-12; 461-15; 718-21.

yahari/yappari 「やはり / やっぱり」 {矢張り** 559; 2020} ["as (might be) expected"; "still"]: DJG v1 p538; Marx v2 day4.
    Examples: 603-6; 1257-52; 1911-13; 1918-23; 2045-18.

~ ya ina ya 「〜やいなや」 {〜や否や 552} ["no sooner did __ than"]: DJG v3 p706.
    Examples: 552-11; 578-11; 1009-27; 1588-3; 1825-12.

yamu wo enai 「やむをえない」 {止むを得ない 42; 387} ["inevitable"].
    Examples: 387-18.

yamu wo ezu 「やむをえず」 {止むを得ず 42; 387} ["inevitably"].
    Examples: 1890-12.

-yasui 「-やすい」 {-易い* 443} ["easy to __"]: DJG v1 p541; Genki ch20; Marx v1 day61.
    Examples: 82-3; 88-19; 103-5; 443-5.

yatte kuru 「やってくる」 {やって来る 274} ["come (to)", "approach"; "come around"; "turn up"].
    Examples: 90-8; 194-12; 238-11; 266-30.

yatto ~ 「やっと〜」 ["finally __"]: DJG v2 p591.
    Examples: 15-8; 46-17; 70-4.

~ yo 「〜よ」 [assertion]: DJG v1 p46-47 examples 12-13 and 15; Genki ch2; Marx v1 day11.
    Examples: 15-17; 18-5; 19-6; 21-4; 24-6; 47-9; 51-3.

-you 「-よう」 ["way to __"]: DJG v2 p595.
    Examples: 706-40; 1458-9; 2125-7.

-you 「-よう」 [conjecture]: DJG v2 p599.
    Examples: 455-16; 494-4; 679-33.

~ you da 「〜ようだ」 ["looks like __"; "seems (that) __"]: DJG v1 p547; Marx v2 day66.
    Examples: 92-8; 195-6; 386-12; 424-7; 476-7; 517-4; 564-5; 637-3.

~ you na 「〜ような」 ["like __"]: DJG v2 p340 bottom (under -っぽい); Genki ch22.
    Examples: 96-10; 126-26; 141-20; 147-9; 147-11; 173-28; 204-2; 273-22; 344-11.

~ you ni 「〜ように」 ["as __", "as if __"]: DJG v1 p554; Genki ch22; Tobira ch1 #3.
    Examples: 81-3; 84-14; 113-2; 113-4; 182-13; 191-21; 218-10; 273-22; 499-30.

~ you ni 「〜ように」 ["so that __"]: DJG v1 p553; Marx v2 day71; Tobira ch4 #6.
    Examples: 285-10; 448-39; 464-17; 532-35; 679-24; 705-40; 787-21.

~ you ni iu 「〜ようにいう」 {〜ように言う 51} ["tell (someone) to __"]: DJG v1 p556; Tobira ch3 #11.
    Examples: 252-21; 279-12; 373-7; 469-2; 620-7; 698-27; 805-10.

~ **you ni naru** 「〜ようになる」 ["reach the point where __"]: DJG v1 p559; Marx v2 day72; Tobira ch2 #11.
>Examples: 303-13; 327-14; 532-30; 649-20; 683-32; 699-28; 734-10.

~ **you ni omowareru/~ to omowareru** 「〜におもわれる/〜とおもわれる」 {〜ように思われる / と思われる 142} ["seem(s) __"]: DJG v2 p325; Tobira ch4 #2.
>Examples: 357-23; 625-14; 788-28; 978-26; 1009-32; 1057-16.

~ **you ni suru** 「〜ようにする」 ["make sure (that) __"; "(act) so as to __"]: DJG v1 p562; Marx v2 day72; Tobira ch3 #13.
>Examples: 86-15; 87-6; 383-30; 416-8; 580-17; 704-32.

you suru ni ~ 「ようするに〜」 {要するに〜 547} ["in sum, __"]: DJG v2 p541 (under つまり〜).
>Examples: 562-11; 677-25; 1130-51; 1575-11.

-you tomo/-ku tomo 「-ようとも/-くとも」 ["even if __", "no matter __"]: DJG v2 p507.
>Examples: 677-32; 1236-34.

-you to suru 「-ようとする」 ["try to __"]: DJG v1 p246 (under みる).
>Examples: 42-6; 56-6; 67-15; 81-6; 92-6; 139-14; 809-8.

youyaku ~ 「ようやく〜」 {漸く〜** 1705} ["finally __"]: DJG v2 p591 (under やっと〜).
>Examples: 265-2; 953-10; 976-27; 999-4.

~ **yue ni** 「〜ゆえに」 {〜故に* 257} ["therefore", "because of __"]: DJG v3 p745.
>Examples: 257-1; 686-22; 1059-38; 1457-14; 2045-15.

-zaru wo enai 「-ざるをえない」 {-ざるを得ない* 387} ["have no choice but to __"]: DJG v2 p606.
>Examples: 387-6; 387-16; 646-19; 1285-4; 1286-9; 1332-15.

~ **ze** 「〜ぜ」 ["__, I'm telling you"]: DJG v1 p47; Marx v2 day1.
>Examples: 1934-11.

~ **zo** 「〜ぞ」 ["__, I'm telling you"]: DJG v1 p47, v2 p609; Marx v2 day1.
>Examples: 46-8; 113-23; 182-13; 386-10; 578-8; 704-12; 716-12; 917-37.

-zu 「-ず」 ["not __, so __"; "not __, but __"]: DJG v2 p214 & 315 (under -なく and -ぬ).
>Examples: 151-10; 228-13; 274-20.

-zu ni 「-ずに」 ["without __ing"]: DJG v1 p271 (under -ないで); Tobira ch4 #9.
>Examples: 217-2; 138-9; 134-16.

-zurai 「-づらい」 {-辛い* 1462} ["hard to __"]: DJG v2 p52 (under -がたい).
>Examples: 185-10.

-zutsu 「-ずつ」 ["__ each"]: DJG v1 p572; Tobira ch11 #9.
>Examples: 2-8; 15-6; 86-8; 93-4; 113-14.

Original Works

This list identifies the works from which items have been drawn for the KLC Graded Reading Sets series. Note the following:

* The numbers at the left appear at the end of the English version of each exercise to identify the original work from which it was drawn. Exercises having no such number are original.

* "Sources: E10/J8", to give one example, indicates that the source of the English and Japanese versions of an exercise are shown respectively at numbers 10 and 8 of the Sources, which follows immediately after this list of Original Works.

* "Transl.:" precedes the name of the person who translated the English version to Japanese, or vice versa. In instances where the English version was translated from a third language, the name of person who translated the original work into English is given as part of the work's title.

* Names of authors and translators, including one-word pen names (marked with *), are listed precisely as given in their original sources. Japanese names are listed either in kanji or in romaji, according to the original source.

* "[C/I]" indicates collective or institutional authorship (such as of a government edict).

* The materials listed below are available to you freely and directly from the original sources (see "Sources" section below). I encourage you to use the links provided to download these works for your own bilingual reading library, and to support the worthy projects that have made these texts available.

1. *Adventure of the Dancing Men, The*, by Arthur Conan Doyle [暗号舞踏人の謎 / コナン・ドイル 著]; Transl: 三上於菟吉; Sources: E10, J8.

2. *Adventure of the Devil's Foot, The*, by Arthur Conan Doyle [悪魔の足 / アーサー・コナン・ドイル 著]; Transl: 枯葉; Sources: E10, J8.

3. *Adventure of the Empty House, The*, by Arthur Conan Doyle [空家の冒険 / コナン・ドイル 著]; Transl: 三上於菟吉; Sources: E10, J8.

4. *Adventures of Sherlock Holmes, The*, by Arthur Conan Doyle [シャーロック・ホームズの冒険 / コナン・ドイル 著]; Transl: Coderati*; Sources: E10, J8.

5. *Aesop's Fables* (George Fyler Townsend, English trans.), by Aesop [イソップ寓話集 / イソップ 著]; Transl: Hanama*; Sources: E10, J8.

6. *Araby*, by James Joyce [アラビー / ジェイムズ・ジョイス 著]; Transl: Coderati*; Sources: E10, J8.

7. *Around the World in 80 Days*, by Jules Verne [80日間世界一周 / ヴェルヌ、ジュール 著]; Transl: SOGO E-text Library; Sources: E10, J8.

8. *Arrest of Arsene Lupin, The*, by Maurice LeBlanc [アルセーヌ・ルパンの逮捕 / モーリス・ルブラン 著]; Transl: SOGO E-text Library; Sources: E10, J8.

9. *As You Like It*, by Mary Lamb [お気に召すまま / メアリー・ラム 著]; Transl: SOGO E-text Library; Sources: E10, J8.

10. *Basic Japanese Sentence Data and Basic English Sentence Data*, by [C/I] [日本語基本文データ及び英語基本文データ]; Transl: [C/I]; Sources: E8, J3.

11. *Beginning of Ownership, The*, by Thorstein Veblen [所有権の起源 / ヴェブレン、ソースタイン 著]; Transl: 永江良一; Sources: E10, J8.

12. *Biographical Sketch of an Infant, A*, by Charles Darwin [幼児の伝記的スケッチ / チャールズ・ダーウィン 著]; Transl: SOGO E-text Library; Sources: E10, J8.

13. *Black Cat, The*, by Edgar Allan Poe [黒猫 / エドガー・アラン・ポー 著]; Transl: 佐々木直次郎; Sources: E10, J8.

14. *Blue & Green*, by Virginia Woolf [青と緑 / ヴァージニア・ウルフ 著]; Transl: 枯葉; Sources: E10, J8.

15. *Boarding House, The*, by James Joyce [下宿屋 / ジェイムズ・ジョイス 著]; Transl: Coderati*; Sources: E10, J8.

16. *Bolted Door, The*, by Edith Wharton [閉ざされたドア / イーディス・ウォートン 著]; Transl: 陰陽師; Sources: E10, J8.

17. *Botchan (Master Darling)*, by Soseki Natsume [坊っちゃん / 夏目漱石 著]; Transl: Mori, Yasotaro (revised by J. R. Kennedy); Sources: E10, J1.

18. *Overcoat, The*, by Nikolai V. Gogol [外套 / ニコライ・ヴァシリエヴィチ・ゴーゴリ 著]; Transl: 平井肇; Sources: E10, J1.

19. *Constitution of Japan, The*, by [C/I] [日本國憲法]; Transl: [C/I]; Sources: E15, J15.

20. *Constitution of the United States, The*, by [C/I] [アメリカ合衆国憲法]; Transl: Embassy of the United States in Japan; Sources: E2, J2.

21. *Count of Monte Cristo, The*, by Alexandre Dumas [モンテ・クリスト伯 / アレクサンドル・デュマ 著]; Transl: Andrew Scott Conning; Sources: E10, J4.

22. *Creationism in the Science Curriculum?*, by Ian Johnston [科学のカリキュラムで創造説？ / イアン・ジョンストン 著]; Transl: 永江良一; Sources: E10, J8.

23. *Crito (Benjamin Jowett, Eng. trans.)*, by Plato [クリトン / プラトン 著]; Transl: SOGO E-text Library; Sources: E10, J1.

24. *Damned Thing, The*, by Ambrose Bierce [妖物 / アンブローズ・ビヤース 著]; Transl: 岡本綺堂; Sources: E10, J8.

25. *Dead, The*, by James Joyce [死者たち / ジェイムズ・ジョイス 著]; Transl: Coderati*; Sources: E10, J8.

26. *Declaration of Independence, The*, by [C/I] [独立宣言]; Transl: Katokt*; Sources: E10, J8.

27. *Depleted uranium: sources, exposure and health effects*, by World Health Organization [劣化ウラン：原因、被曝および健康への影響 / 世界保健機構 著]; Transl: TriNary*; Sources: E10, J8.

28. *Discourse on the Method of Rightly Conducting the Reason, and Seeking Truth in the Sciences*, by Rene Descartes [もろもろの学問分野で正しく理詰めで真理を探究するための方法についての考察 / ルネ・デカルト 著]; Transl: 山形浩生; Sources: E10, J8.

29. *Dog of Flanders, A*, by Ouida [フランダースの犬 / ウィーダ 著]; Transl: 荒木 光二郎; Sources: E10, J8.

30. *Fad Of The Fisherman, The*, by Gilbert K. Chesterton [知りすぎた男・釣り人の習慣 / ギルバート・キース・チェスタトン 著]; Transl: Wilder*; Sources: E10, J8.

31. *Fall of the House of Usher, The*, by Edgar Allan Poe [アッシャー家の崩壊 / エドガー・アラン・ポー 著]; Transl: 佐々木直次郎; Sources: E10, J8.

32. *First Inaugural Address of William Jefferson Clinton* (January 20, 1993), by William J. Clinton [ビル・クリントン第一期大統領就任演説（1993年1月20日） / ビル・クリントン 著]; Transl: Katokt*; Sources: E10, J8.

33. *Genesis, The Book of*, by [Traditional] [創世記]; Transl: [C/I]; Sources: E16, J16.

34. *Gettysburg Address, The*, by Abraham Lincoln [ゲティスバーグ演説 / イブラハム・リンカーン]; Transl: Katokt*; Sources: E10, J12.

35. *Gloria Scott, The*, by Arthur Conan Doyle [グロリア・スコット号 / コナンドイル 著]; Transl: 三上於菟吉; Sources: E10, J8.

36. *Great Gatsby, The*, by F. Scott Fitzgerald [グレイト・ギャツビー / F・スコット・フィッツジェラルド 著]; Transl: 枯葉; Sources: E10, J8.

37. *Happy Prince, The*, by Oscar Wilde [幸福の王子 / オスカー・ワイルド 著]; Transl: 結城浩; Sources: E10, J8.

38. *Harlem Shadows: The Poems of Claude McKay*, by Claude McKay [ハーレムの影:クロード・マケー詩集 / クロード・マケー 著]; Transl: Andrew Scott Conning; Sources: E11, J4.

39. *Heart Of The Spring, The*, by William Butler Yeats [春の心臓 / ウィリアム・バトラー・イエーツ 著]; Transl: 芥川龍之介; Sources: E10, J1.

40. *Hearts and Hands*, by O. Henry [心と手 / O・ヘンリー 著]; Transl: 枯葉; Sources: E10, J8.

41. *Homesteading the Noosphere*, by Eric S. Raymond [ノウアスフィアの開墾 / レイモンド、エリック・S 著]; Transl: 山形浩生; Sources: E10, J8.

42. *Horse Dealer's Daughter, The*, by D.H. Lawrence [馬商の娘馬商の娘 / デイヴィド・ハーバート・ロレンス 著]; Transl: Yusuke Inatomi; Sources: E10, J8.

43. *Imperfect Conflagration, An*, by Ambrose Bierce [不完全火災 / アンブローズ・ビアス 著]; Transl: 枯葉; Sources: E10, J8.

44. *In Midsummer Days*, by August Strindberg [真夏の夢 / ストリンドベルヒ 著]; Transl: 有島武郎; Sources: E10, J8.

45. *Inaugural Address of John Fitzgerald Kennedy* (January 20, 1963), by John F. Kennedy [大統領就任演説（1963年1月20日） / J．F　ケネディ 著]; Transl: Katokt*; Sources: E10, J8.

46. *Inner Landscape, An*, by Motojiro Kajii [ある心の風景 / 梶井基次郎 著]; Transl: Tony Gonzalez; Sources: E10, J8.

47. *Instinct of Workmanship and the Irksomeness of Labor, The*, by Thorstein Veblen [ワークマ

ンシップの本能と労働の煩わしさ / ソースタイン・ヴェブレン 著]; Transl: 永江良一; Sources: E10, J8.

48. *Isaiah, The Book of*, by [Traditional] [イザヤ書]; Transl: [C/I]; Sources: E16, J16.

49. *Ivy Day in the Committee Room*, by James Joyce [アイビーデイの委員会室 / ジェイムズ・ジョイス 著]; Transl: Coderati*; Sources: E10, J8.

50. *Japanese Law Translation Database System*, by [C/I] [日本法令外国語訳データベースシステム]; Transl: [C/I]; Sources: E7, J7.

51. *Little Cloud, A*, by James Joyce [小さな雲 / ジェイムズ・ジョイス 著]; Transl: Coderati*; Sources: E10, J8.

52. *Lykkens Kalosker*, by Hans Christian Andersen [幸福のうわおいぐつ / ハンス・クリスティアン・アンデルセン 著]; Transl: 楠山正雄; Sources: E10, J8.

53. *Manager FAQ, The*, by Peter Seebach [管理職のためのハッカーFAQ / シーバック、ピーター 著]; Transl: Yomoyomo*; Sources: E10, J8.

54. *Manifesto of the Communist Party*, by Karl & Engels Marx [共産党宣言 / カール・マルクス、フリードリッヒ・エンゲルス 著]; Transl: 永江良一; Sources: E10, J1.

55. *Mermaid, The*, by Hans Christian Andersen [人魚のひいさま / ハンス・クリスティアン・アンデルセン 著]; Transl: 楠山正雄; Sources: E10, J8.

56. *Minnie's Sacrifice*, by Frances Harper [ミニーが払った犠牲 / フランセス・ハーパー 著]; Transl: Andrew Scott Conning; Sources: E10, J4.

57. *Monday or Tuesday*, by Virginia Woolf [月曜日か火曜日 / ヴァージニア・ウルフ 著]; Transl: 枯葉; Sources: E10, J8.

58. *Mother, A*, by James Joyce [母親 / ジェイムズ・ジョイス 著]; Transl: Coderati*; Sources: E10, J8.

59. *Narrative of the Life of Frederick Douglass, an American Slave*, by Frederick Douglass [フレデリック・ダグラス自叙伝；アメリカの奴隷 / フレデリック・ダグラス 著]; Transl: Andrew Scott Conning; Sources: E15, J15.

60. *Nighthawk's Star, The*, by Kenji Miyazawa [よだかの星 / 宮沢賢治 著]; Transl: Tony Gonzalez; Sources: E10, J8.

61. *Nose, The* (John Cournos, Eng. trans.), by Nikolai V. Gogol [鼻 / ニコライ・ヴァシリエヴィチ・ゴーゴリ 著]; Transl: 平井肇; Sources: E10, J1.

62. *On Liberty*, by John Stuart Mill [自由について / ジョン・スチュアート・ミル 著]; Transl: 永江良一; Sources: E10, J8.

63. *Our Nig: Sketches from the Life of a Free Black*, by Harriet E. Wilson [うちのニッグ / ヘリエット・ウィルソン 著]; Transl: Andrew Scott Conning; Sources: E15, J15.

64. *Peter Pan*, by James Matthew Barrie [ピーターパンとウェンディ / J．M　バリ 著]; Transl: Katokt*; Sources: E10, J8.

65. *Poems on various subjects, religious and moral*, by Phillis Wheatley [宗教や道徳に関する詩 / フィリス・ホウィートリー 著]; Transl: Andrew Scott Conning; Sources: E10, J4.

66. *Poker*, by Zora Neale Hurston [ポーカー / ゾラ・ニール・ハーストン 著]; Transl: Andrew Scott Conning; Sources: E15, J15.

67. *Prince, The* (W.K. Marriott, Eng. trans.), by Nicolo Machiavelli [君主 / ニッコロ・マキ

ャヴェリ 著]; Transl: 永江良一; Sources: E10, J8.

68. *Principles of Scientific Management, The*, by Fredrick Winslow Taylor [科学的管理法の原理 / フレデリック　ウィンスロー　テイラー 著]; Transl: 大阪市立大学商学部、プロジェクト杉田玄白、参加メンバー; Sources: E10, J8.

69. *Progress Against the Law: Fan Distribution, Copyright, and the Explosive Growth of Japanese Animation*, by Sean Leonard [法に抗っての進歩：アメリカにおける日本アニメの爆発的成長とファン流通、著作権 / ショーン・レナード 著]; Transl: 山形浩生; Sources: E10, J8.

70. *Prussian Officer, The*, by D.H. Lawrence [プロシア士官 / デイヴィド・ハーバート・ロレンス 著]; Transl: Inatomi, Yusuke; Sources: E10, J8.

71. *Restaurant of Many Orders, The*, by Kenji Miyazawa [注文の多い料理店 / 宮沢賢治 著]; Transl: Tony Gonzalez; Sources: E10, J8.

72. *RMS Lecture at KTH*, by Richard M. Stallman [RMS スウェーデン王立工科大学講演 / リチャード・M・ストールマン 著]; Transl: 山形浩生; Sources: E10, J8.

73. *Scandal in Bohemia, A*, by Arthur Conan Doyle [ボヘミアの醜聞 / コナン・ドイル 著]; Transl: 大久保ゆう; Sources: E10, J8.

74. *Second Inaugural Address of Abraham Lincoln* (March 4, 1865), by Abraham Lincoln [アブラハム・リンカーン第2期大統領就任演説（1865年3月4日）]; Transl: Katokt*; Sources: E10, J12.

75. *Selfish Giant, The*, by Oscar Wilde [わがままな大男 / オスカー・ワイルド 著]; Transl: 結城 浩; Sources: E10, J8.

76. *Sense of History, A*, by Gerald W. Schlabach [歴史学における常識 / シュラバック、ジェラルド・W 著]; Transl: SOGO E-text Library; Sources: E10, J8.

77. *Shadow and the Flash, The*, by Jack London [影と光 / ジャック・ロンドン 著]; Transl: 枯葉; Sources: E10, J8.

78. *Souls of Black Folk, The*, by W.E.B. DuBois [黒人たちの心 / W・E・B・デュボイス 著]; Transl: Andrew Scott Conning; Sources: E15, J15.

79. *Spider's Thread, The*, by Ryunosuke Akutagawa [蜘蛛の糸 / 芥川龍之介 著]; Transl: Tony Gonzalez; Sources: E10, J8.

80. *Sport of the Gods, The*, by Paul Laurence Dunbar [神様の嘲り / ポール・ローレンス・ダンバー 著]; Transl: Andrew Scott Conning; Sources: E10, J4.

81. *Status of Forces Agreement between Japan and the United States*, by [C/I] [日米地位協定]; Transl: [C/I]; Sources: E6, J6.

82. *Story of Mimi-Nashi Hoichi, The*, by Lafcadio Hearn [耳無芳一の話 / 小泉八雲 著]; Transl: 戸川明三; Sources: E10, J8.

83. *Story of the Three Little Pigs, The*, by Joseph Jacobs [三匹の子ぶたのお話 / ヨセフ・ヤコブ 著]; Transl: SOGO E-text Library; Sources: E10, J8.

84. *Strange Case of Dr. Jekyll and Mr. Hyde, The*, by Robert Louis Stevenson [ジキルとハイド / ロバート・ルイス・バルフォア・スティーヴンソン 著]; Transl: Katokt*; Sources: E10, J8.

85. *Tale of the Fatty Coon, The*, by Arthur Scott Bailey [寝つかせ話：ふとっちょあらいぐまの物語 / アーサー・スコット・ベイリー 著]; Transl: Kameo*; Sources: E10, J8.

86. *Tales of Troy: Ulysses the Sacker of Cities*, by Andrew Lang [トロイア物語：都市の略奪者ユリシーズ / アンドリュー・ラング 著]; Transl: 永江良一; Sources: E10, J8.

87. *Tatoeba Corpus*, by [C/I] [Tatoeba コーパス]; Transl: [C/I]; Sources: E13, J13.

88. *The Stock-Broker's Clerk*, by Arthur Conan Doyle [株式仲買店々員 / コナンドイル 著]; Transl: 三上於菟吉; Sources: E10, J8.

89. *Time Machine, The*, by H.G. Wells [タイムマシン / ハーバート・ジョージ・ウェルズ 著]; Transl: 山形浩生; Sources: E10, J8.

90. *Treasure Island*, by Robert Louis Stevenson [宝島 / ロバート・ルイス・バルフォア・スティーヴンソン 著]; Transl: Katokt*; Sources: E10, J8.

91. *Treaty of Mutual Cooperation and Security between Japan and the United States of America*, by [C/I] [日本国とアメリカ合衆国との間の相互協力及び安全保障条約]; Transl: [C/I]; Sources: E15, J15.

92. *Treaty of San Francisco*, by [C/I] [日本国との平和条約]; Transl: [C/I]; Sources: E15, J15.

93. *Truck, The*, by Ryunosuke Akutagawa [トロッコ / 芥川龍之介 著]; Transl: Tony Gonzalez; Sources: E10, J8.

94. *Twelve Years a Slave*, by Solomon Northup [奴隷としての12年間 / ソロモン・ノーサップ 著]; Transl: Andrew Scott Conning; Sources: E5, J4.

95. *Universal Declaration of Human Rights, The*, by [C/I] [世界人権宣言]; Transl: [C/I]; Sources: E14, J14.

96. *Usable GUI Design: A Quick Guide for F/OSS Developers*, by Benjamin Roe [使えるGUIデザイン / ベンジャミン・ロウ 著]; Transl: 柴田正明; Sources: E10, J8.

97. *Waiting for the Knock*, by Richard M. Stallman [ノックを待ちながら / リチャード・ストールマン 著]; Transl: 結城 浩; Sources: E10, J8.

98. *What the Moon Saw*, by Hans Christian Andersen [絵のない絵本 / クリスチャン・アンデルセン 著]; Transl: Katokt*; Sources: E10, J8.

99. *Wonderful Wizard of Oz, The*, by L. Frank Baum [オズの魔法使い / L・フランク・ボーム 著]; Transl: 武田正代・山形浩生; Sources: E10, J8.

100. *Wordnet 3.0 and Japanese Wordnet* (lemmata file), by [C/I] [WordNet・日本語WordNet（見出し語ファイル）]; Transl: [C/I]; Sources: E9, J8.

101. *Wordnet 3.0 and Japanese Wordnet* (sentences file), by [C/I] [WordNet・日本語WordNet（例文ファイル）]; Transl: [C/I]; Sources: E9, J8.

102. *Work of Art in the Age of Mechanical Reproduction, The*, by Walter Benjamin [複製技術の時代におけるアート作品 / ヴァルター・ベンヤミン 著]; Transl: 佐藤魚; Sources: E10, J8.

Sources

The author wishes to thank the organizations listed below for licensing their copyrighted materials and/or helping to disseminate public domain materials. Title to copyright in all materials not in the public domain remains with the organizations listed below. All licenses listed below extend also to the reader, under the same conditions provided at each license's linked webpage.

1. **Aozora Bunko** [青空文庫]: All cited materials are in the public domain. To access, visit aozora.gr.jp.

2. **Embassy of the United States in Japan**: All cited materials are in the public domain. To access, visit japan.usembassy.gov.

3. **Kurohashi/Kawahara Lab at Kyoto University** [京都大学黒橋・河原研究室]: All cited materials are used under the Creative Commons Attribution 3.0 Unported license (creativecommons.org/licenses/by/3.0). To access, visit nlp.ist.i.kyoto-u.ac.jp.

4. **Andrew Scott Conning**: The author donates his Japanese translations (covering original works #21, 38, 56, 59, 63, 65, 66, 78, 80, and 94) to the public domain.

5. **Librivox.org**: All cited materials are in the public domain. To access, visit librivox.org.

6. **Ministry of Foreign Affairs, Japan**: All cited materials are in the public domain. To access, visit mofa.go.jp/region/n-america/us/q&a/ref/2.html.

7. **Ministry of Justice, Japan**: All cited materials are in the public domain. To access, visit japaneselawtranslation.go.jp/index/terms_of_use/?re=02.

8. **National Institute of Information and Communications Technology (NICT), Japan** [情報通信研究機構]:

   Basic English Sentence Data [英語基本文データ] used under the Creative Commons Attribution 3.0 Unported License (creativecommons.org/licenses/by/3.0). To access, visit nlp.ist.i.kyoto-u.ac.jp.

   Japanese Wordnet used under public license granted by NICT. To access, visit nlpwww.nict.go.jp/wn-ja/index.en.html.

   All other cited materials used under the Creative Commons Attribution 1.0 License. To access, visit nict.go.jp.

9. **Princeton University**: Wordnet 3.0 used under public license granted by Princeton University. To access, visit wordnet.princeton.edu/wordnet.

10. **Project Gutenberg**: All cited materials are in the public domain. To access, visit gutenberg.org.

11. **Saylor.org**: All cited materials are in the public domain. To access, visit saylor.org.

12. **Sugita Genpaku Project** [プロジェクト杉田玄白]: Free public license granted for all cited materials. To access, visit genpaku.org/sugitalist01.html.

13. **Tatoeba.org**: All cited materials are used under the Creative Commons Attribution 2.0 license (creativecommons.org/licenses/by/2.0/). To access, visit tatoeba.org.

14. **United Nations**: All cited materials are in the public domain. To access, visit:

   (English text): un.org/en/universal-declaration-human-rights

   (Japanese text): ohchr.org/en/udhr/pages/language.aspx?langID=jpn.

15. **Wikisource.org**: The English and Japanese versions of the Treaty of San Francisco, and the English version of the Treaty of Mutual Cooperation and Security between Japan and the United States of America, are used under the Creative Commons Attribution-ShareAlike License (creativecommons.org/licenses/by-sa/3.0/). All other cited materials are in the public domain. To access these materials, visit wikisource.org.

16. **Wordplanet.org**: All cited materials are in the public domain. To access, visit wordplanet.org.

About the Author

Andrew Scott Conning is the founder of PlusOne Learning. He has previously been active as a research scholar at Harvard University, Peking University, the University of Tokyo, the Escuela Nacional de Antropología e Historia, and the Weatherhead Center for International Affairs.

Andrew created the Kanji Learner's Course series because it was the kind of tool he wished had existed when he was studying kanji himself. He sincerely hopes that it will help you on your way toward a more direct and profound understanding of Japan and its people.

Connect with Andrew and the growing community of KLC users at the Kanji Learner's Course User Group on Facebook.

Thank You

Thank you very much for reading this book. If you found it helpful, won't you please take a moment to leave a brief rating at your favorite retailer and/or share your experience with other learners? Please note that Amazon now allows quick one-tap ratings for verified buyers.

ありがとうございます

Printed in Great Britain
by Amazon